Enhancing Adult
Motivation to Learn

Revised Edition

Raymond J. Wlodkowski

Enhancing Adult Motivation to Learn

Revised Edition

A Comprehensive Guide for Teaching All Adults

Jossey-Bass Publishers
San Francisco

Jossey-Bass books and products are available through most bookstores. To contact Jossey-Bass directly, call (888) 378-2537, fax to (800) 605-2665, or visit our website at www.josseybass.com.

Substantial discounts on bulk quantities of Jossey-Bass books are available to corporations, professional associations, and other organizations. For details and discount information, contact the special sales department at Jossey-Bass.

 Manufactured in the United States of America on Lyons Falls Turin Book. This paper is acid-free and 100 percent totally chlorine-free.

Credits appear on page 376.

Library of Congress Cataloging-in-Publication Data

Wlodkowski, Raymond J.
    Enhancing adult motivation to learn : a comprehensive guide for teaching all adults / Raymond J. Wlodkowski. — 2nd ed.
        p. cm. — (the Jossey-Bass higher and adult education series)
    Includes bibliographical references and index.
    ISBN 0-7879-0360-4 (cloth : acid-free paper)
    1. Motivation in adult education. I. Title. II. Series.
LC5219.W53 1998
374'.001'9—ddc21
                                                        98-25427

SECOND EDITION
HB Printing   10 9 8 7 6 5 4 3 2

Contents

Preface

When I wrote the first edition of this book thirteen years ago, I began with the statement that forty million adults in the United States participate in learning activities. Today, it is more accurate to state that for most adults, formal learning—whether through workplace training, a college class, an Internet site, or an elderhostel course—is a way of life. Adults in modern society are on a lifelong educational journey. Although technology has changed some of the tools of instruction, the purpose of the instructor remains largely the same—to help adults learn. However, the challenge is far greater now because we have come to appreciate how culturally diverse adults in this society are and how their perspectives, experiences, and ways of understanding vary. We know that to be effective, instructors and learning environments have to accommodate this remarkable diversity.

Considering the range of possible differences among them, how do we help *all* adults learn? The response in this book, as in the previous edition, is to go to the source, to the energy—to human motivation. All adults want to make sense of their world, find meaning, and be effective at what they value. This is what fuels their motivation to learn. The key to effective instruction is to evoke and encourage this natural inclination—the propensity in all adults, whatever their background or socialization, to be competent in matters they hold to be important.

Like the original text, the revised edition of *Enhancing Adult Motivation to Learn* is designed to be a practical and immediately usable resource for educators, trainers, and staff developers whose primary task is instructing adults in business, industrial, and educational settings. It will also be useful to people who have occasional responsibility for teaching adults, such as administrators, tutors, community workers, medical personnel, coaches, and others in similar professions.

As before, deepening learner motivation and helping adults *want* to learn are the topics that receive continual and major emphasis throughout this text. The number of books available on teaching adults has increased, but this is the single volume devoted to the use of motivation as a constant positive influence during learning activities. In the pages that follow, you will find out how to make the deepening of intrinsic motivation an essential part of instructional planning. Four chapters are devoted to describing in detail sixty tested strategies for eliciting and stimulating learner motivation. You can choose from among them based on how well these strategies apply to your content and learning situation.

What's new to this book is a motivational framework more responsive to the influences of race, ethnicity, gender, and class on adult learning. The inseparability of motivation and culture is described in detail. You can learn how to plan for and establish inclusion in a learning environment. Drawing from the fields of motivation, cultural and ethnic studies, cognitive psychology, constructivist learning, systems theory, and multiple intelligences and from my experience and research, I have attempted to make this book a realistic resource for effectively teaching or training *all* adults. The revised edition has greatly benefited from what I have been able to learn in the last thirteen years from instructors who have used the original text. Their experience, their suggestions, and their criticisms have, I believe, made this edition a better book, a more complete book. The assessment section is much stronger, and instructional planning from beginning to end is based not only on motivation but also on content structure. This edition offers a motivationally based theory of instruction for adults.

I still believe that any instructor who has searched for a straightforward, true-to-life, and useful book on how to enhance adult motivation for learning will find this book helpful. Because the focus of the book is on motivation and instruction, it does not widely discuss such areas as physical development, philosophy, and curriculum. However, there are ample references to allow interested readers to pursue further study in most of these areas. This book is mainly about face-to-face instruction. It can be used for distance education formats because the motivational framework and strategies are applicable. However, I do not use distance education examples.

Here are some promises to you:

A minimal amount of jargon, although I may be swimming against the tide. If anything has grown in the last thirteen years, it's jargon, especially in the social sciences.

A little bit of humor. I love to have fun when I'm teaching.

Many examples. Instructors have said this was one of the strongest qualities of the original book. I agree.

A practical and consistent way to design instruction that can enhance adult motivation to learn any content or skill. I've spent twenty-five years learning how to do this; professionally it's my raison d'être.

Motivational theory and methods positively supported by my own experience. Instructors have said this was a strong point in the original edition as well. Anything I suggest, I have personally tried. Nevertheless, please consider the limits of my own perspective and experience.

A way to teach that respects the integrity of every learner. Although I continue to learn to do this more effectively, I have attempted to make the learner's history, experience, and perspective an essential consideration that permeates this approach to instruction.

Overview of the Contents

This book is organized to give you the most important ideas and information I have found to make effective instruction a motivationally consistent process that enables optimal achievement and offers an inherently rewarding experience for culturally diverse adult learners and their instructors. Chapter One discusses the relationship of culture to adult learning. It describes how an understanding of intrinsic motivation enables us to make instruction more responsive to the influence of culture on learning. It presents the theory and research supporting how motivation contributes to competent adult learning.

Chapter Two discusses the core characteristics—expertise, empathy, enthusiasm, clarity, and cultural responsiveness—that are fundamentally necessary for a person to be a motivating instructor. The chapter outlines each characteristic according to performance criteria so that you can comprehend, assess, and learn these behaviors that are prerequisites to enhancing learner motivation.

Chapter Three introduces the four motivational conditions—inclusion, attitude, meaning, and competence—that substantially enhance adult motivation to learn. These motivational conditions are dynamically integrated into the Motivational Framework for Culturally Responsive Teaching, a model of motivation in action. This model is also an organizational aid for designing instruction. The framework provides guiding questions for creating instruction that continually elicits motivation to learn among diverse adults.

Chapters Four through Seven provide the central content of this book. Each of these chapters is devoted to the comprehensive treatment of a major motivational condition: inclusion is covered in Chapter Four, attitude in Chapter Five, meaning in Chapter Six, and competence in Chapter Seven. These chapters describe in pragmatic terms how each of these motivational conditions has been found to be a positive influence on learning among culturally

diverse adults. They also describe and exemplify specific motivational strategies to engender each of the motivational conditions.
These four chapters contain a total of sixty motivational strategies.
Where applicable, I discuss each strategy in terms of its cultural relevance and how it relates to adult learners. In most instances the
strategies are referenced to further readings that provide research
support and examples of their use in educational settings.

Chapter Eight summarizes the previous chapters by means of a
detailed outline of all the motivational strategies as well as their
specific purposes. In addition, it explains two methods of instructional planning, the superimposed method and the source method.
This chapter also includes four concrete illustrations of instructional
planning and guidelines for assessment of learner motivation. By
carefully considering the growing literature on self-regulated learning and learning transfer, this concluding chapter presents useful
suggestions for increasing an adult's capacity for lifelong learning.
The book ends with an epilogue addressing the moral responsibility of being an effective instructor of adults.

Acknowledgments

This revision owes its development and many of its improvements
to those friends, colleagues, instructors, and students who gave voice
to their observations of how the original book did not adequately
serve the ideals it set out to achieve. Although they had faith in its
merits, they could speak to its flaws. I am particularly grateful to Gale
Erlandson, senior editor of Higher and Adult Education at Jossey-
Bass, for her faith in this project and for her patience and wisdom.
In addition, I want to thank Bill Husson, dean of the School for
Professional Studies at Regis University, and Tom Kennedy, vice
president of New Ventures at Regis University, for their unwaver-
ing goodwill and support for all my educational endeavors. I am
also appreciative to Steve Jacobs for earnestly considering my ideas

and being always available with wit and insight. Finally, I wish to thank Margie, Matthew, and Danny for bringing light to my eyes and warmth to my soul throughout this and many other adventures.

Denver, Colorado   Raymond J. Wlodkowski
November 1998

The Author

Raymond J. Wlodkowski is research professor in the School for Professional Studies at Regis University, Denver. He is a licensed psychologist who has taught in universities for three decades. He specializes in motivation, adult learning, diversity, and professional development. He received his B.S. degree (1965) in social science and his Ph.D. degree (1970) in educational psychology, both from Wayne State University in Detroit.

Wlodkowski conducts seminars for colleges and organizations throughout North America and abroad. Three of the books he has authored have been translated into Spanish, Japanese, and Chinese. The first edition of *Enhancing Adult Motivation to Learn* received the Phillip E. Frandson Award for Literature. Wlodkowski also coauthored *Diversity and Motivation* (1995). He has worked extensively in video production and is the author of five professional development programs, including *Motivation to Learn*, winner of the Clarion Award as the best training and development video program of 1991. He has been the recipient of the Award for Teaching Excellence from the University of Wisconsin, Milwaukee, and the Faculty Merit Award for Excellence from Antioch University, Seattle.

Enhancing Adult
Motivation to Learn

Revised Edition

1

How Motivation Affects Instruction

None of us are to be found in sets of tasks or lists of attributes; we can be known only in the unfolding of our unique stories within the context of everyday events.

Vivian Gussin Paley

Like the national economy, human motivation is a topic that people know is important, continuously discuss, and would like to predict. We want to know why people do what they do. But just as tomorrow's inflationary trend seems beyond our influence and understanding, so too do the causes of human behavior evade any simple explanation or prescription. We have invented a word to label this elusive topic—*motivation*—but even its definition continues to baffle the most scholarly of minds. Most scientists can agree that motivation is a concept that explains why people think and behave as they do (Weiner, 1992). Beyond that very general understanding, any more specific discussion of the meaning of motivation brings in a cornucopia of differing assumptions and terminology.

One of the problems with understanding motivation is that we can neither see it nor touch it. It is what is known in the social sciences as a hypothetical construct, an invented definition that provides a possible concrete causal explanation of behavior (Baldwin, 1967). Because we can neither observe motivation directly nor measure it precisely, we can only infer it from what people say and do. We look for signs—effort, perseverance, completion—and we listen for words: "I want to . . . ," "We will . . . ," "You can count on it." And as long as this state of affairs lasts, there will be many different opinions about what motivation really is. Nonetheless, we do know that understanding why people behave as they do is vitally important to helping them learn. We also know that culture, that deeply learned mix of language, beliefs, values, and behaviors that pervades every aspect of our lives, significantly influences our motivation. In fact, social scientists today regard the cognitive processes as inherently cultural (Rogoff and Chavajay, 1995). The language we use to think, the way we travel through our thoughts, and how we communicate cannot be separated from cultural practices and cultural context. Roland Tharp (Tharp and Gallimore, 1988) tells the story of an adult education English class in which Hmong students themselves would supply a known personal context when the instructor did not. For example, when the teacher used fictional Hmong names during language practice, the students invariably stopped the lesson to check with one another about who this person might be in the Hmong community. With a sense of humor, these adults brought, as all adults do, their personal experience to the classroom. We are the history of our lives, and our motivation is inseparable from culture.

If we keep culture in mind, a useful functional definition of motivation is to understand it as a natural human process for directing energy to accomplish a goal. We are purposeful. We use such processes as attention, concentration, imagination, and passion, to name only a few, to pursue goals, such as learning. How we arrive at those goals and how processes like our passion for a subject take shape are, to some extent, culturally bound to what we have learned in our families and communities.

Seeing human motivation as purposeful allows us to create a knowledge base about effective ways to help adults begin learning, make choices and give direction to their learning, sustain learning, and complete learning. Thus, when we as instructors ask such questions as, What can I do to help these learners get started? or, What can I do to encourage them to put more effort into their learning? or, How can I create a relevant learning activity? we are dealing with issues of motivation. However, because of the impact of culture on motivation, the way we answer these questions will likely vary depending on the different cultural backgrounds of the learners.

Although there have been some attempts to organize and simplify the research knowledge regarding motivation to learn (Pintrich and Schunk, 1996), instructors have received very few practical suggestions as to how to consistently and sensitively influence the motivation of culturally different adult learners (Wlodkowski and Ginsberg, 1995). As a result, they have had to rely on what has been traditionally used to enhance motivation for learning—intuition, common sense, and trial and error. Unfortunately, this approach sometimes leads to a rigid dependency on curriculum guides and an increased interest in a "bag of tricks" approach to instruction—the use of unrelated and often manipulative devices to spark learner interest in learning. Without a unifying motivational theory or model with which to organize and assess their motivational practices, instructors cannot easily refine their teaching. What they learn about motivation from experience on the job as well as from formal courses often remains fragmented and, at best, only partially relevant to the increasing diversity they find in their classrooms and training sessions. However, there are a significant number of well-researched ideas and findings that can be applied to learning situations according to motivation principles. The following chapters thoroughly discuss many of these motivational strategies and present a method to organize and apply them in a manner sensitive to cultural differences.

Why Motivation Is Important

Even without specific agreement on how to define motivation, we know motivation is important, because we know that if we match two people of identical ability and give them the identical opportunity and conditions to achieve, the motivated person will surpass the unmotivated person in performance and outcome. We know this from our experience and observation. We know this as we know a rock is hard and water is wet. We do not need reams of research findings to establish this reality for us. When we do consult research, we find that it generally supports our life experience regarding motivation. To put it quite simply, when there is no motivation to learn, there is no learning (Walberg and Uguroglu, 1980). However, this extreme situation rarely occurs, because motivation is not an either-or condition. It is often present to some degree, but when motivation to learn is very low, we can generally assume that potential learning achievement will to some extent be diminished.

Although there are numerous research studies of adult motivation to participate in structured adult education programs (Deshler, 1996), there are no major research studies that thoroughly examine the relationship between adult motivation and learning. If we define *motivation to learn* as a person's tendency to find learning activities meaningful and to benefit from them (Brophy, 1988), the best analyses of the relationship of motivation to learning continue to be found in youth education. In this field of research, there is substantial evidence that motivation is consistently positively related to educational achievement.

Uguroglu and Walberg (1979) performed a benchmark analysis of 232 correlations of motivation and academic learning reported in forty studies with a combined sample size of approximately 637,000 students in first through twelfth grades. They found that 98 percent of the correlations between motivation and academic achievement were positive. We can reasonably assume that if motivation bears such a consistent relationship to learning for students as old as eighteen years of age, it probably has a similar relationship to adult learning. In support of this assumption, these researchers found that the relationship between motivation and learning increased along with the age of the students, with the highest correlations being in the twelfth grade.

It may be that scholars of adult education have been reluctant to examine the relationship of learning to motivation because the bond seems so obvious. As other researchers have found (Pintrich, 1991), people motivated to learn are more likely to do things they believe will help them learn. They attend more carefully to instruction. They rehearse material in order to remember it. They take notes to improve their subsequent studying. They reflect on how well they understand what they are learning and are more likely to ask for help when they are uncertain. One needs little understanding of psychology to realize that this array of activities contributes to learning.

Motivation is important not only because it apparently improves learning but also because it mediates learning and is a consequence of learning as well. Historically, instructors have known that when learners are motivated during the learning process, things go more smoothly, communication flows, anxiety decreases, and creativity and learning are more apparent. Instruction with motivated learners can actually be joyful and exciting, especially for the instructor. Learners who complete a learning experience and leave the situation feeling motivated about what they have learned seem more likely to have a future interest in what they have learned and more likely to use what they have learned. It is also logical to assume that the more that people have had motivating learning experiences, the more probable it is that they will become lifelong learners.

To maintain a realistic perspective, however, we need to acknowledge that although motivation is a necessary condition for learning, there are other factors—ability and quality of instruction, for example—that are also necessary for learning to occur. If people are given learning tasks that are beyond their ability, no matter how motivated they are, they will not be able to accomplish them. In fact, there is a point of diminishing returns for all of these mandatory factors, including motivation. For example, if learners are involved in a subject that is genuinely challenging and for which they have the necessary capabilities, there will come a point at which effort (motivation) is necessary, whether this takes the form of extra practice or increased study time, to make further progress. Conversely, outstanding effort can be limited by the learner's ability or by the quality of instruction. Sports are a common example. There are many athletes who make tremendous strides in a particular sport because of exemplary effort but finally reach a level of competition at which their coordination or speed is insufficient for further progress. An example of the influence of the quality of instruction might be a learner who wants to do well in math and has the ability and motivation but is limited by a complicated, obtuse textbook with culturally irrelevant examples and an instructor who is unavailable for individual assistance. It is unwise to romanticize or expect too much of motivation. Such a view can limit our resourcefulness and increase our frustration.

It is difficult to understand through any scientific means exactly how motivation enhances learning and achievement. One of the most commonly measured indicators of motivation is persistence (Keller, 1983; Schunk, 1991). People work longer and with more intensity when they are motivated than when they are not (especially if there are obstacles). Academic learning time—time spent actively and successfully involved in learning—is strongly related to achievement (Fisher and others, 1980). These visible manifestations of motivation enable learning and foreshadow how important it is for adults to feel a sense of competence while they are extending effort. Also, motivated learners care more and concentrate better while they expend that effort, and they are more cooperative. They are therefore more psychologically open to the learning material and better able to process information. It is much easier to understand what you want to understand. As Freud (1955, p. 435) said, "One cannot explain things to unfriendly people." Finally, motivated learners probably get much more out of an instructor than unmotivated learners do. As instructors, we are usually more willing to give our best effort when we know our learners are giving their best effort, a wonderful reciprocity for everyone.

Adult Learning, Culture, and Intrinsic Motivation

Brookfield (1996, p. 379) emphasizes the need for a culturally relevant perspective of adult learning: "the differences of class, culture, ethnicity, personality, cognitive style, learning patterns, life experiences, and gender among adults are far more significant than the fact that they are not children or adolescents . . . it is necessary to challenge the ethnocentrism of much theorizing . . . which assumes that adult learning . . . is synonymous with the learning undertaken in university continuing education classes by White American middle-class adults in the postwar era." Theories of intrinsic motivation respect the influence of culture on learning. According to this set of motivational theories, it is part of human nature to be curious, to be active, to initiate thought and behavior, to make meaning from experience, and to be effective at what we value. These primary sources of motivation reside in all of us, across all cultures. When adults can see that what they are learning makes sense and is important according to their values and perspective, their motivation emerges. Like a cork rising through water, intrinsic motivation surfaces because the environment elicits it. Intrinsic motivation is an evocation, an energy called forth by circumstances that connect with what is culturally significant to the person.

Intrinsic motivation is governed to a large extent by emotions. In turn, our emotions are socialized through culture. And emotions influence task engagement, the visible outcome of learner motivation. For example, one person working at a task feels frustrated and stops, whereas another person working at the task feels joy and continues. Yet another person, with a different set of cultural beliefs, feels frustrated at the task but continues with increased determination. What elicits that frustration, joy, or determination may differ across cultures, because cultures differ in their definitions of novelty, hazard, opportunity, and gratification and in their definitions of appropriate responses (Kitayama and Markus, 1994). Thus, a person's response to a learning activity reflects his or her culture.

From this viewpoint, for us to effectively teach all adults requires culturally responsive teaching. Even though the internal logic by which learners do something may not coincide with our own, it is present nonetheless. And to be effective we must understand that perspective. Rather than try to know what "to do to" learners, we work with them to deepen their existing intrinsic motivation and knowledge. Seeing learners as unique and active, we emphasize communication and respect, realizing that through understanding and sharing our resources together we create greater energy for learning.

Beyond providing a sound theoretical foundation for a culturally relevant perspective, theories of intrinsic motivation expand understanding of adult learning along several other strata.

Interaction of Emotion and Cognition

In theories of intrinsic motivation, emotions are critical to learning. Understanding how their emergence is due to cultural meaning can help us understand why we witness such a variety of intensity and arousal among any group of adult learners. Optimal emotional states for learning, such as *flow*, have been extensively studied and documented across and within cultures (Csikszentmihalyi and Csikszentmihalyi, 1988). Emotion is a valid and important topic for understanding the differences we find in learning among adults.

Need for a Social and Interdisciplinary Construction of Knowledge

Jarvis (1987), Cunningham (1989), and Wlodkowski and Ginsberg (1995) emphasize the limitations of a dominantly psychological interpretation of adult learning. Theories of intrinsic motivation presume that each of us constructs his or her own reality; we do this by interpreting perceptual experiences of the external world on the basis of our unique set of experiences with the world and our beliefs about those experiences. In this light, such influences as religion, myth, ethnicity, and regional and peer group norms have powerful motivational force. The responses adults have to learning reflect this complexity. Psychology, at best, has only an incomplete understanding of this remarkable intricacy (Hall, 1997). By using a multidisciplinary approach to adult learning that includes but is not limited to the social sciences, philosophy, political theory, spiritual studies, and linguistics, we can be more flexible and interpretive; the conceptual framework of intrinsic motivation allows for a synthesis of much of this information.

Location of Responsibility for Learning Within Both the System of Education and the Learner

The U.S. system of education continues to be dominated by an extrinsic orientation to motivation; the "carrot and stick" is its most popular metaphor. From this extrinsic perspective, the focus for learning is on the use of extrinsic rewards such as grades, eligibility, and money. When learners do not respond to these incentives, they are often seen as responsible for their lack of motivation. They are likely to be described as lacking ambition, initiative, or self-direction. In fact the question, How do I motivate them? is commonly asked, as though the adults in mind are inert. Such a question implies that these learners are in an inferior position, somehow less able and certainly less powerful than the instructor. They need motivation! This attitude dims the instructor's awareness of the learners' own determination and tends to keep them "less than"—dependent and in need of further help.

Using an intrinsic approach to motivation, the instructor considers the learners' perspective fundamental. "Seek first to understand" is our watchword. We can then see that some learners' socialization may not accommodate extrinsic rewards such as grades and money. Asking ourselves the question, How might this learning environment and system of incentives diminish the motivation of some learners? is a viable means to finding clues for improving the learning situation. We know there is an interaction between learner motivation and the dynamics of the classroom, and we must take the responsibility to foster an optimal environment for everyone. Crucial to educational equity is the understanding that the most favorable conditions for learning vary among people. Because learning is the human act of making meaning from experience, our involving all learners requires us to be aware of how they make sense of their world and how they interpret their learning environment.

How Motivation Relates to Adult Learners

It is a bit frustrating but understandable that the field of adult education cannot agree on a definition of *adult* (Tuijnman, 1996; Merriam and Brockett, 1997). The term is culturally and historically relative. Some cultures regard puberty as entry into adulthood, whereas others use legal codes to permit and promote adult behavior. In the United States, people can vote at eighteen but cannot drink until twenty-one and, in particular instances, can be tried in court as adults at fourteen.

However, the two criteria for adulthood offered by Knowles (1980) are motivationally insightful. First, a person is adult to the extent that she or he is performing social roles typically assigned by our society to those it considers adults—the roles of worker, spouse, parent, responsible citizen, soldier, and the like. Second, a person is adult to the extent that she or he perceives herself or himself to be essentially responsible for her or his own life. Responsibility is a cornerstone of adult motivation. Society's deep value for responsibility among adults is why being effective at what one values looms so large and consistently across most cultures as a force for learning among adults. Cultures hold adults more responsible for their actions than they do children. For adults this is an inescapable fact.

Although there is no unified comprehensive theory of adult learning, there are concepts that are part of the history of adult education and add insight in working with adult learners. Malcolm Knowles's ideas about andragogy (adult learning) have contributed key assumptions and methods for helping adults learn (Merriam and Brockett, 1997). Two assumptions that add particular insight to understanding adult motivation are these: (1) "Adults have a self-concept of being responsible for their own lives . . . they develop a deep psychological need to be seen and treated by others as being capable of self-direction," and (2) "Adults become ready to learn those things they need to know or . . . to cope effectively with their real-life situations" (Knowles, 1989, pp. 83–84). These two assumptions reflect the social norms of society in the United States, a largely individualist and pragmatic culture. Most business and educational institutions value and reward self-directed competence. Most adults are socialized with these values. This accounts for one of the most widely accepted generalizations in adult education: *adults are highly pragmatic learners*.

In keeping with these norms, most adults choose to learn through self-directed learning. Allen Tough's seminal work, *The Adult's Learning Projects* (1979), indicated that more than two-thirds of all learning activities were planned, implemented, and evaluated by adults themselves. Replications with diverse samples of adults have largely supported Tough's findings (Brockett and Hiemstra, 1991).

However, self-directed learning as a personal means to further knowledge (for example, learning how to repair household items) can be extremely different from a required college course in philosophy. Adults from more collectivist cultures, in which success may be attributed to the help of others, and emphasis on harmony within the group and personalized relationships is keen, may have difficulty with self-directed learning in formal educational settings (Triandis, 1995). Self-direction in formal learning settings is thus likely to be more valued by adults who are socialized to value achievement for the self. Although self-directed learning is regarded as central to adult education practice, it is often resisted by adults and has not been adequately addressed from a cultural perspective (Hiemstra and Brockett, 1994). It seems reasonable to suggest that as an instructional approach, self-directed learning may need to be more often negotiated as an option than mandated.

Research consistently shows that adults choose vocational and practical education that leads to knowledge about how to do something more than they choose any other form of learning (Merriam and Caffarella, 1991). Whereas adults have a strong need to apply what they have learned and to be competent in that application, institutions and employers have a pressing need for more knowledgeable and skilled workers. The largest and most rapidly growing category of continuing education, probably in all societies, is that directed toward upgrading the knowledge and skills of people in their jobs (Duke, 1996). In this instance we can see how the reciprocal needs of adults and their institutions interact to produce a powerful desire for learning that increases personal competence.

Adults by social definition, individual need, and institutional expectation are responsible people who seek to enhance their *identity* through learning that further develops their competence. *For adult learners to experience intrinsic motivation, they need to connect who they are with what they learn.* This understanding of adult motivation is linked to a socioconstructivist view of learning; in this view, competence is the prominent adult need. Thought, feeling, and action are directed toward the constructing of meaning. Interest, involvement, and a search for understanding characterize adults' intrinsic motivation. Although adults make sense with their individual minds, this understanding of their motivation pays close attention to the ways meaning is generated culturally and collectively through language and social interactions (Vygotsky, 1978).

If most adults are responsible people who want to increase their competence in useful learning activities, what can we do as instructors to make this a reality? Answering this question is what this entire book is about. To move more clearly in this direction, we can look at what motivation means from the instructor's perspective as well as from the adult learner's perspective. Without some idea of what we want to happen motivationally speaking during the process of instruction, it is difficult to organize ourselves because we have no clear motivational purpose. And if our purpose does not complement what the adult learners want to happen motivationally speaking, we have a potential conflict.

At the bare-bones level, most instructors want adult learners who will responsibly begin, continue, and complete learning activities with a reasonable amount of effort and with successful achievement. If all adults were to learn this way, we would not be concerned about motivation. The adult learner's perspective on motivation is a bit more complicated but fundamentally parallels the instructor's perspective. Adults want to be successful learners. This goal is a constant influence on them, because success directly or indirectly indicates competence. If adults have a problem experiencing success or even expecting success, their motivation for learning will usually decline. Although the meaning of success for adults may vary depending on socialization (for example, personal recognition or family pride), all adults pay keen attention to indicators of success while they are learning (Mordkowitz and Ginsburg, 1987).

Adult motivation can operate on integrated levels, with multiple feelings and thoughts occurring simultaneously. The first integrated level for instructors to take notice of is success + volition. For their motivation to be sustained, adults must experience choice or willingness along with their success in the learning activity. This is the most critical and basic level of positive adult motivation for learning. There is almost no limit to the number of specific reasons why an adult might want to learn something, but unless he or she feels a sense of choice, motivation will probably become problematic (Knowles, 1980). That is because it is difficult to feel responsible unless one has a choice to hold oneself accountable for. Much more will be said about this later. Choice is also very important because without the learner's "voice" in such matters as the selection of topics and assignments, cultural relevance is stifled. At the very minimum, instructors who are concerned about motivation can strive to make success + volition part of their instructional purpose for teaching adults.

A higher level of motivational integration is success + volition + value. At this level, the adult learner does not necessarily find the learning activity pleasurable or exciting but does take the activity seriously, finds it meaningful and worthwhile, and tries to get the intended benefit from it (Brophy, 1983). Adults feel much better when they have successfully learned something they wanted to learn and something they value. This separates superficial learning from relevant learning and deeply anchors the learning process in intrinsic motivation.

The highest level of this progression is success + volition + value + enjoyment. Simply put, at this level the adult has experienced the learning as pleasurable. To help adults successfully learn what they value and want to learn in an enjoyable manner is the sine qua non of motivating learning and motivating instruction. I have never found an adult to be dissatisfied with the level of instruction that engenders this level of emotional integration. It is the kind of teaching that receives awards and is long remembered and appreciated. I do not state this as an incentive for you but as the exposition of a reality. Instructors who teach in this manner are truly masterful because they have made the difficult desirable. Every adult wants to be joyful in the pursuit of valued learning, especially in the realms of life where competence is cherished but formidable to obtain. And for instructors who want adult learners who successfully achieve with a reasonable amount of effort, such teaching is the most challenging and rewarding route to follow.

Participatory Research

Having generalized about the motivational perspective of adults toward the instructional process, we can also look to a number of research findings about adult learners' specific attitudes and characteristics that are clearly informative for improving the overall motivational quality of instruction. There have been many studies exploring why adults choose to participate in various kinds of learning activities. As mentioned earlier, most adults give practical, pragmatic reasons for learning. However, the possibility of forecasting adult interest in learning according to chronological age or a phase of development seems remote. As Tennant and Pogson (1995, p. 5) point out, "the obsolescence of knowledge and skills during work life is a powerful force for distributing learning opportunities across the life span, and learning is now firmly entrenched as a key element of every stage and phase of life." Social and historical influences—gender shifts in the workforce, political change, migration trends, aging professions, family dysfunction, international economic competition, chemical dependence—affect adults and their need for learning. These forces often precipitate the life concerns of adults and lead to their desire for more learning, the range of which can include beginning a new language, becoming more literate, or seeking a job-related skill. Although most adults have multiple reasons for learning, social circumstances and the personal concerns that emanate from them are a dominant part of what brings most adults into group learning situations.

There is also a considerable amount of research regarding barriers to adult learning—reasons why adults do not participate in learning activities. Social as well as psychological barriers exist. Among studies that use self-report surveys, adults most frequently mention cost and lack of time as barriers to participation (Van der Kamp, 1996). Deshler (1996) uses the expression *educationally deformed* to describe some adults who resist formal education not only because of the poor instruction they received in the past but also because of the failure and disrespect they endured due to class, gender, or racial bias while in elementary and secondary schools. From a sociological viewpoint, unequal access to wealth and power is the foremost explanation for the diminished educational aspirations found among some low-income adults. There is little doubt that such social factors as unemployment, market trends, home background, government support or neglect of education, and the provision of education in languages other than English combine to powerfully affect the consideration of formal learning for adults. For many, the path to adult education is a steep hill. The revision of this book particularly addresses the issue of inclusion to respond to the understanding that the initial motivation to participate of many adult learners may be very vulnerable.

Aging

It was once thought that aging was a real barrier to learning. This seems less so than ever before. Advances in sanitation, nutrition, and medical knowledge have continued to increase life expectancy in most industrialized countries; the average life expectancy is now approaching eighty years (Schaie and Willis, 1996). In the United States, people remain more active and more satisfied, and feel physically better for longer in their older years (Smolak, 1993). As more and more adults live into their eighties, sixty may no longer seem old. (This seems ever so true as I enter my mid-fifties.)

There are significant culturally related differences in life expectancy. For example, according to the U.S. Department of Commerce (1990), on the average women live longer than men (about seven years), and European Americans live longer than African Americans (about six years). These statistics signal the vast array of individual differences we see in age-related decline in our families and workplaces. Considering the divergence among people in personal habits, living environments, accident rates, disease exposure, genetic predisposition, and available medical care, these differences are not surprising. Although the odds of occurrence are higher as people age, old age certainly does not mean automatic physical, emotional, or mental deterioration.

Most physical and cognitive skills have peaked by early or middle adulthood; they maintain a plateau until a person's fifties or early sixties and then begin to decline (Schaie and Willis, 1996). Beginning slowly, this decline usually accelerates by the late seventies. Compensation can offset this deterioration. Eyeglasses, hearing aids, medications, increased illumination, and increased time for learning are some of the ways to equalize learning opportunities for older adults.

Older learners often require more time for learning new things because, on the average, they perceive, think, and act more slowly than younger learners. This is due to progressive impairment of the central nervous system. However, there are substantial individual differences, and speed of response by itself should not prevent anyone from learning what he or she wants to learn (Schaie, 1989). When adults can control the pace of educational experiences and their exposure to educational materials, most of them in their forties and fifties have about the same ability to learn as they had in their twenties and thirties (Knox, 1977).

Some people believe that because of the decline in vision, reading is a serious problem for older adults. However, in the absence of disease or serious impairment, the normal physical changes of the eyes can be accommodated through the use of eyeglasses and increased illumination. Older adults do have more difficulty rapidly processing visual information and should be allowed more time and control for extracting information from materials, computer screens, films, photographs, and overhead projections (Kosnik and others, 1988).

Hearing has also been well researched (Olsho, Harkins, and Lenhardt, 1985). There is a hearing loss as people become older and a translation problem as well. Rapid speech is more difficult for older adults to decipher. In addition, adults over fifty usually have some impairment in discerning very soft sounds and high-pitched sounds. Attending to the acoustic environment and moderating the speed of presentation and verbal delivery can directly assist older adults in adjusting for this sensory loss.

Intelligence

In terms of intelligence, we can summarize that normal, healthy adults can be efficient and effective learners well into old age. As far as using standardized intelligence tests for effective guidance is concerned, the narrow framework, cultural bias, and low correlation with work performance of these tests militate against their use with most adults (Tennant and Pogson, 1995). If we understand intelligence as the ability to solve problems or to fashion products that are valued by one's culture or community, we realize intelligence cannot be conceptualized apart from the context in which people live. There is always an interaction between individuals' biological proclivities and the opportunities for learning that exist in their culture. Thus there exist multiple ways to be capable and to demonstrate intelligence. According to Howard Gardner (Checkley, 1997) people have the capacity for at least eight intelligences (see Table 1.1). People differ in the strength of these intelligences. Some perform best when asked to manipulate symbols of various sorts (linguistic and logical-mathematical), whereas others are better able to demonstrate their understanding through a hands-on approach (spatial and bodily-kinesthetic). Rather than possessing a single intelligence, people have *a profile of intelligences* that combine to complete different tasks. This means that tools and techniques are part of one's intelligence and its use. The keen ability of the Inupiat hunter to discern sea, stars, and ice from a small boat on the Arctic Ocean meets an intellectual challenge as profound in its own way as that faced by a systems analyst deciphering a federal budget at a computer terminal. The crucial question, then, is not, How intelligent is one? but, How is one intelligent?

There are *mechanics of intelligence*—the way people process information, form classifications, perceive relationships, and extract logical conclusions—that are important for conventional academic learning (Dixon and Baltes, 1986). There are losses to this domain as people age. However, we may produce needless casualties if we are inflexible about accommodating adult learners who would be able to exhibit their understanding but cannot because the learning environment restricts them to paper-and-pencil assessments. For example, there are adults who lack facility with formal examinations but can display relevant comprehension when problems arise in natural contexts. Teacher and medical educators bear daily witness to this phenomenon.

Table 1.1. Gardner's Multiple Intelligences.

Intelligence	Example	Core Components
Linguistic	Novelist Journalist	Sensitivity to the sounds, rhythms, and meanings of words; sensitivity to the different functions of language written and spoken
Logical-mathematical	Scientist Accountant	Sensitivity to and capacity to discern logical and numerical patterns; ability to handle long chains of inductive and deductive reasoning
Musical	Composer Guitarist	Abilities to produce and appreciate rhythm, tone, pitch, and timbre; appreciation of the forms of musical expressiveness
Spatial	Designer Navigator	Capacities to perceive the visual-spatial world accurately and to perform transformations on one's initial perceptions and mental images
Bodily-kinesthetic	Athlete Actor	Abilities to know and control one's body movements and to handle objects skillfully
Interpersonal	Therapist Politician	Capacities to discern and respond appropriately, to communicate the moods, temperaments, motivations, and desires of other people
Intrapersonal	Philosopher Spiritual leader	Access to one's own feelings and inner states of being with the ability to discriminate among them and draw on them to guide behavior; knowledge of one's own strengths, weaknesses, desires, and intelligences
Naturalist	Botanist Farmer	Capacity to recognize and classify plants, minerals, and animals, including rocks, grass, and all variety of flora and fauna

Source: Adapted from Gardner and Hatch, 1989; Checkley, 1997.

In fact, what is called *practical intelligence* may be the centerpiece of intelligence during the adult years. Tennant and Pogson (1995, p. 42) describe practical intelligence as that which emphasizes "practice as opposed to theory, direct usefulness as opposed to intellectual curiosity, procedural usefulness as opposed to declarative knowledge, and commonplace, everyday action or thought with immediate, visible consequences. Practical thinking thus has a real-life end in mind: it seeks to do, to move, to achieve something outside of itself, and works toward that purpose." When applied in a particular domain, practical knowledge is often referred to as *expertise*. As such, practical intelligence is often largely nonanalytical and is based on prior experience. In their particular area of expertise, most experts show quick, economic problem solving and superior memory (Chi, Glaser, and Farr, 1988). Who has ever visited an older professor, seamstress, or farmer and not marveled at the wit and wisdom of what they still do? In these days we don't retire, we become consultants. The understanding of intelligence as fixed and unalterable, especially as a capacity doomed to inevitable decline with age, is giving way (Chapell, 1996). We realize that intellectual capacity during adulthood is a multidimensional combination of experience and knowledge that displays its continuing growth and highest potential in culturally relevant, real-life situations.

Memory

Memory has received a good deal of attention by researchers in learning. Secondary memory, a short-term store where considerable processing takes place, seems to be more of a problem for older adults than long-term (tertiary) memory (Salthouse, 1991). This explains why older adults might have more difficulty remembering several new names at a party than they would remembering the names of high school classmates in a graduation picture. When material is learned well, and new information is integrated with previously learned material, memory appears to remain stable during most of adulthood. LaBouvie-Vief and Schell (1982) argue that older people are more focused on the relevant. Their memory functioning seems geared toward the pragmatic. Age differences in memory are far less dramatic when material is familiar and meaningful.

Older adults have their greatest problems memorizing meaningless, rote, or complex material. This may be due to decreases in mental capacity and to slowed information processing (Schneider, 1996). There is also the possibility that short-term memorization of complex material may take older adults longer because they have to scan large stores of previously stored information to find proper associations. Generally, older learners are likely to have the most problems with initial learning and subsequent recall when learning activities are fast paced, complex, or unusual.

Cross (1981, p. 164) has some very practical suggestions to help older adults with memorization: "First, the presentation of new information should be meaningful, and it should include aids to help the learner organize it and relate it to previously stored information. Second, it should be presented at a pace that permits mastery in order to strengthen the original registration. Third, presentation of one idea at a time and minimization of competing intellectual demands should aid original comprehension. Finally, frequent summarization should facilitate retention and recall."

Personality

In terms of personality, most people show consistency throughout adulthood. The limited change that does occur seems largely to take place in young adulthood, during the shift from student to employed status (Kogan, 1990). Traits, habits, modes of thinking, and the ways by which people cope and interact remain largely stable through old age. We tend to resist change because, as is the case in any deeply organized system, change in one aspect of our personality would require change in other interrelated parts. For example, becoming less absolute in certain religious beliefs may require us also to become more flexible in certain beliefs about people and morality, something we might not desire or feel ready to do. As people grow older, they increasingly depend on previously learned solutions (Cross, 1981). Youthful learners are more likely to engage in problem solving that involves higher-risk behavior and trial-and-error solutions. Some elderly learners become more introverted as they age. Instructional processes that are flexible and nonthreatening are more likely to engage them and prevent withdrawal.

We can make numerous other generalizations about adult development and characteristics related to motivating instruction; these are distributed throughout this book to accentuate their relationship to specific motivational strategies and to enhance your practice of these strategies.

Two Critical Assumptions for Helping Adults Want to Learn

Hypothetical constructs as broad and as complex as motivation invite controversy and argumentation. One of the most likely causes of misunderstanding and reduced communication is for the receiver of a message to be unclear about the assumptions of the sender. It is this lack of clarity, rather than a lack of logic, that increases the likelihood of disagreement. I offer the following assumptions so that you can better understand why I've chosen the suggestions for motivational instruction that follow. These assumptions form a substantial part of the foundation and rationale for the approaches advocated in this book.

The first assumption is that *if something can be learned, it can be learned in a motivating manner*. People must be motivated to some degree to formally learn anything, even if the influence of that motivation is limited merely to their paying attention (Walberg and Uguroglu, 1980). Once we have someone's attention, we can use a myriad of possible influences to sustain that attention and interest. In a perverse way, commercial advertising is a testimony to the human ability to make anything attractive and appealing. If something is worth an instructional effort, one believes there is some degree of worth to the material. It must meet some kind of valid need, or there would be no reason for making it the purpose of instruction. Finding that need, affirming it, and engagingly developing it through instructional processes that are culturally responsive are challenges, no doubt, but not impossible ones.

The second assumption is that *every instructional plan also needs to be a motivational plan*. More often than not, the variables that interfere with and complicate learning are human variables—the needs, emotions, impulses, attitudes, expectations, irrationalities, beliefs, and values of people. Not surprisingly, these are motivational variables as well. Whatever the subject matter, it is usually rather stable and controllable. Often it has a logical structure and sequence. Finding an instructional design format for most subject matter is not an enormous problem (Rothwell and Kazanas, 1992). There are many to choose from, but most do not adequately deal with the human variables just mentioned. However, motivational theories are vitally concerned with these variables and offer many methods and principles to deal with them. The challenge, then, is to integrate these methods and principles with instruction into a cohesive framework. Most instructors do this, but through intuition and spontaneous decision making. Their difficulties arise when motivation seems low or to be diminishing. They have no formal plan for solving problems and often lack exact methods to revise, refine, or build on. This lack of formal plans and methods often leaves them feeling helpless, hopeless, and prone to blame the learners themselves. When they turn to books on motivation, the vast array of competing and conflicting theories often leaves them only more confused. There is no structure to ensure consistent application, especially in working with diverse adult learners. Probably one of the most helpful aspects of any plan is that it reminds us of what to do and when to do it and shows us where we might possibly flex and adjust along the way. If we have no plan to enhance learner motivation, our efforts too often become trial-and-error affairs lacking cohesion and continuity.

The research and literature on motivation has many constructive suggestions for instructors to implement while teaching adults; however, without some method of planning for those suggestions, instructors will probably apply them weakly and inconsistently. This book is a means to resolve this dilemma; so instructors may not only wonder about but act on Csikszentmihalyi's challenging realization (1997, p. 13) that "it is how we choose what we do, and how we approach it, that will determine whether the sum of our days adds up to a formless blur, or to something resembling a work of art."

Characteristics and Skills
of a Motivating Instructor

There is a place where differences and commonalties,
unity and diversity, can be seen as the poles around
which beauty revolves. The axis between these poles
is called empathy.

Herbert Muschamp

Consider for a moment a motivating instructor who helped you as an adult to genuinely want to learn, who was able to influence you to go beyond another course finished, another credit earned. See that person, and remember what learning was like with that individual. Pleasant? Exciting? Startling? Absorbing? There are many possible reactions but seldom the ordinary. Most of us have had at least one such instructor. And every one of us has the potential to be such an instructor to other adults. Let's start with the basics.

Motivating instructors are not entirely magical. They *are* unique; they do have their own style and strengths. But research, observation, and common sense all point to common elements that are the foundation of their instruction. These core characteristics can be learned, controlled, and planned for by anyone who instructs adults. I see them as the five pillars on which rests what we as instructors have to offer adults. If we lack any one of them, there will be far less support for responding effectively to the many complexities that can strain an instructional relationship with adults.

These five pillars are *expertise, empathy, enthusiasm, clarity,* and *cultural responsiveness*. Our most advantageous approach as instructors is to see these pillars as skills and not as abstractions or personality traits. They can be learned, and they can be improved on through practice and effort.

Instruction is a pragmatic art, a craft. We create, compose, and perform for the benefit of learners. Every professional artist has a practice regimen, and fundamentals make up a considerable portion of it. Just as exercise is an inherent part of the lives of fine dancers, and daily practice is a continual ritual for outstanding musicians, so too are these basic elements the foundation for motivating instruction. If we use them steadily and strive always to refine them, they can be developed and enriched. They are achievable.

Offering Expertise: The Power of Knowledge and Preparation

For many people, the pillar of expertise may have other names. Some people prefer to call it substance, knowledge, or competence (Shulman, 1987). Whatever the title, the practical definition of expertise for those of us who instruct adults boils down to three essential parts: (1) we know something beneficial for adults, (2) we know it well, and (3) we are prepared to convey or construct it with adults through an instructional process. Adhering to these three criteria will render our expertise most effective.

1. We know something beneficial for adults.

Watch a group of uninterested adults in any kind of learning activity—an in-service training session, a lecture, a business seminar. (You have probably been a participant, at least a few times, in such a dreary experience yourself.) Their voices aren't shouting, but their minds and bodies are: "Don't waste my time." "Who are you kidding?" "I wish I could get out of here!" "I don't need this." It's almost palpable. As learners, adults are demanding, and rightfully so.

An instructor of adults is quite unlike a teacher of children or adolescents. This person is an adult among adults. He or she cannot count on the customary advantages of age, experience, and size for extra leverage or added influence as an elementary school teacher might. Many adults will have had experiences that far surpass the background of their particular instructor. As a group, they have out-traveled, out-parented, out-worked, and out-lived any of us as individual instructors. Collectively, they have had more lovers, changed more jobs, survived more accidents, moved more households, faced more debts, achieved more successes, and overcome more failures. It is highly unlikely that we can simply impress them with our title, whether it be trainer or professor.

Also, most adults come to learn for a definite reason. They are pragmatic learners. They want their learning to help them solve problems, build new skills, advance in their jobs, make more friends—in general, to do, produce, or decide something that is of real value to them. The dominant question and request of adult learners to anyone who instructs them is, "Can you really help me?"

We begin to answer this question by determining whether we indeed have something beneficial to offer adult learners. We have to ask ourselves, What do I know that this group can understand, use, or apply that will help them? Once we have answered this question with *concrete examples* of the knowledge, skills, or awareness that we can offer this group, we will also have taken the first step in avoiding the classic mistake that many so-called experts make when instructing adults—thinking that simply knowing a lot about a subject is enough to teach it effectively. Colleges abound with knowledgeable professors who teach quite poorly. In many instances, they have not considered what students might know and be able to contribute. They have not taken the step of connecting their knowledge to the daily needs and lives of their students. For this reason, there is no bridge to common understanding or means to construct knowledge collectively.

When we instruct a particular group for a lengthy period of time, we eventually become quite naked: our words and actions continuously strip away the camouflage of our announced degrees and experience to tell learners whether what we know really makes a difference. Connecting our expertise to learners' perspectives and knowledge, before we begin to instruct, builds our confidence that we do have something of value to share and that time is on our side.

2. We know our subject well.

There is no substitute for thoroughly knowing our topic. Nothing beats it. Whatever experience, reading, reviewing, or practice it takes, its payoff far outweighs its cost.

By asking yourself the questions that follow, you can determine for yourself whether you know something well enough to be able to instruct others.

1. Do I myself understand what I am going to teach? Can I explain it to myself in my own words?

2. Can I give more than one good example of what I am teaching? A story, a joke, a fact, a piece of research, an analogy—there are many different types of examples. The main thing is to have more than one. This demonstrates the depth and breadth of your understanding and increases your ability to reach learners for whom a single example would not have enough explanatory power.

3. Can I personally demonstrate the skill (if you are teaching a skill)? Being able to do so gives you real credibility, in your own eyes and in the eyes of others. If you are not able to demonstrate, or if this is inappropriate, are there models, films, or videotapes that can do the job?

4. Do I know the limits and consequences of what I am teaching? Say, for instance, that you are explaining a managerial technique. Do you know what types of employees it may not

work with or under what conditions it would be wise not to use it? What are its effects on production and morale? Does it entail any personal risk for the manager? Your consideration of possible limits and future consequences reveals the sensibility of your expertise.

5. Do I know how to bridge what I am teaching to the world of the learners—their knowledge, experience, interests, and concerns? Do I know where and how to let what they know inform what I know? If you do not, your knowledge may be irrelevant or misapplied.

6. Do I know what I don't know? Where are the boundaries of my own knowledge and skill? How far am I from the cutting edge of my discipline? To be aware of your limits is a very intelligent modesty. Adults don't expect instructors to know everything, but they do want an honest appraisal of the usefulness of what they are learning because they may apply so much of it. Instructors who know their own frontiers can better qualify and temper their instruction. Learners are therefore less likely to become disillusioned or to misapply what they have learned, and instructor and learner alike can better see the direction of future needed learning.

Knowing our subject matter well enhances our confidence, flexibility, and creativity as instructors. We may still have learners who are difficult to reach, but our fund of knowledge will not be what fails us. We can count on it. We can also be more open to questions and new directions that may come from our learners. When a person is really adept with a concept or a skill, he or she can play with it. Spontaneity and improvisation are more possible for the competent. Consummate artists and scientists base their experiments on knowledge. As Zinker (1977, p. 22) writes, "The creative process begins with one's appreciation of what is there—the essence, the clarity and the impact of what is around us."

3. We are prepared to convey or construct knowledge with adults through an instructional process.

The emphasis of this criterion is on the *immediate* planning and organization of instruction and materials for any given lesson or learning activity—the intensive preparation just before the instructional moment. Brilliant and scholarly people at the zenith of their respective professions have been notorious for poorly prepared instruction. Albert Einstein was known for burying his eyes in his notes, with his words haltingly emerging through his monotone as well as his mustache. It is difficult to imagine, but some people actually engaged in small talk while he lectured.

Being well prepared for instruction culminates at two essential points: we have a relaxed familiarity with our materials, and we can look at our learners most of the time. We can actually have a conversation with them. This makes them living participants in moment-to-moment communication with us rather than a cardboard audience of faces. If we are tied to our notes, if we cannot put our manuals down, if we do not know what the next step is, our chances of being motivating instructors are nil.

Vital instruction flows. There has to be a union of sorts between the instructor and the learners so that both parties feel part of a single process. Effective instructors set the stage for this fluid enterprise by knowing their material well enough to read learner cues, watching for signs of interest, insight, and possible boredom. This ability allows the instructor to change qualities of voice, emphasis, and direction at will. Learners feel that this type of instructor is talking with them rather than at them, because the instructor's responsiveness to them is so apparent. They can see these reactions in the instructor's eyes and facial expressions. Questions and give-and-take between the instructor and the learners seem integrated into the stream of the lesson. Like an expert navigator on a familiar ship on foreign waters, the instructor has the touch and feel of the material to sail a steady course.

The type of immediate preparation that allows for motivating instruction is whatever it takes for us to know that when the time for instruction comes, we will spend most of it being with the learners themselves and being able to talk with them. For the experienced instructor, this preparation may mean a few moments of quiet reflection; for the novice, it may entail hours of review, rehearsal, and organization. The range is wide. Notes, index cards, outlines, and even textual materials are appropriate to use as long as we don't always refer to them and can interact with our learners. If any section of our material seems insurmountable (occasionally this will happen to the best of instructors), we can make sure our learners can at least look with us. Visual aids, overheads, chalkboard outlines, and handouts are some possibilities. For computer-based training or distance education, there is usually far less dependency on face-to-face involvement with the instructor.

Any significant achievement demands some degree of immediate readiness. Speakers collect their thoughts. Actors reflect on their roles. Athletes psych up. As motivating instructors, we can be no less prepared in our quest for involved learners. The time we spend mobilizing our knowledge and abilities just prior to instruction is probably the final step of our preparation. How we feel about the instruction we are about to convey will carry over to how we feel when we meet our learners. The commitment to readiness enhances our confidence, the emotion that gives us the most access to our best talents.

Having Empathy: The Power of Understanding and Compassion

Alice, a woman in her mid-thirties, decides to take a communications course in the extension program at her local college. For the last six years she has committed herself to the role of homemaker. Now that her children are older and more independent, she is considering college or full-time employment. This course will be the first step. Her friends have encouraged her to take a basic communications class because it would be a reasonable but not too difficult introduction to current educational practices as well as a means to help her gain some useful skills for the job market. She is motivated.

The class meets once a week in the evening for two and a half hours. At the first class session, the instructor introduces himself, has the students introduce themselves to one another, and lists the requirements for the course—the reading of the course textbook and four assigned articles, a midsemester and final exam, and a term paper. He mentions that he is a tough marker and a real stickler for the use of appropriate English grammar in student papers. After a number of questions from the class regarding these requirements, he dismisses them early so that the students can get a head start on their required reading for the next week. Alice is a bit intimidated but determined.

At the second class session, the instructor lectures on the history of communications theory and outlines a number of research studies that demonstrate the significant effect of different communication innovations. Alice is impressed by her instructor's knowledge but finds her interest waning. The third class session is a lecture on postmodernism and the politics of media influence.

Alice decides to drop the course and get a percentage of her tuition back before it's too late for any compensation. When her friends ask her why she didn't finish the course, she looks at them with a perplexed expression and replies, "It just didn't seem like something I needed right now. The course was about communication, but it wasn't what I expected."

There are a number of different ways to look at this scenario. One way might be to consider what Alice could have done to have helped herself in the course or to have avoided this particular course altogether. Perhaps she should have been more careful in selecting the class; she should have found out more about both the instructor and the course content before she signed up for it. She also might have talked with the instructor and made her needs and expectations more clear to him.

From another vantage point, we could say that the instructor should have taken some time to know his students, to gauge their feelings, and to find out what their personal goals and expectations were. Then he could have modified his course objectives and content accordingly. Wherever we place the responsibility, the same core issue remains: *adults' goals and expectations for what they are taught will powerfully influence how they motivationally respond to what they are taught.* In general, the more their goals and expectations are met by what and how they learn, the more likely they are to be motivated to learn.

As mentioned earlier, most adults come to learning activities for specific reasons. These reasons are based on what they think they need or want. These desires translate into *personally relevant goals* (Ford, 1992). These goals may be social interaction, new skills, some type of certification, or simply relief from boredom. However, if the content or process of instruction does not in some way meet these goals, the learning will have very little meaning for adults. Involving adults in a learning process that does not seem to fulfill any of their personal goals eventually leads them to an inevitable conclusion: "This is a waste of time."

In this book I often use the terms *goals* or *personal goals* to recast what adults in everyday language often refer to as their needs, wants, desires, or motives. I specifically mention this partly because Maslow's theory (1970) and the hierarchy of needs the theory describes—physiological, safety, belongingness and love, esteem, and self-actualization—have been so influential in adult education. However, aside from physiological and safety needs, there is very little empirical support for Maslow's hierarchy (Whaba and Bridwell, 1976; Pintrich and Schunk, 1996), especially across cultures. People do need to feel physically well and personally safe before they can commit to learning. Once these two needs have been satisfied, people respond to the rest of the needs in the hierarchy as well as others on a situational and cultural basis.

Another problem with a needs-based theory is that it implies that a *lack* of something is necessary for human energy to emerge, whereas goals may emerge from basic human functioning, such as the goal to explore or the goal to understand. Using the language of goals also allows for more facile use of knowledge about how people and their cultures construct relevant and valued goals.

Instructors of adults face the challenge of seeing the learners' world and what they want from it as the learners see it. Adults learn in response to their own goals and perceptions, not those of their instructors. Empathy is the skill that allows instructors to meet this formidable requirement for motivating instruction.

Carl Rogers (1969, p. 111), one of the foremost proponents of the use of empathy, defined empathy this way: "when the teacher has the ability to understand the student's reactions from the inside, a sensitive awareness of the way the process of education and learning seem *to the student*." Daniel Goleman (1995, p. 96) calls empathy the fundamental people skill and defines it as "the ability to know how another feels." Other writers have used words like *compassion, consideration,* and *understanding* with similar intent. Researchers have found consideration to be a major dimension in effective leadership (Vaill, 1982).

For those of us who instruct adults, the pillar of empathy is most readily useful when it is organized into the following three parts: (1) we have a realistic understanding of the learners' goals, perspectives, and expectations for what is being learned; (2) we have adapted our instruction to the learners' levels of experience and skill development; and (3) we continuously consider the learners' perspectives and feelings. These three criteria will help us know when we have reached a level of empathy that meets a standard capable of laying the foundation for motivating instruction.

1. We have a realistic understanding of the learners' goals, perspectives, and expectations for what is being learned.

As a process, comprehending the learners' goals, perspectives, and expectations involves our answering two important questions: How do I best find out what the learners' goals, perspectives, and expectations are? and, When do I know I realistically understand their goals, perspectives, and expectations?

Caffarella (1994) describes eight widely used methods for gathering information about adult learners; these compose a helpful guide to answering our first question. Table 2.1 summarizes these methods.

At the beginning of the learning experience, it may be a good idea to talk with the learners about the information you have collected through the use of some of the methods cited in Table 2.1. You might say, for example, "As a result of conducting these interviews, I'd like to know more about . . ."; or, "Having spent a day in your school, I better understand . . ." Such commentary and related dialogue can enhance your communication with learners and give learners a deeper understanding of the care that has gone into the creation of their learning experience.

The second question, When do I know I realistically understand the learners' goals, perspectives, and expectations? has no final answer. My experience as a teacher is that instruction is nearly always a work in progress, a living composition. The learning objectives we take into a classroom are our vision of what we wish to accomplish. But the learners in that room have their own vision and related goals. Remaining flexible, being open to learners' input, and in some instances, creating learning goals with them are ways to keep our composition vital and relevant. This approach is especially important when the learning group is culturally different from us. Taking some time in the beginning of a course to hear comments and suggestions from learners regarding the course objectives shows

Table 2.1. Methods for Understanding Learners' Goals, Perspectives, and Expectations Prior to the Learning Experience.

Method	Description	Guideline
1. Experience	Spending time with the learners in their community, work, or learning settings—if possible, while they are involved in activities related to the purpose of the learning experience.	Learners should represent the gender and racial and ethnic composition of the learning group.
2. Written surveys	Using paper-and-pencil formats that gather opinions, attitudes, needs, goals, strengths, preferences, concerns, and perceptions.	You should consider the potential limitations of reading and writing proficiencies among the learners. Some for whom English is not a first language may have difficulty with this format. See Rothwell and Kazanas (1992) for extensive ideas for developing needs assessments.
3. Interviews	Talking with people either in person or by phone.	Your role, status, and perceived trustworthiness will have a great deal to do with the kind of information you receive. This is an excellent method to probe for deeper goals and concerns.
4. Group sessions	Identifying, analyzing, and using narratives, such as stories and folklore, to understand learners' ideas, issues, and goals. Can include brainstorming, focus groups, general group discussion, and so forth.	Group size is usually four to eight members. Group members should represent the gender and racial and ethnic composition of the learning group.

Table 2.1. Methods for Understanding Learners' Goals, Perspectives, and Expectations Prior to the Learning Experience, cont'd.

Method	Description	Guideline
5. Job or task analysis	Analyzing and assessing the tasks, activities, and procedures related to the learning goals as they are performed on the job or in professional settings. This method is probably most applicable in workshops and training.	Because this analysis is so important for ensuring transfer of learning and relevance as well as for comprehending prerequisite skills for the training, collected information has to be valid.
6. Performance tests and tasks	Assessing learners' knowledge, skills, attitudes, and values that are significantly related to the learning goals.	Measures should be valid and reliable and conducted with enough time prior to the learning experience to allow for adjustments based on the performance results.
7. Written materials	Analyzing information from reports, manuals, newsletters, community media, and evaluation studies to better understand the context and proficiencies of the learning group.	Documents and media should be up-to-date and relevant.
8. Conversations with colleagues and friends who know the learning group	Engaging in informal discussions to gain insights and ideas about how to design your course or training.	This is like a consultation and can expand the creativity and effectiveness of the learning experience.

Source: Adapted from Caffarella, 1994, pp. 73–74.

our respect for the learners and their experience and perspective. However, unless this is an exceptional situation—for example, a visiting teaching assignment, a crisis workshop, a Freirean problem-posing, or the like—the objectives we have set for our course or module should include most of the goals and concerns that our learners bring with them to the first meeting of our instructional program. By making the effort to understand learners prior to the first instructional meeting, we are more likely to face only moderately refining our instructional plan rather than seriously revising it.

Another type of expectation that is crucial for us to understand is what the adult learner anticipates in the way of course requirements. Learners bring strongly felt expectations with them when it comes to what and how much we ask them to do. In our learners' eyes, our fairness and our humanity will significantly depend on how our requirements measure up against their own expectations for this critical element. Usually, this is an issue of time. All course and training requirements take some time to do, whether they involve reading, writing, practice, or problem solving. Many studies have found time constraints to be a major obstacle to participation in adult education (Darkenwald and Valentine, 1985). Sometimes instructors think that learners want fewer requirements because they want the easy way out. I think it is much more helpful to see requirements in terms of the time they demand and to recognize that adult learners want to make sure they have enough time to fully demonstrate their real abilities. The issue is not "give me a break." It's "let's make sure I really have a chance to show you what I can do." Our understanding of the type of learners we have and the amount of time they can realistically afford is a necessary consideration to explore *before* we create our course and training requirements.

2. We have adapted our instruction to the learners' levels of experience and skill development.

Did you ever have the experience of being in a course or training program where you didn't have the skills or background necessary to do what you were asked to do? Were you ever in such a program and couldn't leave it? Maybe it was in the military, in secondary school, or worse yet, in something you volunteered for. It's a special kind of misery, a mixture of fear, embarrassment, and infuriation. If there's no hope of learning, we usually try to get out of the situation. Our motivation is to escape, and when that's not possible, at best to endure and to avoid depression.

As instructors, we don't want to make people fail. In terms of empathy, *this means giving learners things to do that are within their reach*. If we give them assignments that are too easy or for which they have had too much experience, they will be bored and disinterested. We must strike a delicate balance. The instructional goal is to match the learning process, whether it be materials, activities, assignments, or discussions, to the abilities and experience of our learners. We don't want to assign books our learners cannot read or to expect them to be very interested in things they have done many times.

If we are unfamiliar with our learners or if our subject matter is rapidly changing, we may want to use diagnostic or formative evaluation procedures to better understand their capabilities and experiences related to our subject area. We can use interviews, paper-and-pencil tests, simulations, exercises, or whatever helps us know what our learners can or cannot do relative to what we are offering them. The purpose of these assignments is not to categorize learners but to help us create instructional procedures for better adult motivation and learning. Even among professional athletes, coaches begin training camps with exercises and tests that are basically diagnostic. They know from years of hard-earned experience that you cannot take anyone from anywhere unless you start somewhere near where they are.

3. We continuously consider the learners' perspectives and feelings.

More than ever before, technology and electronic media are allowing education to be conducted across vast distances and widely different cultures. Distance education, accelerated courses, and teleconferencing are just part of an array of seemingly more efficient but also potentially more insensitive methods of delivering educational services. The need for compassion on the part of the instructor is probably greater than it has ever been.

The more we transmit instruction technologically, the more adult learners need to know we care about them and reasonably understand them as human beings. Hand in hand with this understanding is Saint-Exupéry's marvelous maxim, "What is essential is invisible to the eye" (1943, p. 70). There are countless important things that go on between an instructor and a learner during instruction that no single human sense, no global standardized test, no amazing electronic equipment will ever pick up. In some ways, I wish this were not so. To some extent, this "invisibility" makes incomplete all the ideas and strategies found in this book. And yet anyone who has ever really been an instructor knows that Saint-Exupéry's maxim is true. That is why empathy is as much an attitude as a skill. It is a constant desired awareness of what our learners are living and experiencing with us as they know and feel it.

Of the skills necessary for empathy, listening is most important. It is the single most powerful transaction that occurs between us and another person that conveys our acceptance of his or her humanity. The way we listen tells learners more than anything else does how much consideration we are really giving them. Do we understand? Do we interrupt? Do we look over that person's shoulder? Do we change the subject? Do we really know what that person is feeling?

When we *listen for understanding*, learners are more likely to feel understood and respected, making it safer for them to listen to us (Mills, 1995). Listening for understanding is preferable in teaching because it avoids judging people according to a conceptual framework of our own devising and allows us to become fascinated with how things look to learners. We can be genuinely intrigued by how learners make meaning out of ideas and experience. Such respectful interest is more likely to elicit deeper dialogue and mutual understanding.

If we can also *attune* our responses to learners, we have a chance to connect with them emotionally (Goleman, 1995). Attunement occurs tacitly and involves tone of voice, body language, and words conveying to the listener a reciprocal understanding of his or her feelings. A mother does this with an infant when she responds to the child's squeals of delight with a gentle shake, a smile, and a higher-pitched voice expressing glee. An instructor does this with a learner when he or she responds to a student's frustration with a knowing nod, a furrowed brow, and words communicating a willingness to listen further.

Validation may also be important. Sometimes learners need to know that we can accept how they are feeling given what they have experienced or how they understand the world: "I see you're upset; having lived through the kind of discrimination you've just described probably doesn't leave much choice in the matter. I appreciate the courage it took to tell us about this. Thank you."

Listening for understanding, attunement, and validation are skills that help convey empathy. To use these skills effectively takes practice. They can best be learned and rehearsed during encounters that are not stressful; they will then be more accessible to you during the emotional heat of conflict or controversy.

Empathy is not simply an altruistic notion. It's a dynamic process, involving people's ability to express their thoughts and feelings to each other in ways that often change the relationship and, most important, continue the relationship. Combined with expertise, empathy makes the instructor a more nurturing person in the eyes of the learner. Whenever an instructor can contribute to fulfilling the goals of a learner, the learner can identify with that instructor. The learner may begin to take on some of the attitudes and behaviors of the instructor, literally to act in some ways like the instructor. We identify to some degree with almost any leader who

significantly meets our needs, whether it is a parent, a political figure, or an instructor. This process is part of the reason we often feel
a profound sorrow when such a person dies. A Mother Teresa, a former coach—any leader important to us can have this effect on us.
We have not just lost someone who meant something to us; we
have lost a part of ourselves as well.

Identification allows each of us as motivating instructors to leave
a legacy. And enthusiasm for our subject can be a noble inheritance.

Showing Enthusiasm:
The Power of Commitment and Expressiveness

To instill an awareness of the importance of enthusiasm in an
instructor, I often ask people in my courses and workshops to
remember a motivating teacher they have had as an adult: someone
who taught in a way that evoked their passion for what they were
learning and gave value to it. (You may wish to follow along with
me.) I ask them to say the teacher's name; to see the teacher's face;
to remember what it was like to be in that course, workshop, or seminar; and to remember the feeling they would have as they came
into the class and as they left it. After they have had a chance to
share their recollections among themselves, I ask them to raise their
hands if the teacher they remembered was enthusiastic about what
he or she was teaching them. If I were to count all the people who
did not raise their hands in the twenty years I've done this activity,
there would be less than thirty individuals. With groups as large as
five hundred people, it is the norm to have a unanimous show of
hands.

I think I inadvertently realized the importance of enthusiasm as
a characteristic of teachers when I was a sophomore in high school.
Struggling to learn geometry and feeling the steady diminishment
of my will and effort, I remember the day the teacher came in with
a cart full of plastic circles, squares, and triangles. As usual, she
looked listless, dispirited, and withdrawn, qualities her teaching

reflected as constants. Bob, the boy next to me whose career in geometry was headed in the same direction as mine, dryly observed as he nodded toward her, "See what geometry can do to you." That was it! To my fifteen-year-old brain, he was right. We could suffer the same fate. Though we both did poorly in geometry, we never felt bad about it. It's unavoidable: we are what we teach. And every learner knows it.

The word *enthusiasm* originates from the Greek noun *enthousiasmos*, which in turn comes from the Greek verb *enthousiazein*, meaning to be inspired or possessed by a god. Other dictionary meanings include "strong excitement" or "feeling on behalf of a cause or subject." In discussing instruction, I prefer a definition that includes the person's inner feelings as they are expressed in outward behavior.

Enthusiastic instructors are people who care about and value their subject matter. They teach it in a manner that expresses those feelings with the intent to encourage similar feelings in the learner. Emotion, energy, and expressiveness are outwardly visible in their instruction.

If we care about our instructional topic, we will be naturally inclined to be expressive about it. If we do not care about our subject, we will find it more difficult to produce feelings and gestures. We might be able to act out or invent such expressions for a particular occasion but to maintain such zeal would be laborious. Without a source of inspiration, it is difficult to be inspirational. The goal of encouraging in the learner our value for our subject matter is important as well. This goal motivates us to have rapport with our students and to express our feelings in a way that engages our learners to share in our enthusiasm. Otherwise, we could become so involved in our own emotions that we might teach for our own benefit rather than for the benefit of our learners. Arrogant instructors often display this shortsightedness.

In educational research, enthusiasm has long been linked to increased learner motivation and achievement. According to

Cruickshank and his associates (1980), all other things being equal, a teacher who presents materials with appropriate gestures and expressiveness will have students who achieve better on tests than will the teacher who does not gesture, reads in a monotone, and generally behaves in an unenthusiastic manner. The eminent researcher Gage (1979) sees enthusiasm as a possible "generic" teaching behavior that is useful at all grade levels, in all subject areas, and for all types of students. From the field of managerial studies, it has been reported that leaders of high-performing systems have *very strong feelings* about the attainment of the system's purposes. Vaill (1982) believes this characteristic appears 100 percent of the time in the actions of these leaders.

Enthusiastic instruction has such a powerful influence on the motivation of learners for reasons both physical and psychological (Perry, Magnusson, Parsonson, and Dickens, 1986). The first and foremost reason is that instructors are sellers. We are advocates. We say, "Learn this; it's good for you." Some of us sell math or technical skills, others training programs or social skills. Our subject matter is our sales product. Whatever the content, the message is still the same: "Learn it. It's worth it." Whenever an individual, especially an adult, is being sold something, he or she performs a keen intuitive scan of the salesperson, asking, in effect, "What does this product do for *you?*" If we cannot show by our own presence, energy, and conviction that this subject matter has made a positive difference for us, the learner is forewarned. If we appear bored, listless, and uninvolved with what we are asking the adult to learn, his response will be, "If that's what knowing this does for you, by all means, keep it away from me." That is self-protection. No one wants to buy what has not done its own seller any good. This inherent learner wisdom makes enthusiasm an absolute necessity for motivating instruction. For learners, *how* instructors say it will always take priority over *what* instructors say.

Enthusiastic instructors are potent models (Feldman, 1997). I have discussed expertise and empathy *before* the pillar of enthusiasm for this reason. When adults see an instructor as competent and compassionate, they tend to imitate the instructor's own behavior and attitudes toward the subject matter. If these two influential characteristics are missing, the spirited instructor could simply be dismissed as an enthusiastic jerk! Without personal proficiency and a rapport with learners, the zealous instructor appears foolish, more a person to be ridiculed than a person to be admired. Learners can see that when a knowledgeable, caring instructor displays such expressiveness about the subject matter, this person's enthusiasm is the natural emotional outcome of justified commitment. Such an instructor can be an inspiration to adult learners.

Enthusiasm by its very nature is energy, and energy attracts. It is not easy to disregard an expressive person. Enthusiastic instructors are constantly producing stimulation by the way they act. Learners are more likely to pay attention and therefore understand what is said or demonstrated. Greater alertness produces better learning, which makes future stimulation more likely and rewarding. And on it goes. Thus a constant self-perpetuating chain of events is established. It is no wonder learners "can't wait" for the next course session with an inspiring instructor.

One more quality that enthusiastic instructors effortlessly embody is believability. Because of their commitment to and involvement with their subject, they tend to use their own vital words and expressions. "Wow!" "Who could imagine?" and, "That's incredible!" may seem corny, but they are undeniably authentic. Such instructors also are somewhat vulnerable to their own emotions. They would actually have a hard time hiding their feelings about what they teach. Learners can't help but be aware that enthusiastic instructors are speaking from their hearts as well as their minds. This awareness accentuates instructors' credibility, and learners more easily embrace their instruction.

The pillar of enthusiasm has two basic criteria: (1) we value what we teach for ourselves as well as for the learner, and (2) we display our commitment with appropriate degrees of emotion and expressiveness. Attending to these two criteria will not only give us some indication of our enthusiasm but also have the added benefit of helping us sustain it in our instruction.

1. We value what we teach for ourselves as well as for the learner.

Our own interest in our subject is probably the surest indicator that we value it. Do we devote time to understanding it better? Are we active members of organizations that specialize in our discipline? Do we follow and learn from the best practitioners in our field? Do we read the magazines, journals, or newsletters of our subject area?

What is our area of specialty? Almost every artist, professional, and scholar has one, something unique she knows or does better than most others in her field—a genuine source of pride. Be it the local chef who creates a celebrated entrée or the Nobel laureate who engages in esoteric research, people who value their work usually try to develop a particular aspect of their skill or knowledge. It's our way of personalizing and showing appreciation for what we do. Our specialty transforms us: we are not merely an ordinary practitioner in the field but a vital part of our subject matter—a person who adds a singular contribution or style to the realm of our work. Enthusiastic instructors distinguish themselves by knowing they possess such exceptional pursuits. Just as we might know of some exotic faraway island, we have discovered something out of the ordinary to share with our learners.

Understanding the effects of what we teach helps us care about our subject area. Knowing which "firsts" our learners will experience with us can be a powerful influence on our enthusiasm. The first time I ever read one of Shakespeare's sonnets was with a teacher. The first time I ever used a computer was at a workshop under the guidance of an instructor. The first time I ever learned how to prepare my own media displays was with a trainer. The list is very long and very important to me. Please consider the first-time experiences and skills you bring to learners. They form an inventory likely to be savored.

2. We display our commitment with appropriate degrees of emotion and expressiveness.

Displaying our commitment to our subject matter is the exhilarating quality that makes instruction enthusiastic. In some ways, we are like cheerleaders. We root for what we believe in.

Allowing ourselves to have feelings about what we teach is the key. Here are some examples: getting excited about new concepts, skills, materials, and future events related to our subject; showing wonder about discoveries and insights that emerge from learners; and sincerely expressing emotions as we are learning with our students—"I feel frustrated by these problems myself"; "I became sad as I read this essay"; "I'm happy to see the progress you're making."

A little bit of dramatization may help as well. Whatever the actor in us will allow is a good rule of thumb. We can tell interesting stories about what we teach; role-play our subject matter (by becoming historical figures, delivering quotations and speeches, simulating characters in problems, and so forth); and use the arts and media, such as music, slide shows, and film excerpts, to demonstrate and accentuate our subject matter.

Showing our interest in the world as it relates to what we teach is another very attractive way to display our enthusiasm. It not only vividly demonstrates our commitment but also broadens the importance of our subject matter. We can bring in articles and newspaper clippings about current events that relate to what we teach; take field trips; invite credible guest speakers who work in areas related to our subject matter; self-disclose interesting personal experiences we have had as we learned about our field; and share any new learning that we might be carrying on at the moment. Be cautious about using these last two ideas, however. Being too extreme with them could be interpreted as self-centered, which would then be more harmful than helpful with adult learners.

Although emotional involvement, dramatization, and showing interest are ways to display our enthusiasm, how do we really know if our instruction expresses this quality? The following are some indicators (Larkins, McKinney, Oldham-Buss, and Gilmore, 1985) commonly found in instruments designed to measure teacher enthusiasm:

Speaking with some variation in tone, pitch, volume, and speed

Gesturing with arms and hands

Moving about the room to illustrate points and to respond to questions

Making varied, emotive facial expressions as called for

Displaying energy and vitality

How people express and perceive enthusiasm varies across cultures. Currently, there is no instrument to measure teacher enthusiasm that is both precise and culturally sensitive. Nor is there an ideal model for enthusiastic teaching. A flamboyant and dynamic speaker who might do well at a corporate training seminar might be stylistically very ill suited for a rural school board meeting.

However, the indicators noted in the preceding list are excellent categories to consider for assessing your own enthusiasm while teaching. A possibly effective method would be to videotape a few of your instructional experiences and to evaluate yourself in the five categories just listed, considering your subject area, the learners you normally teach, and another instructor who successfully enhances the motivation of similar learners. That way, you would have a sensitive context for your self-assessment and a model for comparison. If you prefer, you might ask a respected colleague to observe you teaching and to give you feedback about your enthusiasm using the five categories as focal points for discussion. I personally favor the latter approach, especially if it is reciprocal, because I have found the discussion that results from these observations to be enormously informative.

As instructors, we are sometimes faced with solving the problem of *loss of enthusiasm*. There are six potential destroyers of enthusiasm.

Whether you are a novice or a more experienced instructor of adults, you may find the following descriptions of these hazards beneficial.

1. *Satiation.* You seem to be doing the same thing over and over again. The feeling is one of boredom. There is nothing fresh or new in your instruction. You feel you may be in a rut, and B. B. King's anthem is far too clear to you: "the thrill is gone." One of the best antidotes for this condition is *change.* Change the content, process, environment, or population of your instructional situation. Ask yourself which aspect of your instruction would benefit from such an alteration and take the necessary steps. We know from systems theory that one significant change in a system can change everything. This principle may be positively applicable to your situation.

2. *Stress.* You feel burned out, psychologically drained, and physically near exhaustion. Perhaps you are somewhat depressed as well. Instruction is taking too much out of you. If this is the case, make up your mind to control the stress and not let it control you. Stress does kill. There are myriad books and programs that offer realistic assistance. Contact your professional organization, local health department, or physician for appropriate references.

3. *Lack of success.* You are just not getting the job done. You feel some degree of incompetence. Maybe your learners are not learning well enough, or they seem poorly motivated, or they are not applying what they learn. There may even be discipline problems and personality conflicts between you and the learners. To a large extent, this book is devoted to resolving these issues. A realistic additional intervention would be to discuss the matter with a respected and trusted colleague. Have yourself a consultation. Almost all professionals do so when problems or questions come up in their work. Doctors, lawyers, therapists, and managers readily and wisely seek the counsel of fellow practitioners to resolve the many dilemmas common to anyone who provides a service to human beings.

4. *Loss of purpose.* The ultimate values for which you instruct adults seem vague and distant, possibly forgotten. You no longer feel

the pride you once had in your craft. Instruction has become an ordinary, mundane task. You're surviving but not feeling pride in your work. This is a common malady to almost anyone who does something frequently for long periods of time. It is often a form of taking one's occupation for granted. (This happens in marriages as well.) Some combination of distance, reflection, and the company of other enthusiastic practitioners can often be helpful. Vacations, conferences, conventions, and retreats are some means to consider for self-renewal.

5. *Living in the past.* You are having an attack of the good-old-days bug. The learners aren't as good as they used to be. The instructional conditions have deteriorated. You see things as they once were. You see things as they are now. You feel depressed. You tell yourself things will not get better. You feel even more depressed. This can lead to cynicism. And if you associate with other cynics, feeding off one another's hopelessness can produce an endless cycle. Break this pattern by seeing your situation as you would like it to be. Allow yourself to imagine how it can happen. Begin to take the necessary steps. Associate with others who are willing to work toward these goals with you.

6. *Plateauing.* Your instruction may be effective, but you no longer believe you can get better. You feel stagnant. Personal and professional growth on the job seems dead-ended. There is very little challenge to your work. You feel resigned rather than committed. If you cannot leave this situation, you may feel trapped. Whether you go or not, the beneficial alternative is the same: create another challenge for yourself. This means setting a desired concrete goal in your professional life for which the outcome is not certain. There will be some risk of failure, but that is where the exhilaration comes from. Your challenge could be to raise your instructional goals, try a new training process, or become a mentor to a less experienced instructor. Whatever it is, make it a moderate risk, meaning that the odds for whatever you do are clearly in your favor. Then plan for the challenge and act on it. The results will speak for themselves.

Demonstrating Clarity:
The Power of Organization and Language

You are a trainee in a special program your employer has developed. You are attending your first training seminar to gain the appropriate skills for your new position. It is the first hour of the session, and things seem to be going smoothly. Materials have been passed out. The leader has introduced himself. He seems well qualified, experienced, and enthusiastic. In fact, he has just told you that one of the most important prerequisites for success in your new job will be a positive attitude toward your colleagues.

A trainee raises her hand and asks, "I've often heard how important a positive attitude is. But what does that really mean? I think where I get confused is just understanding what an attitude is. Could you tell me what that word means?"

You had not considered it before, but you now realize you are not too sure what an attitude is either. The instructor waits a moment and begins his answer. "Well, ah . . . an attitude is, um . . . sort of like a way of looking at something or maybe thinking about what you see, or feeling a certain way, so that you end up . . . no, let me say, act, uh . . . better yet . . . judge the situation and that makes you behave in a certain way. Like, if you don't like someone, you won't talk to them. Or . . . if you respect something, you'll take better care of it."

The instructor moves on. You are confused, and you notice by the expressions on their faces that most of your peers seem to be feeling the same way, too. Trainee motivation has seriously slipped in the seminar. You feel a bit worried that you will not be able to understand this instructor.

Adult learners endure this situation all too frequently. They have expert, well-intentioned, enthusiastic instructors who do not communicate clearly. In the example just cited, the instructor could have said, "An attitude is the combination of a perception with a judgment that results in an emotion that influences our behavior.

For example, you see a neighbor at a party. You like this person. You feel happy to see him. You decide to walk over and say hello." At the very least, the instructor should have asked the trainee if she needed more explanation or examples. This would have allowed for further clarification and might have saved the day.

No matter how expert, empathic, and enthusiastic an instructor is, the fourth pillar—instructional clarity—is still necessary for motivating instruction. People seldom learn what they cannot understand. Worse yet, it is frustrating to be in the presence of someone who seems to know and care about something but cannot convey what that something is.

Instructional clarity is teaching something in a manner that is easy for learners to understand and that is organized so that they can smoothly follow and participate in the intended lesson or program. But there is a catch—what may be easy for one person to understand may not be so for another. There is a dynamic between what the instructor does and what the learner brings to the instructional situation. This is the interaction of the instructor's language and teaching format with the learner's language and experience. For a simple illustration of a breakdown in this interaction, suppose that an instructor is teaching a concept and uses an example with which some learners are unfamiliar. Perhaps he refers to the sport of hockey. One learner in the group has never seen a hockey game, and another is learning English and cannot translate the word. Rather than being enlightened, both learners are only confused by the example.

Adult learners are especially baffled by a lack of instructional clarity because so often they bring with them a history of having been able to learn what they needed to know in order to survive and prosper. They know they have the ability to learn, but if the instructor's language or methods are vague and confusing, adult learners are left feeling unable to learn—an extremely frustrating situation. Increasing this tension is most adult learners' real need for new learning to perform their jobs or advance in their careers.

There are many studies confirming that instructional clarity is positively associated with learning (Land, 1987; McKeachie, 1997). Berliner (1988) found that *expert teachers*, effective teachers who have developed fluid and often masterful solutions to common classroom problems, were extremely well organized and thoughtful about teaching procedures. More recently, the concept of instructional clarity seems to be evolving in at least two directions: the first, influenced by cognitive psychology, focuses on how instructors can organize knowledge so that it is acquired and integrated with prior knowledge (Marzano, 1992); and the second, influenced by multicultural and linguistic studies, focuses on how instructors can use communication skills to promote the learning and participation of English-language learners (Kinsella, 1993).

It is difficult to prescribe what an instructor can do to guarantee instructional clarity. Significant research continues in this area, and much evidence is still coming in. However, there are two helpful performance standards that current data tend to support: (1) we plan and conduct instruction so that all learners can follow and understand; and (2) we provide a way for learners to comprehend what has been taught if it is not initially clear. Following these two criteria as guidelines will help us establish and develop instructional clarity for learners.

1. We plan and conduct instruction so that all learners can follow and understand.

This guideline emphasizes our organization and language. Organization is the logical connection and orderly relationship between each part of our instructional process. Are we like a good map—that is, can learners follow us from one learning destination to the next? Do we properly emphasize and note the most important concepts and skills, just as a road map highlights the larger cities?

Beyond good outlining, planning for instructional clarity includes the following:

- Anticipating problems learners will have with the material and having relevant examples and activities ready to deepen their understanding.

- Creating the best graphics, examples, analogies, and stories to make ideas easier to understand. (Much more information about this idea is found in Chapters Five and Six.)

- Including checkpoints with questions or problems to make sure learners are able to understand and follow the lesson.

- Knowing the learning objective and preparing a clear introduction to the lesson so that students know what they will be learning.

- Considering the use of *advance organizers* and *visual tools*. These are graphics, examples, questions, activities, and diagrams that support understanding of new information by directing learners' attention to what's important in the coming material, highlighting the relationships of the ideas to be presented, and reminding learners of relevant information or experience. (For extensive discussion and examples, see Chapter Six.)

- Rehearsing directions for such learning activities as simulations, case studies, and role playing so that learners are clear about how to do the activities and can experience their maximum benefits.

We can enhance clarity during instruction by using *explanatory links*—such words as *if, then, because,* and *therefore*—that tie ideas together and make them easier to learn (Berliner, 1987). Consider the difference in clarity when an instructor says, "Thomas Jefferson owned slaves. Some historians question his greatness as a president," as opposed to, "Some historians question Thomas Jefferson's greatness as a president because he owned slaves."

When we *signal transitions* from one major topic to another, we greatly help learners follow along. Using such phrases as *the next step*, *the second phase*, and *now we turn to . . .* tells learners that we are changing the focus of our discussion.

Most important is continually to use words and descriptions that are familiar to learners. If we are talking about something as simple as a smell or an odor, we would be wise to avoid the words *effluvium* or *redolence* to get across our meaning, unless we choose first to define them. When traveling with learners into new areas of knowledge, we can use examples and analogies that are clear to them. To feel like Cleopatra in Rome is much more comprehensible to most people than to feel like Alcibiades in Athens. We have to decide what is appropriate. The main goal is to avoid being vague. As long as we remain vigilant of the expressions on learners' faces, we have a reasonable chance of staying attuned to how well learners understand.

Obvious from this discussion is the importance of language. Comprehension for English-language learners can be extremely challenging because so much advanced learning is abstract and context-reduced, lacking real objects or the visual and social clues (such as pictures, facial expressions, and feedback from others) one might have during a conversation. Kinsella (1993) offers helpful suggestions for increasing clarity for English-language learners during instruction:

- Pair less proficient English users with sensitive peers who can clarify concepts, vocabulary, and instructions in the primary language.

- Increase wait time (by three to nine seconds) after posing a question to allow adequate time for the learner to process the question effectively and formulate a thoughtful response.

- Make any corrections indirectly by mirroring in correct form what the learner has said. For example, suppose a student says, "Majority immigrants San Francisco from Pacific Rim." You can repeat, "Yes, a majority of the immigrants in San Francisco come from the Pacific Rim."

- Use these conversational features regularly in class discussions, lectures, and small-group work:

Confirmation checks	"Is this what you are saying?"
	"So you believe that . . . "
Clarification requests	"Will you explain your point so that I can be sure I understand?"
Comprehension checks	"Is my use of language understandable to you?"
Interrupting	"Excuse me, but . . . "
	"Sorry for interrupting . . . "

- Write as legibly as possible on the board or on overhead transparencies, keeping in mind that students educated abroad may be unfamiliar with cursive writing.

- Allow students to use a tape recorder for repeated listening to comprehend and retain information.

- Modify your normal conversational style to make your delivery as comprehensible as possible: use a slightly slower speech rate, enunciate clearly, limit idiomatic expressions, and pause adequately at the end of a statement to allow time for learners to clarify their thoughts and to take notes.

- Relate information to assigned readings whenever possible and give the precise place (page numbers) in the text or selection so that learners can later find the information for study and review.

- Allow learners to compare notes near the end of class or training and to ask you any questions they could not answer among themselves.

2. We provide a way for learners to comprehend what has been taught if it is not initially clear.

We can meet this criterion in many different ways, depending on how and what we teach. The range of possibilities spans reviewing difficult material to having announced office hours for learners who want personal help. The Instructional Clarity Checklist found in Exhibit 2.1 is a way of surveying these many options. It is also a means of using learner feedback to tell us how clearly learners understand us. Those statements that relate directly to guideline two ("We provide a way for learners to comprehend what has been taught if it is not initially clear") are preceded by an X. Statements relating to guideline one ("We plan and conduct instruction so that all learners can follow and understand") are preceded by an O.

The Instructional Clarity Checklist is a concrete way to better understand how clear our instruction really is. If we videotape our-selves during instruction, we can use this checklist to assess the clarity of our instruction while we actually see and hear ourselves interact with learners.

Being Culturally Responsive: The Power of Respect and Social Responsibility

Think of someone who respects you, someone who easily comes to mind and about whose respect you have little doubt. I have two notions about this person. The first is that he or she very seldom, if ever, threatens you in order to make you do something. The second is that *your opinion* matters to this person. Your way of understanding things can influence this person, especially in the way you're treated. These two notions do not amount to a complete philosophical

Exhibit 2.1. Instructional Clarity Checklist.

This is a checklist for learners to complete, but it can also be adapted to become a self-informing survey. In its present form, it can be given to learners for their feedback on your instruction. This will tell you from their point of view what you do well and what you may need to do to improve the clarity of your instruction.

(After each statement, place a check mark under the category that most accurately applies to it.)

As our instructor you:	All of the time	Most of the time	Some of the time	Never	Doesn't Apply
O 1. Explain things simply.	—	—	—	—	—
O 2. Give explanations we understand.	—	—	—	—	—
O 3. Teach at a pace that is not too fast and not too slow.	—	—	—	—	—
O 4. Stay with the topic until we understand.	—	—	—	—	—
X 5. Try to find out when we don't understand and then repeat things.	—	—	—	—	—
O 6. Show graphics, diagrams, and examples to help us understand.	—	—	—	—	—
O 7. Describe the work to be done and how to do it.	—	—	—	—	—
X 8. Ask if we know what to do and how to do it.					
X 9. Repeat things when we don't understand.	—	—	—	—	—
O 10. Explain something and then use an example to illustrate it.	—	—	—	—	—
X 11. Explain something and then stop so we can ask questions.	—	—	—	—	—
O 12. Prepare us for what we will be doing next.	—	—	—	—	—

Exhibit 2.1. Instructional Clarity Checklist, cont'd.

As our instructor you:	All of the time	Most of the time	Some of the time	Never	Doesn't Apply
O 13. Use words and examples familiar to us.	—	—	—	—	—
X 14. Repeat things that are hard to understand.	—	—	—	—	—
O 15. Use examples and explain them until we understand.	—	—	—	—	—
O 16. Explain something and then stop so we can think about it.	—	—	—	—	—
O 17. Show us how to do the work.	—	—	—	—	—
O 18. Explain the assignment and the materials we need to do it.	—	—	—	—	—
O 19. Stress difficult points.	—	—	—	—	—
O 20. Show examples of how to do course work and assignments.	—	—	—	—	—
X 21. Give us enough time for practice.	—	—	—	—	—
X 22. Answer our questions.	—	—	—	—	—
X 23. Ask questions to find out if we understand.	—	—	—	—	—
X 24. Go over difficult assignments until we understand how to do them.	—	—	—	—	—

Source: Adapted from Gephart, Strother, and Duckett, 1981, p. 4.

treatise on respect, but to most of us in our daily lives, they are how we know whether or not we are respected. They are particularly valid in a learning environment, and they demonstrate why respect is essential to the motivation of adults. Without respect, the only reason someone does something for another is out of fear, obedience, ignorance, lust, or love—sometimes of the misguided sort.

As part of the fifth pillar—cultural responsiveness—I stress respect as a *respect for diversity*, an understanding that people are different as a result of history, socialization, and experience as well as biology. Thus learners normally have different perspectives, and all of them have a right to instruction that accommodates this diversity. Social responsibility, the second essential quality of cultural responsiveness, emerges from this respect for diversity. Realizing that all people matter means we must ask the question, What is my teaching ultimately connected to beyond myself and my students? I vitally believe in the interdependence of all people and things. Motivation does not occur in a vacuum. It is energy with a consequence. This understanding obliges me to see my work in the context of an ideal for social justice, because I know better than most that people's motivation to learn is released by a vision of a hopeful future. That means I seek to foster effective learning for all learners with attention to the collective good of society. How I do this may differ or at times conflict with others who have the same intent, whether they are learners, citizens, or colleagues. Therefore, the following guidelines for cultural responsiveness are both necessary and personally relevant: (1) we create a safe, inclusive, and respectful learning environment; (2) we engage the motivation of all learners; and (3) we relate course content and learning to the social concerns of learners and the broader concerns of society.

1. We create a safe, inclusive, and respectful learning environment.

In a safe learning environment, there is little risk of learners' suffering any form of personal embarrassment because of self-disclosure, a lack of knowledge, a personal opinion, or a hostile or arrogant social environment. We can go a long way toward ensuring this kind of security by assuming a nonblaming and realistically hopeful view of people and their capacity to change.

Blame is a classic trap, one in which our normal instincts disable us. When a problem or disagreement emerges, we often seek to assign responsibility. In so doing, we may find fault or label a person, often without validity and with little empathy. Blaming can create a cycle of reciprocally hostile attitudes and actions that damages relationships among people, especially culturally different people (Wlodkowski and Ginsberg, 1995). As ugly as it is to say it, blaming is usually some version of, "Oh, *that's* the way you see it . . . you no good so-and-so!"

Rather than blame, we instructors can model and support increased understanding, mutual problem solving, and taking advantage of these opportunities for further learning. Beverly Daniel Tatum (1992) offers an excellent example of doing this in her course The Psychology of Racism. She explicitly works with the assumption that because prejudice was inherent in her students' environments when they were children, they cannot be blamed for what they were taught, intentionally or unintentionally. She points out that they all have a responsibility to interrupt the cycle of oppression and that understanding and unlearning prejudice may be a lifelong process. She acknowledges that they may not all be at the same point in the process and should have mutual respect for each other, regardless of where they perceive each other to be.

Ridding a learning environment of blame does not mean that we give up our critical reasoning or avoid facing the truth as we understand it. It does mean realizing that a different viewpoint can give us information that leads to shared understanding and a clearer path for communication; that though I may see it differently from you, I do not withdraw my respect for you. A realistically hopeful view of people is not a mask to cover problems or difficulties. We do not ignore human suffering. But we do pay attention to opportunity, give the benefit of the doubt, expect learners to do well, and find joy in the process of working toward the solutions to problems.

The *modus operandi* of an instructor fostering a safe, inclusive, and respectful learning environment is to share the ownership of knowing. This is not a method as much as it is a value and a way of being. It means encouraging all learners to understand their own construction of meaning and to accept the integrity of their own thinking (Oldfather, 1992). It requires us to be responsive to each learner's oral, written, and artistic self-expression. Accordingly, we invite and honor the ideas, feelings, and concerns of every learner in the community.

From this perspective, the learner's *voice* is critical (Lather, 1991). Truth is a process of construction in which the learner participates (Gilligan, 1982; Belenky, Clinchy, Goldberger, and Tarule, 1986). A learner must trust her own thinking if she is to be intrinsically motivated. How many times have we heard an instructor say, "Those people just don't like to think"? Well, if we are the learners and it isn't our own thinking, and if we can't say that we see things differently without fear of rejection or threat, then such thinking is unlikely to be very appealing. Telling and hearing our stories is essential to human nature. Stories are compelling because they are the way we make sense of things. To know we are using our own minds to transcend what we know, to play with ideas, and to realize clearly what was once vastly incommunicable can be ecstasy.

When learners know that the having and sharing of ideas is a sincerely respected norm in the learning environment, they will be more likely to expose their thinking. In fact, it is one of the few ways they can come to realize that there are multiple viewpoints on any issue and to appreciate how others also use the process of construction for their own learning and grasp of truth.

2. We engage the motivation of all learners.

In any course or training, it's pretty easy to absolve ourselves of responsibility for the lack of motivation of some students. Now and then I even hear the excuse, "They have a right to fail." This implies that strenuous efforts on our part to encourage learning among resistant students may deny them their freedom of choice and constitutional legacy. However, my most common experience has been that most instructors of adults are sometimes frustrated, confused, or at a loss as to what to do about those learners who seem reluctant to learn or, more often, reluctant to do enough to learn what the instructor would consider satisfactory. Some of us resolve this issue by teaching to a certain segment of the class: those adults who most easily learn with us, leaving the rest to the hands of fate. Yet we need to be aware there is clear evidence that those learners left at the roadside of adult education are generally culturally different from their teachers, income level being one of the most dominant dissimilarities (Stacey and le To, 1996).

If we accept that students become intrinsically motivated when they can see that what they are learning makes sense and is important to them, we are required as instructors to be respectful of our students' culture, perspectives, concerns, and interests. Our finding salient ways to include these compelling aspects of their lives in the creation of a learning environment or a lesson is the key to engaging the motivation of *all* learners. To a greater or lesser extent, we strive to create the educational experience *with* our learners, interpreting and deepening the meaning we share together. I understand this goal to be an ideal and possibly a never-ending, unfulfilled challenge. But I also believe that to act as though I can reach this ideal is both responsible and wise. I offer the Motivational Framework for Culturally Responsive Teaching (introduced in Chapter Three) as the most realistic means I have found to consistently meet this challenge.

3. *We relate course content and learning to the social concerns of learners and the broader concerns of society.*

Education is inextricably connected to society. It directly contributes to the construction of the individual and society. We are what we learn to be. People and society are developed in one direction or another through education (Shor, 1993). Ethics and politics are inherent in the instructor-learner relationship (authoritarian or democratic), in readings chosen for the syllabus (those left in and those left out), and in the process of learning (for example, which questions get asked and answered, and how deeply are they probed). Because people cannot escape the pervasive human need to invest meaning in their world and must have a hopeful future to feel a deep motivation to learn (Courtney, 1991), the connection of our instruction to broader social concerns that affect how people live, work, and survive is inescapable. As instructors we have a social responsibility to promote equity and justice. In our teaching and training we begin by being sensitive to the social concerns of our learners and the equitable treatment of all people in our courses. I have found Paulo Freire's conception of a critical consciousness (1970) to be an invaluable guide to creating a learning environment in which the integrity of all learners is more effectively supported and where learning seems more likely to contribute to the common good of society—to inform as well as to transform us.

Instructors with a critical consciousness reflect the following qualities (Shor, 1993):

- *Power awareness:* approaching our instruction and content with an understanding that society is constructed by organized groups; realizing who has power and how power is structured and used in society, especially as it influences learners in the course

- *Critical literacy:* using analytic habits of thinking, reading, writing, and discussing that go beneath surface impressions, traditional myths, mere opinions, and routine clichés; understanding the social contexts and consequences of any subject matter; being willing to probe for the deeper meaning of an event, reading, statement, image, or situation, and applying the meaning found to one's own as well as the learner's situation

- *Desocialization:* recognizing and challenging prejudicial myths, values, behaviors, and language, especially those learned in mass culture, such as class bias and excessive consumerism

- *Self-education:* using learning opportunities to initiate constructive social change, ideas, and projects: for example, using action research in a course to inform a local paper, corporation, or community organization about discovered abuses or inequities

---

In this chapter, we examined and discussed the five pillars of motivating instruction—expertise, empathy, enthusiasm, clarity, and cultural responsiveness. They are five necessary, interdependent, and vital building blocks. They form a strong foundation, but they are not a complete structure. We could not consider the material that follows in this book without first acknowledging these core characteristics. In presenting the motivational strategies in this book, I am strongly urging the instructor who uses them to do so in a manner that is expert, empathic, enthusiastic, clear, and culturally responsive. Under these circumstances, the strategies are more likely to be both respectful and effective with adult learners.

3

What Motivates Adults to Learn

*The map of the self is different in each culture, and
each culture could be said to require its own separate
psychological science.*

                                        Andrew Lock

As a discipline, motivation is a teeming ocean. A powerfully
influential and wide-ranging area of study in psychology, motivation at its core deals with *why people behave as they do*. But in
terms of scholarly agreement and tightly controlled boundaries of
application, motivation swarms the field of psychology with abun-
dant and rich and often dissimilar ideas. Theoretical assumptions
relying on a view of human beings as rational, materialistic, pragmatic, self-oriented, and self-directed coexist with views of human
beings as irrational, spiritual, altruistic, community-oriented, and
other-directed (Gergen, Gulerce, Lock, and Misra, 1996).

This state of affairs has been brought about by the complexity
of human behavior, the influence of socialization processes on any
human endeavor, and a growing realization that claims for knowledge in the human domain are relative to the culture in which they
are spawned. Currently, *socioconstructivism* is a growing theoretical
force in understanding ways to improve learning in formal settings
such as schools and professional seminars (Hickey, 1997). Incorporating views from sociology and anthropology, this perspective

acknowledges the impact of collaboration, social context, and negotiation on learning. Critical to this view is the understanding that people learn through their interaction with and support from other people and objects in the world. As psychologists, we are aware that to better understand learning may require us to perceive a person's thinking and emotions as inseparable from each other and from the social context in which the activity takes place. For example, would I have these thoughts (writing clearly about adult motivation) and feelings (mild anxiety—maybe I won't) if I were not in front of a word processor surrounded by research journals and texts and aware of my history as a teacher of adults? It seems unlikely that I would. However, I am still an individual with my own thoughts, guided by personal interests and goals. I live as a socially constructed being with an individual identity. Both ways of being human exist at the same time.

From Piaget to Vygotsky, from Aristotle to Foucault, there are myriad theories to support each of these two major perspectives: a more mechanistic, individualist framework or a more contextual, socially constructed framework. Rather than choosing one to displace the other, I believe that *both* an individualistic worldview and a socioconstructivist worldview can inform educational practice, much as both Eastern and Western views of health inform medical practice. As time passes, these views are likely to become more closely integrated. Already in many instances, originally individualistic ideas, such as personal relevance, fit snugly into a socioconstructivist perspective. What a person finds relevant is often directly related to individual values, which are social constructions.

In general, both of these views can embrace intrinsic motivation and the tenets that human beings are curious and active, make meaning from experience, and desire to be effective at what they value (McCombs and Whisler, 1997). Because promoting learning among all adults is most possible through culturally responsive teaching based on intrinsic motivation, the motivational strategies documented from either of these perspectives are considerable assets to instructors of adults. Motivational strategies are deliberate instructor actions that enhance a person's motivation to learn. *The strategy contributes to stimulating or creating a motivational condition: a mental/ emotional state of being* in which the learner is desirous of information, knowledge, insight, and skill. For example, an intriguing question (strategy) might provoke curiosity (motivational condition); or a relevant example (strategy) might elicit interest (motivational condition) in a person. It is the interest and curiosity—the motivational conditions—that energize the individual's learning and foster engagement in such learning processes as reflection and dialogue.

What is most important to create, then, is a framework that combines essential motivational conditions in a way that is intrinsically motivating for diverse adults in formal learning situations. The strategies from an individualistic or socioconstructivist perspective can then be assigned and understood according to the condition to which they most obviously contribute. Let's begin by discussing the essential conditions; we will then describe the framework and conclude by applying that framework to an actual instructional situation. The descriptions of the specific strategies that contribute to creating each of the essential motivational conditions will follow in the chapters ahead.

Numerous social science theories and their related research have shown at least four motivational conditions to be substantially enhancing of adult motivation to learn—inclusion, attitude, meaning, and competence.

How Inclusion Fosters Involvement

Inclusion is the awareness of learners that they are part of an environment in which they and their instructor are *respected by and connected to one another.* Social climate creates a sense of inclusion. Ideally, learners realize that they can consider different, possibly opposing, perspectives as part of their learning experience. At the same time, there is a mutually accepted, common culture within the learning group and some degree of harmony or community. The atmosphere encourages learners to feel safe, capable, and accepted.

Respect is not a well-developed concept in psychology. Mentioned but seldom defined, *respect* rarely appears in the indexes of most psychology textbooks. Nonetheless, its importance to human beings is irrefutable. As we discussed in Chapter Two, to be free of undue threat and to have our perspective matter in issues of social exchange are critical to our well-being and learning. Unless learners know that they can express their true selves without fear of threat or humiliation, they will not be forthcoming with their perceptions of their own reality. In such circumstances, an instructor does not find out learners' understanding of the world or their true ideas. If there is no meaningful dialogue and if no relevant action is possible, learners become less motivated, as well they should.

Connectedness in a learning group is perceived as a sense of belonging for each individual and an awareness that each one cares for others and is cared for. There is a shared understanding among group members that they will support each other's well-being. In such an environment, people feel trust and an emotional bond with at least a few others; because of this, there exists a spirit of tolerance and loyalty that allows for a measure of uncertainty and dissent. When the attribute of connectedness is joined with respect, it creates a climate in a learning group that invites adults to access their experience, to reflect, to engage in dialogue, and to allow their histories to give meaning to particular academic or professional knowledge—all of which enhance motivation to learn.

Telling and hearing our stories is essential to human nature. It is the way we make sense of things. It is compelling. With a sense of inclusion, most adults can publicly bring their narratives to their learning experiences. They can personalize knowledge—use their own language, metaphors, experiences, or history to make sense of what they are learning (Belenky, Clinchy, Goldberger, and Tarule, 1986). They can be involved knowledge builders rather than alienated knowledge resisters. When learners are encouraged by the learning atmosphere to use their own social and cultural consciousness, they can construct the cognitive connections that make knowledge relevant and under their personal control (Vygotsky, 1978).

Aside from research (Poplin and Weeres, 1992) and our common sense, which tell us that learners who feel alienated achieve less than those who do not, consider your own experience of being a minority. On those rare occasions when I have been, even when it's not a matter of ethnicity but when I simply have a different point of view, I remember my own struggle to make myself heard and understood as I wanted to be understood. My anxiety was usually palpable. I also remember those occasions when the instructor created an atmosphere that allowed my differences to be respectfully heard. I spoke more easily, learned more, and was certainly more open to learning more. Unless we are the ones discounted, we are often unaware of how motivationally debilitating feeling excluded can be to adults. Ask any group of adults about their motivation in a course where they felt excluded. The answers are searing.

The foundation of any learning experience resides in the nature of the teacher and student relationships. On a moment-to-moment basis, probably nothing is quite as powerful. We are social beings, and our feelings of inclusion or exclusion are enduring and irrepressible.

How Attitudes Influence Behavior

In general, an *attitude* is a combination of concepts, information, and emotions that results in a predisposition to respond favorably or unfavorably toward particular people, groups, ideas, events, or objects (Johnson, 1980). For example, an accountant is required by her company to take an in-service training course. A colleague who has already taken the training tells her that the instructor is authoritarian and arrogant. The accountant finds herself a little anxious as she anticipates the new training. At her first training session, the instructor matter-of-factly discusses the course and its requirements. The accountant judges the instructor's neutral style to be cold and hostile. She now fears the instructor and resents the mandatory training. This accountant has combined information and emotions into a predisposition to respond unfavorably to a person and an event. If the accountant's colleague had told her the instructor was helpful and caring, it is less likely that the same outcome would have occurred.

Attitudes powerfully affect human behavior and learning because they help people make sense of their world and give cues as to what behavior will be most helpful in dealing with that world. If someone is going to be hostile toward us, it is in our best interest to be careful of that person. Attitudes help us feel safe around things that are initially unknown to us. Attitudes also help us anticipate and cope with recurrent events. They give us guidelines and allow us to make our actions more automatic, making life simpler and freeing us to cope with the more unique and stressful elements of daily living. In psychology, this is called the *least effort principle:* whenever possible, apply past solutions to present problems or, whenever possible, apply past reactions to present experiences. This kind of reacting not only helps us cope but also to be consistent in our behavior, which is a vital need for human beings.

Needs influence attitudes because they make certain goals more or less desirable. For example, if managers are taking a training seminar because they feel a need to improve relations with workers, they will more likely have a positive attitude toward the learning experience than those who believe their relations with employees are completely satisfactory. Also, whenever physical or safety needs are under threat, as in the case of hungry or exhausted students or workers facing an imminent layoff, adults are not usually in the mood for learning unless it will concretely and immediately resolve these concerns.

Although attitudes can be influenced by such situational factors as strong needs, drugs, or illness, they are, for the most part, learned.

They are acquired through such processes as experience, direct instruction, identification, and role behavior (teacher-student, parent-child, employer-employee, and so forth). Because attitudes are learned, they can also be modified and changed. New experiences constantly affect our attitudes, making them shift, intensify, weaken, or reverse. They are part of a dynamic process in which people, the media, and life in general constantly impinge on them. Attitudes can be personally helpful, as in the case of a positive expectancy for success, or they can be personally harmful, as in the case of an intense fear of failure. Attitudes are with us all the time, and they constantly influence our behavior and learning.

Attitudes are of great importance in understanding adult development because they predispose one's choices of activities, companions, and environments across the life span. Strongly related to adult attitudes and adaptation are *change events*, events in people's lives that affect their cognitive representations of themselves and others (Costa and McCrae, 1989). These change events alter previous goals, attitudes, and behaviors, transforming the quality of adult life. Education introduces many change events as people adjust to new ideas, challenging courses, and the consequences of acquired degrees and related career shifts.

New learning is usually risky business; the outcome is seldom a certainty. For adults, this risk may be even higher because the new learning is required for a job, a promotion, or some important personal goal. In unpredictable situations, people's attitudes are very active, because they help people feel more secure. As an instructor of adults, you can be quite assured that students' attitudes will be an active influence on their motivation to learn from the moment instruction begins. Adult learners will immediately make judgments about you, the particular subject, the learning situation, and their personal expectancy for success. However, beyond knowing that their attitudes are a constant influence on learners' motivation and learning, it is difficult to make broad generalizations about the attitudes of adults with respect to learning in general.

Hayes and Darkenwald (1990) found that women and people with a higher level of initial education show a more positive attitude toward adult education than do men and the less formally educated. However, we need to keep in mind that many less traditionally educated adults are marginalized learners for reasons of race, ethnicity, or class. They may distrust "education" because of having encountered difficulties in their earlier education, brought about in part by being denied their own interests, history, and ways of knowing. Because so many adults have had previous negative experiences with formal education, two of the most important criteria for developing a positive attitude among *all* learners are *relevance* and *choice*. Irrelevant learning can startle, annoy, or frighten us. We not only find such learning unimportant or strange but also implicitly know we are doing it because of someone else's domination or control. This knowledge triggers or develops a negative attitude. If we had some degree of choice in the learning situation, we might alter its irrelevant aspects to better accommodate our perspectives and values.

Personal relevance is not simply familiarity with learning based on the learners' prior experience. Because of media saturation, people could be familiar with a particular television program or magazine yet find it totally irrelevant. People perceive personal relevance when their learning is contextualized in their personal and cultural meanings, allows their voice to remain intact, and reflects their construction of reality. In other words, the learning is connected to who they are, what they care about, and how they perceive and know. In this process, the instructor and learners figuratively become coauthors, taking neither their own view nor the view of the other to be specially privileged but entering into a genuine dialogue, with each standpoint having its own integrity (Clifford, 1986).

When learners can act from their most vital selves, their curiosity emerges. They want to make sense of things and seek out challenges that are in their range of capacities and values. This leads to what human beings experience as interest, the emotional nutrient for a continuing positive attitude toward learning. When we feel interested, we have to make choices about what to do to follow that interest. Such choosing or self-determination involves a sense of feeling free in doing what one has chosen to do (Deci and Ryan, 1991). For the process of learning—thinking, practicing, reading, revising, studying, and other similar activities—to be desirable and genuinely enjoyable, adults must see themselves as personally endorsing their own learning. Global history and social science merge to support this observation: people consistently struggle against oppressive control and strive to determine their own lives as an expression of their deepest beliefs and values. Learning is no exception.

How Meaning Sustains Involvement

According to Mezirow (1997, p. 5), "a defining condition of being human is that we have to understand the meaning of our experience." Making, understanding, and changing meaning are fundamental aspects of adult development that continuously take place in a sociocultural context (Gilligan, 1982; Tennant and Pogson, 1995). But what is meaning from a motivational perspective? In relationship to learning, what is the meaning of meaning itself?

There are a number of ways to unravel this concept. One way to understand meaning is to see it as an increase in the complexity of an experience or idea that relates to people's values or purposes. This meaning may be beyond articulation, as in the realm of the creative or spiritual. Emotion, art, and spirituality are essential to human experience and have incontestable meaning that is often inaccessible in words. For example, as I grow older, the meaning of friendship increases in conceptual complexity (different types of friendship) as well as in emotional and spiritual impressions I cannot easily describe in words.

Deep meaning implies that the experience or idea increasing in complexity is connected to an important goal or ultimate purpose, such as family survival or the meaning of life. As the philosopher Susanne Langer (1942) has posited, there is a human need to find significance. Across many cultures, achieving purpose appears fundamental to a satisfying life (Csikszentmihalyi and Csikszentmihalyi, 1988). When we assist learners in the realization of what is truly important in their world, they access more passionate feelings and can be absorbed in learning. Emotions both give meaning and influence behavior. If, for example, learners become troubled as they discover that certain tax laws create economic inequities, the complexity of their understanding has increased, and they may now find their agitation propelling them toward further reading about tax legislation. In general, however, because many adults prefer to avoid distress, more positive emotions, such as wonder and joy, are often more likely to deepen interest and nurture involvement.

Another way to understand meaning is to conceive of it as the ordering of information that gives identity and clarity, as when we say that the word *castle* means a large fortified residence or when we recognize our telephone number in a listing. This kind of meaning embraces facts, procedures, and behaviors that contribute to our awareness of how things relate or operate or are defined but do so in a way that doesn't deeply touch our psyche. In the words of Whitehead (1979), this is "inert knowledge." A good deal of foundational and professional knowledge is inert knowledge. It easily becomes boring. By recasting this knowledge in a context of goals, concerns, and problems relevant to adults, we can infuse it with deeper meaning. There are also motivational strategies that enhance the meaning of initially irrelevant information by stimulating learners' curiosity and insight. We will discuss these at length in Chapter Six.

Adults can feel included and have a positive attitude toward learning, but their involvement will diminish if they do not find learning meaningful. By making their goals, interests, and perspectives the context of learning, we create a system that evokes meaning and involvement in learning. A challenging learning experience in an engaging format about a relevant topic is intrinsically motivating because it increases the range of conscious connections to those interests, applications, and purposes that are important to learners. The enhancement of meaning is at the core of learning and motivation because human beings by their very nature need to maintain an ordered state of consciousness (Csikszentmihalyi, 1997), a harmony within themselves and with others.

How Competence Builds Confidence

Competence theory (White, 1959) assumes people naturally strive for effective interactions with their world. We are genetically programmed to explore, perceive, think about, manipulate, and change our surroundings to promote an effective interaction with our environment. Practicing newly developing skills and mastering challenging tasks engender positive emotions, *feelings of efficacy* that are evident even in early infancy. Researchers have demonstrated that babies as young as eight weeks old can learn particular responses to manipulate their environment. In one such study (Watson and Ramey, 1972), infants were placed in cribs with a mobile above their heads. By turning their heads to the right, they activated an electrical apparatus in their pillows, causing the mobile to move. These children not only learned to "move" the mobile but also displayed more positive emotions (smiling, cooing) than did the infants for whom the mobile's movement was controlled by the experimenter.

This innate disposition to be competent is so strong that we will risk danger and pain to accomplish a more able relationship with our environment. Consider the one-year-old who continually falls attempting to walk and, while still crying from a recent tumble, strives to get up and go at it again. Or the adult who, on gaining proficiency at one level of skiing, swimming, climbing, or running, "naturally" moves on to the next level, often putting body or being in jeopardy. The history of the human race is a continuous, colorful catalogue of bold scientists and adventurers who have relentlessly reached out to explore their world. We humans are active creatures who want to have a part in shaping the course of our lives.

As adults, we most frequently view competence as the desire to be *effective at what we value*. Our socialization and culture largely determine what we think is worth accomplishing (Deci and Ryan, 1991). As we move from childhood to adulthood, our feeling competent more and more involves social input. Parents and teachers and schools and jobs, the unavoidable stuff of growing up, increasingly replace independent play and toys.

Because awareness of competence is such a powerful influence on human behavior, adults who are learning and can feel an actual sense of progress are usually well motivated to continue their efforts in a similar direction. Because adults enter educational programs with a strong need to apply what they have learned to the real world, they are continually attentive to how effectively they are learning. They know their families, jobs, and communities will be the arenas in which they test this new learning. Therefore, they are more motivated when the circumstances under which they assess their competence are *authentic* to their actual lives.

In formal learning situations, adults feel competent when they know they have attained a specified degree of knowledge or a level of performance that is acceptable by personal standards, social standards, or both. This sense of competence usually comes when adults have had a chance to apply or practice what they are learning. When they have evidence (through feedback) of how well they are learning and can make internal statements, such as "I really understand this" or "I am doing this proficiently," adults experience feelings of efficacy and intrinsic motivation because they are competently performing an activity that leads to a valued goal. This experience of effectiveness affirms their innate need to relate adequately to their environment.

The process and the goal are reciprocal—one gives meaning to the other. If someone wants to learn how to use a computer because it is a valued skill, that awareness of how valuable computer skills are will evoke his motivation as he makes progress in learning computer skills. However, the gained competence, the progress itself, will increase the value of the goal, making computer skills more valuable; the person could eventually enter a career that was before unimaginable (perhaps prompting that common existential question, How did I get here?).

When people know with some degree of certainty that they are adept at what they are learning, they feel confident. This confidence comes from knowing that they have *intentionally* become proficient. Their self-confidence emanates from such internal statements as, "I know this well," or, "I will be able to do this again."

The relationship between competence and self-confidence is mutually enhancing. Competence allows a person to become more confident, which provides emotional support for an effort to learn new skills and knowledge. Competent achievement of this new learning further buttresses confidence, which again supports and motivates more extensive learning. This can result in a spiraling dynamic of competence and confidence growing in continued support of each other. To feel assured that one's talents and effort can lead to new learning and achievement is a powerful and lasting motivational resource. It is also the mark of a true expert or champion in any field. Instructors can help adults learn to be confident by establishing conditions that engender competence. It is a wonderful gift.

Organizing the Essential Motivational Conditions: The Motivational Framework for Culturally Responsive Teaching

We have seen how important and complex the relationship of motivation and culture is to adult learning. Instructors need a model of teaching and learning that respects the inseparability of motivation and culture. The Motivational Framework for Culturally Responsive Teaching provides this understanding (Wlodkowski and Ginsberg, 1995). It dynamically combines the essential motivational conditions that are intrinsically motivating for diverse adults (see Figure 3.1). It provides a structure for planning and applying a rich array of motivational strategies. Each of its major conditions is supported by numerous theories and by related research that documents that condition's powerful influence on learner motivation.

The Motivational Framework for Culturally Responsive Teaching is respectful of different cultures and capable of creating a com-

Figure 3.1. The Motivational Framework for Culturally Responsive Teaching.

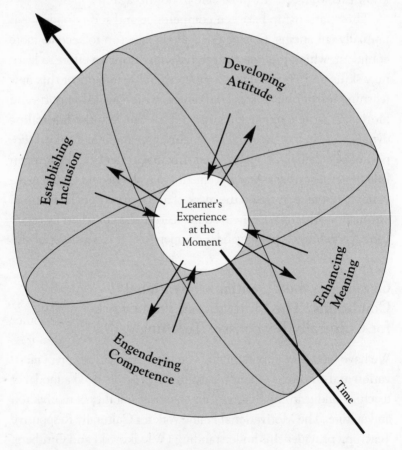

Source: Wlodkowski and Ginsberg, 1995, p. 29.

mon culture that all learners in the learning situation can accept. It is a holistic and systemic representation of four intersecting motivational conditions that teachers and learners can create or enhance. The essential conditions are as follows:

1. *Establishing inclusion:* creating a learning atmosphere in which learners and teachers feel respected and connected to one another

2. *Developing attitude:* creating a favorable disposition toward the learning experience through personal relevance and choice

3. *Enhancing meaning:* creating challenging, thoughtful learning experiences that include learners' perspectives and values

4. *Engendering competence:* creating an understanding that learners are effective in learning something they value

People experience motivational influences polyrhythmically—that is, as a simultaneous integration of intersecting realities on both conscious and subconscious levels. You meet a friend you have not seen for many years. As you embrace your friend, many emotions rush through you—joy, sorrow, love, perhaps regret. In that moment, your perceptions of your friend intersect with a history of past events recalled in your mind. A number of feelings arise from this dynamic network. How many of them affect you at this or any given moment? No one really knows.

From Buddha to Bateson, scholars and thinkers have understood life and learning to be *multidetermined.* As we have discussed earlier, researchers increasingly view cognition as a social activity that integrates the mind, the body, the process of the activity, and the ingredients of the setting in a complex interactive manner (Lave, 1988). Meeting your friend alone in an airport might be a very different emotional experience from meeting this same person in her home with her family present. Scholars in the field of situated cognition understand human beings to frequently act without deliberation; our perception and action arise together, each coconstructing the other (Bredo, 1994). *Much of the time we compose our lives in the moment.*

The conventional psychological model—perceiving, thinking, acting—describes a linear process that may occur far less often than earlier theorists have imagined. Understanding how the social and historical can be so vital to a person's thinking and learning helps us realize why dialogue and reflection may not be enough to change adult attitudes and behavior, why we need to remain humble as we attempt to unravel the mystery of adult learning, and why we need to do motivational planning. Because the four motivational conditions work in concert and exert their influence on adult learning in the moment as well as over time, instructors would be wise to plan how to establish and coordinate these conditions when possible.

Motivational planning can be integrated with instructional planning, or it can be used in addition to instructional planning. Motivational planning helps us avoid a serious pitfall common to teaching: blaming the learners for being unresponsive to instruction. With no motivational plan to analyze for possible solutions to motivational difficulties that arise during instruction, especially with adults who are culturally different from ourselves, we are more likely to place responsibility for this state of affairs on them. It is difficult for us to be openly self-critical. Defense mechanisms like rationalization and projection act to protect our egos. Motivational planning helps us keep our attention on the learning climate and on how we instruct and what we can do about that instruction when it is not as vital as we would like it to be. This focus diminishes our tendency to blame, which is a common reaction to problems that seem unsolvable.

Applying the Motivational Framework for Culturally Responsive Teaching

Let us take a look at the Motivational Framework for Culturally Responsive Teaching in terms of the teaching-learning process. Because most instructional plans have specific learning objectives, they tend to be linear and prescriptive: instructors sequence learn-ing events over time and predetermine the order in which concepts and skills are taught and when they are practiced and applied. Although human motivation does not always follow an orderly path, we can plan ways to evoke it throughout a learning sequence. In fact, because of motivation's emotional base and natural in-stability, we need to painstakingly plan the milieu and learning ac-tivities to enhance adult motivation, especially when we face a time-limited learning period. For projects, self-directed learning, and situational learning (as in the case of problem posing), we may not be so bound to a formal plan.

The most basic way to begin is to transform the four motiva-tional conditions from the framework into questions to use as guide-lines for selecting motivational strategies and related learning activities to include in the design of your instructional plan:

1. *Establishing inclusion:* How do we create or affirm a learning atmosphere in which we feel respected by and connected to one another? (Best to plan for the *beginning* of the lesson.)

2. *Developing attitude:* How do we create or affirm a favorable disposition toward learning through personal relevance and choice? (Best to plan for the *beginning* of the lesson.)

3. *Enhancing meaning:* How do we create engaging and challeng-ing learning experiences that include learners' perspectives and values? (Best to plan *throughout* the lesson.)

4. *Engendering competence:* How do we create or affirm an under-standing that learners have effectively learned something they value and perceive as authentic to their real world? (Best to plan for the *ending* of the lesson.)

Let us look at an actual episode of teaching in which the instruc-tor uses the motivational framework and these questions to compose an instructional plan. In this example, the teacher is conducting the first two-hour session of an introductory course in research. The class takes place on Saturday morning. There are twenty adult learners ranging in age from twenty-five to fifty-five. Most hold full-time jobs. Most are women. Most are first-generation college students. A few are students of color. The instructor knows from previous experience that many of these students view research as abstract, irrelevant, and oppressive learning. Her instructional objective is as follows: *students will devise an in-class investigation and develop their own positive perspectives toward active research*. Using the four motivational conditions and their related questions, the instructor creates the sequence of learning activities found in Exhibit 3.1.

Let's look at the narrative for this teaching episode. The teacher explains that much research is conducted collaboratively. The course will model this approach as well. For a beginning activity, she randomly assigns learners to small groups and encourages them to discuss any previous experiences they may have had doing research and their expectations and concerns for the course (*strategy: collaborative learning*). Each group then shares its experiences, expectations, and concerns as the teacher records them on the overhead. In this manner, she is able to understand her students' perspectives and to increase their connection to one another and herself (*motivational condition: establishing inclusion*).

The teacher explains that most people are researchers much of the time. She asks the students what they would like to research among themselves (*strategy: relevant learning goal*). After a lively discussion, the class decides to investigate and predict the amount of sleep some members of the class had the previous night. This strategy engages adult choice, increases the relevance of the activity, and contributes to the emergence of a favorable disposition toward the course (*motivational condition: developing attitude*). The students are learning in a way that includes their experiences and perspectives.

Five students volunteer to serve as subjects, and the other students form research teams. Each team develops a set of observations and a set of questions to ask the volunteers, but no one may ask

Exhibit 3.1. An Instructional Plan Based on the Four Questions from the Motivational Framework for Culturally Responsive Teaching.

Motivational Condition and Question	Motivational Strategy	Learning Activity
Establishing inclusion: How do we create or affirm a learning atmosphere in which we feel respected by and connected to one another? (Beginning)	Collaborative learning	Randomly form small groups in which learners exchange concerns, experiences, and expectations they have about research. List them.
Developing attitude: How do we create or affirm a favorable disposition toward learning through personal relevance and choice? (Beginning)	Relevant learning goals	Ask learners to choose something they want to research among themselves.
Enhancing meaning: How do we create engaging and challenging learning experiences that include learner perspectives and values? (Throughout)	Critical questioning and predicting	Form research teams to devise a set of questions to ask in order to make predictions. Record questions and predictions.
Engendering competence: How do we create or affirm an understanding that learners have effectively learned something they value and perceive as authentic to their real world? (Ending)	Self-assessment	After the predictions have been verified, ask learners to create their own statements about what they learned about research from this process.

them how many hours of sleep they had the night before. After they ask their questions, the teams rank the five volunteers in order of the amount of sleep each had, from the most to the least (*strategy: critical questioning and predicting*). When the volunteers reveal the amount of time they slept, the students discover that no research team was correct in ranking more than three volunteers. The students discuss why this outcome may have occurred and consider questions that might have increased their accuracy, such as, "How much coffee did you drink before you came to class?" The questioning, testing of ideas, and predicting heighten the engagement, challenge, and complexity of this learning for the students (*motivational condition: enhancing meaning*).

After the discussion, the teacher asks the students to write a series of statements about what this activity has taught them about research (*strategy: self-assessment*). Students then break into small groups to exchange their insights. Their comments include such statements as, "Research is more a method than an answer," and, "Thus far, I enjoy research more than I thought I would." Self-assessment helps the students extract from this experience a new understanding they value (*motivational condition: engendering competence*).

This snapshot of teaching illustrates how the four motivational conditions constantly influence and interact with one another. Without establishing inclusion (small groups to discuss concerns and experiences) and developing attitude (students choosing a relevant research goal), the enhancement of meaning (research teams devising questions and predictions) might not occur with equal ease and energy, and the self-assessment to engender competence (what students learned from their perspective) might have a dismal outcome. Overall, the total learning experience encourages equitable participation, provides the beginning of an inclusive history for the students, and enhances their learning about research.

In this class session, the strategies and their related activities work together holistically as well as systemically. Removing any one of the four strategies and the motivational condition it evokes would likely affect the entire experience. For example, would the students' attitude be as positive if the teacher arbitrarily gave them the task of researching sleep among themselves? Probably not, and this mistake would likely decrease the research teams' efforts to devise questions.

One of the values of the Motivational Framework for Culturally Responsive Teaching is that it is not only a model of motivation in action but also an organizational aid for designing instruction. By continually attending to the four motivational conditions and their related questions, the instructor can select motivational strategies from a wide array of theories and literature to apply throughout a learning unit. The teacher translates these strategies into a set of sequenced learning activities that continuously evoke adult motivation (as well as teach).

Exhibit 3.1 is an example of a fully planned class session in which the learning activities are derived from and aligned with motivational strategies. To use this framework, *pedagogical alignment*—the coordination of approaches to teaching that ensures maximum consistent effect—is critical. The more harmonious the elements of the instructional design, the more likely they are to sustain intrinsic motivation. That's why one strategy—cooperative learning or self-assessment, for example—is alone unlikely to evoke intrinsic motivation. It is the mutual influence of a combination of strategies based on the motivational conditions that elicits intrinsic motivation.

As Exhibit 3.1 shows, there are four sequenced motivational strategies, each based on one of the four motivational conditions. Each strategy has been translated into a learning activity. The Motivational Framework for Culturally Responsive Teaching allows for as many strategies as the instructor believes are needed to complete an instructional plan. The instructor's knowledge of the learners' motivation and culture, the subject matter, the setting, the technology available, and the time constraints will determine the nature of and quantity of the motivational strategies. This framework provides a holistic design that includes a time orientation, a cultural perspective, and a logical method of fostering intrinsic motivation from the beginning to the end of an instructional unit.

For projects and extended learning sessions, such as problem solving or self-directed learning, the sequence of strategies may not include all four motivational conditions. For example, inclusion and attitude often have been established earlier through previous work, advising, or prerequisite classes. These conditions may need less cultivation, and the conditions of meaning and competence may be most important to foster. Chapter Eight specifically deals with how to compose motivating lessons and uses four extensive case examples to illustrate effective instructional designs.

The Motivational Framework for Culturally Responsive Teaching is the foundation for a pedagogy that crosses disciplines and cultures to respectfully engage *all* learners. It reflects the value of human motivation and the principle that motivation is inseparable from culture. The framework is a means to create compelling learning experiences in which adults can maintain their integrity as they attain relevant educational success.

Each of the next four chapters focuses on an essential motivational condition and its specific motivational strategies, including examples of related learning activities. These strategies are realistic teaching methods. Your understanding of these strategies and how to use them can significantly increase the creativity, skill, and impact of your motivational planning. That the strategies primarily stress what *you* can do does not mean that adult learners bear no responsibility for their own motivation or are dependent on you for feeling motivated while learning. The purpose of this book is to respectfully evoke, support, and enhance the motivation to learn that all adults possess by virtue of their own humanity and to make you a valuable resource and vital partner in their realization of a motivating learning experience.

4

Establishing Inclusion
Among Adult Learners

*When a system of oppression has become institutional-
ized it is unnecessary for individuals to be oppressive.*
                                            Florynce Kennedy

When we are teaching, exclusion is usually an indirect act, an omission of opportunity or of someone's voice. We're usually not mean-spirited but, more likely, unaware that a perspective is missing, that a biased myth has been perpetuated, or that we aren't covering topics of concern to certain adults. In fact, most adult learners, usually those who have been socialized to accommodate our method of instruction, may like our course or training. Things seem pretty pleasant. Why go looking for trouble?

We need to be mindful about our instruction because, as Adrienne Rich (1984) has so eloquently said, "there is no way of measuring the damage to a society when a whole texture of humanity is kept from realizing its own power." When it comes to the perspective of this book, I believe that enabling people to realize their own power relates to our obligation to create an equitable opportunity to be motivated to learn as well as to have the right to an equitable education. The two are inseparable. To begin, I believe we have to be vigilant about the patterns we see in our courses and training. Are some people left out? Do particular income groups or ethnic groups do less well than others? Who are the people whose motivation to learn is not emerging or seems diminished among the adults we teach or train? How might we be responsible for or contribute to these trends?

My experience is that teaching or training begins with relationships, respectful relationships. For most adults, the first sense of the quality of the teacher-student relationship will be a feeling, sometimes quite vague, of inclusion or exclusion. Upon awareness of exclusion, adult learners will begin to lose their enthusiasm and motivation. If you'd like to appreciate this tendency by working directly with adults themselves, try the exercise called Marginality and Mattering (Frederick, 1997). Ask adults to remember a moment in the recent past (a week to a month) when they felt marginal, excluded, or discounted—"the only one like me in a group, not understood or, perhaps, unaccepted." Ask them to reflect on this and then to pair off and discuss the following questions: How did you know? How did you feel? How did you behave? Then ask them to remember a moment when they felt that they mattered, were included, or were regarded as important to a group. Ask the adults to reflect on this and then to pair off again to discuss the questions, How did you know? How did you feel? How did you behave? Ask the adults to reflect on both situations and to discuss the patterns of thinking, feeling, and behaving that emerged, the influence of those patterns on their motivation and enthusiasm, and how the changes in motivation and enthusiasm might relate to learning and teaching. As this exercise will demonstrate, our motivation is constantly influenced by our acute awareness of the degree of our inclusion in a learning environment.

Feelings of cultural isolation often cause adult motivation to learn to deteriorate. In a course or training seminar, a sense of community with which all learners can identify establishes the foundation for inclusion. Our challenge as instructors is to create a successful learning environment for all learners that (1) respects different cultures and (2) maintains a common culture that all learners can accept. We are fortunate, because adults are community-forming beings. Our capacity to create social coherence is always there (Gardner, 1990). We need community to find security, identity, shared values, and people who care about us and about whom we care. As more and more adults sandwich their education between work and family, adult education settings provide critical opportunities to experience community and a sense of belonging. But mere contact with those different from us does little to enhance intercultural appreciation. Mutual respect and appreciation evolve from the nature of our contact. The norms we set as instructors and the strategies we use to teach will largely determine the quality of social exchange among our learners. Those norms should be supportive of equity, collaboration, and the expression of each learner's perspective (Wlodkowski and Ginsberg, 1995). It simply makes sense to set a tone in which learners can come together in friendly, caring, and respectful ways.

The strategies that follow contribute to establishing a *climate of respect*. In this atmosphere, intrinsic motivation is more likely to emerge because learners can voice the things that matter to them. Their well-being is more assured. They can begin to develop trust. Relevant learning is possible. These strategies also enable learners to *feel connected* to one another. This feeling of connection draws forth learners' motivation because their social needs are met. Feeling included, people are more free to risk the mistakes true learning involves as well as to share their resources and strengths. Before we discuss these strategies, we need to look at the dimensions of cultural variation often critical to effective intercultural communication. Your understanding of these important dimensions should increase your capacity to sensitively apply the strategies to establish inclusion. To describe these dimensions, I have summarized an essay by Peter Andersen (1997, pp. 244–256).

Understanding Dimensions of Cultural Variation

As we enter the third millennium, contact between people from various cultures is increasing. International migration is at an all-time high. International trade increased 400 percent between 1965 and 1995 (Brown, Kane, and Roodman, 1994). The amount of intercultural contact in today's world is unprecedented, making the study of intercultural communication more important than ever.

Two of the most fundamental nonverbal differences in intercultural communication involve space and time. Time frames of cultures may differ so dramatically that if only these differences existed, intercultural misunderstandings could still be considerable. In general, time tends to be viewed in the United States as a commodity that can be wasted, spent, saved, managed, and used wisely. Many cultures have no such concept of time. In many traditional cultures and in many cultures in developing countries, time moves to the rhythms of nature, the day, the seasons, the year. Human inventions like seconds, minutes, and hours may have no real meaning.

Research has documented that cultures differ substantially in their use of personal space, the distances they maintain, and their regard for territory (Burgoon, Buller, and Woodall, 1989). Considerable intercultural differences have been reported in people's *kinesic* behavior, including their facial expressions, body movements, gestures, and conversational regulators. Stories abound in the intercultural literature of gestures that signal endearment or warmth in one culture but are obscene or insulting in another. Differences in kinesic behavior come into play in a learning environment; they can determine how one gets the floor in conversation, shows deference or respect, indicates agreement or disagreement and approval or disapproval. For the teacher, these norms of participation may seem obvious and their derivation from European American norms of conduct unimportant, but to a learner from another culture, such expectations may be alienating or exhausting (because of the relentless anxiety of determining how to behave appropriately), especially if learners are directly called on to recite and are graded for oral participation in class.

Along with genetics, culture is the most enduring, powerful, and invisible shaper of our communication behavior. Initial research has shown that cultures can be located along dimensions that help explain intercultural differences in communication. Most of the adult learners we work with will probably not be international students; however, they will often have ethnic backgrounds and histories of immigration that make the dimensions discussed in the sections that follow quite informative about their differences in communication and nonverbal behavior.

Immediacy, Expressiveness, and Contact Cultures

Immediacy behaviors are actions that simultaneously communicate warmth, closeness, and availability for communication and approach rather than avoidance (Hecht, Andersen, and Ribeau, 1989). Examples of immediacy behaviors are smiling, touching, making eye contact, being at closer distances, and using more vocal animation. Some scholars have labeled these behaviors *expressive* (Patterson, 1983). Cultures that display considerable interpersonal closeness or immediacy have been labeled *contact cultures,* because people in these cultures stand closer and touch more (Hall, 1996). People in *low-contact cultures* tend to stand apart and touch less.

It is interesting that contact cultures are generally located in warmer countries, low-contact cultures in cooler climates. Considerable research has shown that high-contact (more expressive and immediate) cultures are found in most Arab countries, the Mediterranean region, the Middle East, Eastern Europe, Russia, and virtually all of Latin America (Jones, 1994). Low-contact (less expressive and immediate) cultures are found in most of Northern Europe and virtually every Asian country; white Anglo-Saxons (whose culture is the primary culture of the United States) and traditional American Indians also have low-contact cultures. These findings are painted with a fairly broad brush; they will become more detailed as we review the other dimensions of cultural variation.

Individualism and Collectivism

One of the most fundamental dimensions along which cultures differ is their degree of individualism as opposed to collectivism. The main cultures of Europe, Australia, and North America north of the

Rio Grande tend to be individualistic. The main cultures of Latin America, Africa, Asia, and the Pacific Islands tend to be collectivist. Individualists are oriented toward achieving personal goals, by themselves, for purposes of pleasure, autonomy, and self-fulfillment (Triandis, 1995). Collectivists are oriented toward achieving group goals, by the group, for the purposes of group well-being, relationships, togetherness, and the common good.

The United States is considered the most individualistic country on earth (Hofstede, 1982). As Bellah and his associates (1985, p. 142) have written, "Anything that would violate our right to think for ourselves, judge for ourselves, make our own decisions, live our lives as we see fit, is not only morally wrong, it is sacrilegious." Many people in the United States find it difficult to relate to a culture in which interdependence may be the basis of a sense of self. Although individualism has been argued to be the backbone of democracy, it has also been considered to be largely responsible for problems of crime, alienation, loneliness, and narcissism in U.S. society.

Different ethnic groups in the United States vary along the dimensions of individualism and collectivism. For example, most African Americans tend to be individualistic, whereas most Mexican Americans place greater emphasis on group and relational solidarity (Hecht, Andersen, and Ribeau, 1989).

The degree to which a culture is individualistic or collectivistic affects adult communication and nonverbal behavior. People from individualistic cultures are more remote and distant proximally. People from collectivist cultures tend to work, play, live, and sleep in closer proximity to one another. Lustig and Koester (1993, p. 147) maintain that "people from individualistic cultures are more likely than those from collectivist cultures to use confrontational strategies when dealing with interpersonal problems; those with a collectivist orientation are likely to use avoidance, third party intermediaries, or other face saving techniques." People in collectivist cultures may suppress both positive and negative emotional displays that are contrary to the mood of the group, because maintaining the group is a primary value. Individualistic cultures encourage people to express emotions because individual freedom is a paramount value. In the United States, flirting, small talk, smiling, and initial acquaintance are more important than in collectivist countries, where the social network is more fixed and less reliant on individual initiative.

Gender

The gender orientation of a culture has a major impact on role and communication behavior, including the types of expressions permitted by each sex, occupational status, the ability to interact with strangers or acquaintances of the opposite sex, and all aspects of interpersonal relationship between men and women. *As conceptualized here, rigidity refers to the rigidity of gender rules.* In rigid cultures, masculine traits are typically such attributes as strength, assertiveness, competitiveness, and ambitiousness, whereas feminine traits are such attributes as affection, compassion, nurturance, and emotionality (Hofstede, 1982). In less rigid cultures, both men and women can express more diverse, less stereotyped sex-role behaviors.

Considerable research suggests that androgynous (both feminine and masculine) patterns of behavior result in more social competence, success, and intellectual development for both men and women (Andersen, 1988). Nonverbal styles through which both men and women are free to express both masculine traits (such as dominance and anger) and feminine traits (such as warmth and emotionality) are likely to be healthier and more effective for lowering stress (Buck, 1984).

Power Distance

The fourth fundamental dimension of intercultural communication is power distance. Power distance, the degree to which power, prestige, and wealth are unequally distributed in a culture, has been measured in a number of cultures using the Power Distance Index

(PDI), developed by Hofstede (1982). In cultures with high PDI scores, power and influence are concentrated in the hands of a few rather than more equally distributed throughout the population. Most African, Asian, and Latin American countries have high PDI scores. The United States is slightly lower than the median in power distance. Cultures differ in terms of how status is acquired. In many countries, such as India, class or caste determines one's status. In the United States, power and status are typically determined by money and conspicuous material displays (Andersen and Bowman, 1990).

Cultures with high power distance will foster and encourage emotions that present status differences: for example, in high power distance cultures, people are usually expected to show only positive emotions to high-status others. The continuous smiles of many Asians are a culturally inculcated effort to appease superiors and to smooth social relations that are appropriate to a culture with a high PDI. As students, many Asians are expected to be modest and deferential in the presence of their instructors. Vocal cues are also affected. A loud voice in a high-PDI culture may be offensive to higher-status members.

Uncertainty

For the purposes of this discussion, uncertainty is a cultural predisposition to value risk and ambiguity (Hecht, Andersen, and Ribeau, 1989). People with intolerance of ambiguity or with high levels of uncertainty avoidance want clear, black-and-white answers. Disagreement and nonconformity are not appreciated. Emotional displays are usually tolerated less in countries with high levels of uncertainty avoidance. Cultures with tolerance of ambiguity and with low levels of uncertainty avoidance are more tolerant, accept ambiguous answers, and see many shades of gray. In general, the higher uncertainty avoidance is among people, the greater their fear of failure and the lower their risk taking in academic situations.

The majority culture of the United States is low in uncertainty avoidance. When people from the United States communicate with people from a country like Japan or France (both high in uncertainty avoidance), the people from the United States may seem excessively nonconforming and unconventional, whereas their Japanese and French counterparts may seem too controlled and rigid (Lustig and Koester, 1993).

High and Low Context

The last dimension of intercultural communication we will discuss is that of context. A high-context (HC) communication is a message in which most of the information is either in the physical context or internalized in the person. Very little is in the coded, explicit part of the message (Hall, 1976). Lifelong friends often use HC messages that are nearly impossible for an outsider to understand. A gesture, a smile, or a glance provides meaning that doesn't need to be articulated. Low-context (LC) messages are just the opposite. Most of the information is in explicit code and must be elaborated and highly specific, like a legal brief. Very little of the communication is taken for granted.

The lowest-context cultures are found in Switzerland, Germany, Canada, and the United States. Placing a high value on Aristotelian logic, these cultures are highly verbal and preoccupied with specifics and details. The highest-context cultures are found in Asia (notably China), Japan, and Korea (Hall, 1984). Strongly influenced by Zen Buddhism, these cultures place a high value on silence, on less emotional expression, and on unspoken, nonverbal parts of communication. American Indian cultures with migratory roots in East Asia are like these cultures in their use of HC communication.

Communication is quite different in HC and LC cultures, and frequently one culture will misattribute the causes for the behavior of the other group. People from LC cultures are often perceived as excessively talkative, belaboring the obvious, and redundant. People from HC cultures may be perceived as secretive, sneaky, and mysterious. The people from HC cultures are particularly affected by contextual cues. Facial expressions, tensions, movements, speed of interaction, location of interaction, and other "subtleties" are likely to be perceived and may have meaning for people from HC cultures that people from LC cultures may remain unaware of.

In addition to these dimensions of cultural variation is the issue of language and dialect. We frequently use our own language as a normative reference; that is, we may consider "standard English," for example, as *the* language rather than *a* language. Thus, as instructors, we may see adults who speak a different version of English as "language deficient." Instead of asking ourselves, How do we respectfully teach these students in the area of standard English where necessary? we may see the learners as impaired. This view can lower our expectations for these adults, leading to their lower motivation and learning, a well-documented self-fulfilling prophecy (Good and Brophy, 1994).

Perhaps, like me, you realize how daunting it is to understand someone from another culture. You may also be joyful about the number of possible ways there are to be human. I benefit (not without anxiety) from knowing that my teaching is shaded by a persona that is more rigidly masculine than I like, fairly expressive with a median PDI, tolerant of ambiguity, low context, and leaning leftward toward collectivism. This self-analysis makes me more mindful of the dimensions of cultural variance and gives me a better chance to provide instruction compatible with the norms and values of learners from other cultures. By being conscious of these tendencies, I believe I'm less likely to impose them on others as expected norms. Continuing to learn and understand these dimensions of cultural variation helps me select educational practices that accommodate the communication styles of those adults whose socialization has been different from my own. The following discussion of the motivational strategies will take into consideration these dimensions of cultural understanding.

Engendering an Awareness and Feeling of Connection Among Adults

As discussed in Chapter Two, the core characteristics of empathy and cultural responsiveness will significantly influence the degree to which we engender a feeling of connection among adults. Raising an awareness of what we have in common and instilling a sense of mutual care are essential. A good place to begin preparing ourselves is to consider the learners we expect to be teaching and our own *positionality* in the group—that is, the cultural group identities we have that may influence our own outlook as well as how these learners will look upon us (Johnson-Bailey and Cervero, 1997). These identities are usually the more visible dimensions of race, gender, age, and physical ability or disability, but they also include ethnicity, class, and sexual orientation as well as some of the cultural variations discussed in the preceding sections.

For example, when I teach an extension course, I need to realize that being a male, middle-class, European American academic gives me a certain perspective that may be quite different from that of the African American, working-class women who are some of the students in my course. I probably have very different experiences regarding such issues as health, education, safety, and economic security. If I merely follow personal opinions and familiar routines, I may give an advantage to one group of students over another in the topics I choose, in the time or opportunity students have to speak, and in the feedback I give. Indeed, for certain groups of students, I may not have the "expertise" in matters of personal psychology and social relations I think I have. Yet if I think only of these sorts of things or that I must know every detail, I can feel overwhelmed and immobilized. I want also to hold in my mind the large strands of life that I and all my students hold in common: the mutual desire for good health, education, and security; the emotions of sorrow, joy, and love; the experiences of family, death, birth, and illness; and the reason we all came together—to learn. That desire, my awareness of difference and common ground, and the knowledge that I can flex and plan make me realistically enthusiastic. And I know where I can begin. I like to start with introductions. (Please note that I have numbered the strategies throughout this book for organizational purposes, not to indicate an order of preference or a particular sequence to follow. The selection of each strategy you use will depend on your philosophy, situation, and goals.)

STRATEGY 1: *Allow for introductions.*

Introduce yourself. This is definitely for the first meeting of the group and seems quite obvious, but it is amazing how many instructors fail to extend this common courtesy. Say a few things about who you are, where you're from, why you're conducting the course or training session, and by all means, welcome the group. This really shouldn't take more than a couple of minutes. It is also a good idea to give the learners a chance to introduce themselves as well. This emphasizes their importance and your interest in them as people. It also helps people start to learn each other's names (name tents are a valuable supplement to this strategy) and significantly reduces the tension so often present at the beginning of most courses and training sessions. Scores of articles (Johnson and Johnson, 1996) have been written describing different exercises for helping people get acquainted in new social situations. My particular favorite among such devices is multidimensional sharing, the next strategy I describe.

STRATEGY 2: *Provide an opportunity for multidimensional sharing.*

Opportunities for multidimensional sharing differ from many icebreakers. They tend to be less game-like and intrusive. For adults from backgrounds that value modesty, introductory activities that require self-disclosure or the sharing of deeper emotions may seem contrived and psychologically invasive. I remember being in a teaching workshop where a well-meaning trainer asked us as part of the introductory activity to "share about one person who loves us." Rather than encourage connection, this request tended to stall the development of mutual care among us.

Opportunities for multidimensional sharing are those occasions, from introductory exercises to personal anecdotes to classroom celebrations, when people have a better chance to see one another as complete, evolving human beings who have mutual needs, emotions, and experiences (Wlodkowski and Ginsberg, 1995). These opportunities give a human face to a course or training, break down biases and stereotypes, and provide experiences in which we see ourselves in another person's world.

There are many ways to provide opportunities for multidimensional sharing, depending on the history, makeup, and purpose of the group. Informal ways include potluck meals, recreational activities, drinks after class, and picnics. For introductory activities, anything that gets people to relax and to laugh together or helps them learn each other's names deserves our serious attention. Here are two introductory activities I have often used.

Learners usually need some time to think before they begin this activity, which can be a small- or large-group process. Each person introduces himself or herself and recommends (1) one thing he has read (such as an article, story, or book) *or* (2) one thing he has seen (such as a TV program, film, or real-life experience) *or* (3) one thing he has heard (such as a speech, musical recording, or song) that has had a strong and positive influence on him. Each person concludes by stating the reasons for recommending his choice.

The second activity, which I learned from Margery Ginsberg, is called Decades and Diversity. People in the group divide themselves into smaller groups according to the decade in which they would have or did graduate from high school (the fifties, sixties, seventies, and so on). Each smaller group brainstorms a list of items in three to five areas of experience at that time: popular music, clothing styles, major historical events, weekend social opportunities (What did you usually do on a Saturday night?), and standards (What was considered significant immoral behavior for you as an adolescent—a no-no in the eyes of your family?). Then each group reports on its list. The activity concludes with a discussion by the members of the entire group about their insights, the possible meanings of the lists, and the process they engaged in. The powerful influence of age and its accompanying time of socialization consistently emerges as part of the groups' perceptions.

These activities are most inclusive and motivating when they validate the experiences of the adults involved and establish a sense of affiliation with you and other learners. The more natural and appropriate such opportunities feel, the more likely a genuine sense of community can evolve.

STRATEGY 3: *Concretely indicate your cooperative intentions to help adults learn.*

Almost everyone who has something to learn from somebody is vulnerable to a nagging fear—what if I really try, and I can't learn it? Adults commonly experience this fear, because so much of what they must learn will directly influence their job performance or family relations. For instructors to let learners know at the outset that there is a concrete means of assistance available will help learners reduce their fear and save face. Be it announcing our availability during office hours or at breaks in a workshop, arranging tutorial assistance by appointment, or creating a device whereby learners who are having difficulty can use special materials or aids—essentially, our message is, "As instructor and learner, we are partners in solving your learning problems. I want to help you, and it's OK to seek help." We are telling the learners that their vulnerability will be safeguarded and that they will have a nonjudgmental and interested response to their requests for assistance (Johnson, 1980). With this strategy, we offer immediate evidence that we do care about the people who learn with us.

STRATEGY 4: *Share something of value with your adult learners.*

The next time you go to hear a professional speaker, whether it is at a banquet or a conference, check to see how much time elapses before that person tells a joke or a humorous anecdote. It will probably be less than three minutes, and it will happen about four out of every five times. Professional speakers know the value of *sharing humor*. It does far more than break the tension between speaker and audience. It says, if you can laugh with me, you can listen to me. You can identify with me. You can see I am a human being and that I have emotions too. All sharing has this potential—to break down images and to allow the learner to experience our common humanity without self-consciousness. Humor is a very efficient means to this end. It also tells the learner that there are at least times when we do not take ourselves too seriously, that we have some perspective on life, and that the way we teach will allow for the vitality of laughter in the learning process.

Another type of effective sharing is to relate a *credible intense experience*. This may be some trouble we have had on the job, a difficult learning experience, a crisis within our family, an unexpected surprise, an accident—something that tells the learners that we have mutual concerns and a shared reality. This form of sharing should relate to the topic at hand, or it will seem forced. I sometimes tell about problems I have had with apathetic learners. I know most of my audience has had similar problems, and this gives me a chance to share what I have learned from these dilemmas. This type of sharing has also taught me how much of this process is a two-way street. Seeing the concerned faces in the audience increases my identification with them as well.

Sharing *your involvement with the subject matter*—problems, discoveries, research, or new learning—is a way to show your enthusiasm as well as your humanity. Adults are interested in seeing how their investment in the subject matter will pay off for them. When we share our involvement with the topic at hand, we model this potential for them and reveal something about our real selves as well.

Another powerful, ongoing form of sharing is to give adult learners *our individual attention*. When we do, we are committing one of our most valuable assets as instructors to our learners—our time. Being available to learners before, during, and after class directly tells them we care about them. Also, one-to-one contact creates a more personal and spontaneous situation.

In general, sharing *something about our real selves*, when done tactfully and appropriately, gives adult learners a chance to see us beyond the image of an instructor. Most people are a bit surprised when they see their instructors in common settings like supermarkets, shopping centers, and theaters. Part of this surprise is due to novelty, but part is also due to how dramatically set apart most learning environments seem from the real world. By wisely self-disclosing our reactions to common experiences—television shows, sporting events, travel, maybe even a little trouble we've had with life along the way—we give adult learners a chance to identify positively with us and become more receptive to our instruction (Jourard, 1964).

STRATEGY 5: *Use collaborative and cooperative learning.*

Although there are a wide variety of *collaborative learning methods*, most emphasize the learners' exploration and interpretation of course material to an equal or greater extent than they do the instructor's explication of it. When everyone participates, working as partners or in small groups, questions and challenges to create something energize group activity. Instructors who use collaborative procedures tend to think of themselves less as singular transmitters of knowledge and more as colearners.

Among the many collaborative learning possibilities, *cooperative learning* represents the most carefully organized and researched approach. More than one-third of all studies comparing cooperative, competitive, and individualistic learning have been conducted with college and adult learners. David Johnson and Roger Johnson (1995) have found in an analysis of 120 of these investigations that cooperative learning significantly promotes greater individual achievement than do competitive or individualistic efforts. When adults learn cooperatively, they tend to develop supportive relationships across different ethnic, language, social class, and gender groups. Cooperative learning groups create a setting in which learners can

Construct and extend understanding of what is being learned through explanation and discussion of multiple perspectives.

Use the shared mental models learned in flexible ways to solve problems jointly.

Receive interpersonal feedback as to how well they are performing procedures.

Receive social support and encouragement to take risks in increasing their competencies.

Be held accountable by peers to practice and learn procedures and skills.

Acquire new attitudes.

Establish a shared identity with other group members.

Find effective peers to emulate.

Discover a "voice" to validate their own learning (Rendon, 1994).

As its practitioners strenuously emphasize, cooperative learning is more than merely placing learners in groups and telling them to work together (Johnson, Johnson, and Smith, 1991). Positive interdependence and individual accountability are fundamental components of effective cooperative learning. Groups lacking either of these two features are properly identified as engaged in a form of collaborative learning, not cooperative learning. To organize lessons so learners do work cooperatively requires an understanding of five components—positive interdependence, individual accountability, promotive interaction, social skills, and group processing—and their rigorous implementation in the group and in the lesson. It is also of paramount importance that a significant amount of cooperative learning take place within the learning environment to permit monitoring by the instructor and to allow groups to initially establish themselves while they can receive needed support.

1. *Positive interdependence.* When learners perceive that they are linked with groupmates in such a way that they cannot succeed unless their groupmates do (and vice versa) and that they must coordinate their efforts with the efforts of their partners to complete a task (Johnson, Johnson, and Smith, 1991), they are positively interdependent. They sink or swim together. Each group member has a unique contribution to make to the group because of his resources, role, or responsibilities. For example, in the popular *jigsaw procedure*, a reading assignment is divided among the group, with each member responsible for comprehending a separate part and explaining or teaching that part to all other members of the group until the entire group has a coherent understanding of the total reading assignment. The following three approaches are additional ways to create positive interdependence in a cooperative learning group.

Positive goal interdependence: the group is united around a common goal, a concrete reason for being. It could be to create a single product, report, or answer, or it could be general improvement on a task so that all members do better this week than they did last week. Outcomes might include a skill demonstration, a media product, an evaluation summary, a problem solution, an action plan, or just about anything that leads to greater learning and that the group members can produce and hold each other responsible for.

Positive resource interdependence: each group member has only a portion of the resources, information, or materials necessary for the task to be accomplished, and the members have to combine resources in order for the group to achieve its goals. The metaphor for this approach is a puzzle, and each group member has a unique and necessary piece to contribute to the puzzle's solution. For example, for an upcoming exam, each member of a group might be responsible for a different study question; when the group convenes, members share their knowledge of the question and check to make sure all groupmates have satisfactorily comprehended this knowledge.

Positive role interdependence: each member of the group selects a particular role that is complementary, interconnected, and essential to the roles of the other group members. Suppose, for example, that the learning goal is the development of some form of skill, such as interviewing. One group member is the person practicing the skill (the interviewer), another person is the recipient of the skill (the interviewee), and a third person is the observer-evaluator. In this manner, each person has an essential contribution to make in terms of either skill practice or feedback. Roles can easily be rotated as well.

In all cooperative learning groups, it is extremely important that the learners are very clear about the assignment, goal, and role involved. Especially with diverse groups of learners, checking for this kind of understanding can make the difference between a satisfying or a confusing learning experience. Positive interdependence works best when all group members understand that each person has a part to do, that all members are counting on each other, and that all members want to help each other do better.

2. *Individual accountability.* This is present when the learning of each individual in the learning group is assessed, the results are shared with the learner, and the learner is responsible to groupmates for contributing a fair share to the group's success. One of the main purposes of cooperative learning is to support each member as a vital, competent individual in his or her own right. Individual accountability is the key to ensuring that all group members are strengthened by learning cooperatively and that they have a good chance to effectively transfer what they have learned to situations in which they may be without a group support.

Some texts emphasize individual accountability as a means to prevent *hitchhiking*, the situation in which a learner contributes little of worth to the total success of a group's learning experience and overly benefits from the contributions of other group members. My experience is that this seldom occurs when cooperative norms are well in place and competitive assessment or grading procedures are eliminated. A powerful extrinsic reward denied to most members of a group will undermine cooperation and encourage individuals to seek the greatest amount of external gain for the least amount of effort. They do not count playing time in the championship game when they hand out those Super Bowl rings: every team member receives one.

Specific ways to enhance individual accountability include the following:

- Keep the size of the groups small. Keep the role of each learner distinct. Typical size is two to four members.

- Assess learners individually as well as collectively.

- Observe groups while they are working.

- Randomly request individuals to present what they are learning, either to you or another group.

- Request periodic self-assessments and outlines of responsibilities from individual group members.

- Randomly or systematically ask learners to teach some-one else or you what they have learned.

A simple and positive way to support individual accountability and prevent related conflict among group members is to brainstorm answers to the question, How would we like to find out if someone in our cooperative learning group thought we were not doing enough to contribute to the benefit of the total group? What are some acceptable ways of letting us know? Then write the possible actions on the chalkboard and discuss them. Such a procedure can go a long way to avoid unnecessary suspicion or shame.

3. *Promotive interaction.* When members of cooperative groups encourage and assist each other with information and emotional support and also deliberate to reach relevant goals, they are engaged in promotive interaction. Mutual care should permeate this inter-action: as it does, for example, when someone in a cooperative writ-ing group hears a fellow member read her own words and offers sincere and helpful suggestions to improve the manuscript. This sort of interaction allows different perspectives and commitments to take hold.

4. *Social skills.* Cooperative work depends on communication that enables group members to reach goals, get to know and trust each other, communicate accurately, accept and support each other, and resolve conflicts constructively (Johnson, Johnson, and Smith, 1991). Even though adults want to cooperate, they may not be able to do so effectively if they lack conventional social skills.

My experience with diverse adults is that when the norms of col-laboration and "no blame" are discussed and made explicit, they cre-ate (along with *ground rules,* discussed later in this chapter) a learning climate that significantly reduces aggressive conflict. There is then far less need for direct training in conventional interpersonal skills, such as *active listening,* which often feel contrived and alien to many people, especially those who do not identify with the dominant culture. It is appropriate for an instructor to intervene in a group, when necessary, to suggest more effective procedures for working together. Yet instructors should not intervene any more than is necessary. I often find that if everyone exercises a little patience, cooperative groups work their way through their own problems and construct not only timely solutions but also methods for solving similar problems in the future. Sometimes, simply asking group members to set aside their task, describe the problem as they see it, and come up with a few solutions and then a decision as to which one to try first is enough to get things moving along satisfactorily.

5. *Group processing.* Cooperative learning benefits from group processing—that is, members' reflecting on their group experience to describe actions that were helpful and unhelpful and to make decisions about what actions to continue or change. When groups with the same members continue over longer periods of time (more than a few hours) or are significantly diverse, discussing group functioning is essential (Adams and Marchesani, 1992). Adults need time to have a dialogue about the quality of their cooperation, to reflect on their interactions, and to learn from how they work together. This *processing time* gives learners a chance to receive feedback on their participation, understand how their actions can be more effective and cohesive, plan for more helpful and skillful interaction for the next group session, and celebrate mutual success. As instructors, we need to allow enough time in the learning environment for this activity to take place and to provide some basic structure for it—for example, by suggesting the group discuss a few things it is doing well and one thing it could improve.

In general, heterogeneous groups tend to work well. Unless projects or special reasons prevail, regularly remixing groups at the beginning of new activities often has a revitalizing affect and makes working with different people a course norm. However, practical reasons may sometimes override the benefits of heterogeneity. Students' interest in a specific topic, accessibility for meetings outside of class, very limited skills, or language acquisition issues might predicate more homogeneous groups. For projects or activities with significant assessment consequences (for example, if they represent a large proportion of a course grade), I usually accept individual completion as an option. I do this to respect the more individualistic or absolutist orientations among class members. In addition, for some activities, I find that letting students form their own groups (ranging from two to four members) allows smaller groups and a greater comfort level for those adults less at ease with cooperative learning.

Once cooperative learning groups start working, our role as the instructor is that of colearner, observer, adviser, and consultant. Without being obtrusive, we should watch cooperative groups, especially as they *begin* their tasks. Sometimes we can see that certain groups will need clarification or guidance. Otherwise we remain available, always keeping in mind that it is the learners themselves who are the major resources for support and assistance to one another.

Exhibit 4.1, an outline for planning cooperative learning activities, is an adaptation of the Cooperative Lesson Planning Guide from *Active Learning* (Johnson, Johnson, and Smith, 1991).

Many different types of groups can be structured as cooperative learning groups. The following is a list of possibilities.

- *Special interest groups:* groups organized according to categories of participants' interests for the purposes of sharing information and experiences and of exploring common concerns.

- *Problem-solving groups:* groups organized to develop solutions to substantive problems of any nature.

Exhibit 4.1. Cooperative Lesson Planning Guide.

Step 1: Select an activity and desired outcome(s).

Step 2: Make decisions.

    a. Group size: _____

    b. Assignment to groups: _____

    c. Room arrangement: _____

    d. Materials needed for each group: _____

    e. Roles: _____

Step 3: State the activity in language your students understand.

    a. Task: _____

    b. Positive interdependence: _____

    c. Individual accountability: _____

    d. Criteria for success: _____

    e. Specific behaviors to encourage: _____

Step 4: Monitor.

    a. Evidence of cooperative and encouraged behaviors: _____

    b. Task assistance needed: _____

Step 5: Evaluate outcomes.

    a. Task achievement: _____

    b. Group functioning: _____

    c. Notes on individuals: _____

    d. Feedback to give: _____

    e. Suggestions for next time: _____

    _____

    _____

Source: Adapted from Johnson, Johnson, and Smith, 1991, pp. 4:35–36.

- *Planning groups:* groups organized to develop plans for activities, such as field trips, guest speakers, resource use, and the like.

- *Instructional groups:* groups organized to receive specialized instruction in areas of knowledge or skill. The instructional task cannot be taught in a large-group setting, such as in a science laboratory, human relations seminar, or machine operation training course.

- *Investigation or inquiry groups:* groups organized to search out information and report their findings to the entire learning group.

- *Evaluation groups:* groups organized for the purpose of evaluating learning activities, learner behavior, or any issue that requires feedback or decision making on the part of the learning group or instructor.

- *Skill practice groups:* groups organized for the purpose of practicing any set of specified skills.

- *Tutoring or consultative groups:* groups organized for the purpose of tutoring, consulting, or giving assistance to members of other groups.

- *Operational groups:* groups organized for the purpose of taking responsibility for the operations of activities important to the learning group, such as room arrangements, refreshments, preparation of materials, operation of equipment, and the like.

- *Learning-instruction groups:* groups that take responsibility for learning all they can about a particular content unit and instructing themselves, the rest of the learning group, or both.

- *Simulation groups:* groups organized to conduct an inter-group exercise to increase knowledge or build skills, such as role playing, a game, or a case study review.

- *Learning achievement groups:* groups organized to produce a learning product that develops the members' knowledge, skills, or creativity.

- *Cooperative base groups:* cooperative learning groups that remain together for the duration of a course, have a stable membership, and foster individual accountability as they provide support, encouragement, and assistance in completing course responsibilities (Johnson, Johnson, and Smith, 1991).

- *Learning communities:* a form of block scheduling that enables college students to take more than one course together to give them an opportunity to work as a study team over a period of a semester or longer (Tinto, 1998).

Considering the length of this section on cooperative learning, you might infer that I think competitive and individualistic learning should be abandoned in adult education and training. On the contrary, I like competitive activities *when my peers and I can freely choose to participate or not to participate.* I fondly remember those movies of the fifties in which the Step Brothers or Fred Astaire and Gene Kelly would engage in a friendly rivalry of dancing, each person topping the other only to see the other person dance to an even more fantastic choreography. That's what good competition is about: choosing to elevate others and oneself to a higher plane of performance, whether it is in dancing, basketball, debate, or making wine—knowing you need each other because achieving your very best vitally depends on someone else accomplishing his or her very best.

Also, for less consequential learning, for drill practice, and for enjoyment, when the stakes are not very high (the most you can win is a round of applause), individual and intergroup competition can be quite effective. For any learning task where students' individual differences and abilities are significant, as in math or writing, an individualized approach may be more helpful to some learners. Also, there are occasions when cooperative learning can take too much time to structure and operate. What matters most is that cooperation is the norm for learning, that we are a community of learners who care about the learning of our peers as we do about our own learning. The more intellectually and socially connected we feel, the more we will persist to learn (Tinto, 1998).

Life's most important goals demand cooperation. The nurturing of our children, the quest for peace, the safeguarding of the environment, and the daily press for a stable economy all rely on mutual goodwill. Whether or not these aspirations are ever met relates profoundly to the way we learn.

STRATEGY 6: *Clearly identify the learning objectives and goals for instruction.*

As soon as adults know the objectives of an instructional unit, they begin to form a personal theory about the choices and competencies necessary for accomplishing those tasks. They ask themselves such questions as, Where do I begin? Am I able to do this? What do the other people in this course seem to know about these objectives? These reflections influence their attitude as well as their sense of inclusion. Academically, the objectives have a unifying force. These goals set the purpose for which the learners are there and show them, at the very least, what they presently hold in common, no matter their background. Objectives provide the mutual bond for learning and are why cooperation makes sense. Learners can more clearly understand and discuss their expectations. For nonnative speakers of English, clear objectives are even more critical.

Entire books have been written about how to construct learning objectives. I understand them to have at least three possible forms: clearly defined goals, problem-solving goals, and expressive outcomes.

1. *Clearly defined goals.* When specific objectives, skills, or competencies are appropriate and meaningful, especially in technical areas such as medicine and engineering, clearly defined goals can heighten learners' sense of control and capability. These goals let learners know what skills they need to acquire and inform them about what is necessary to achieve those skills. The three essential elements (Caffarella, 1994) for constructing a learning objective are *who* (the learners), *how* (the action verb), and *what* (the contents): for example, "As a result of this workshop, participants [the learners] will create [the action verb] a résumé containing their professional achievements [the contents]." Adults studying to be medical technicians are likely to appreciate knowing that they (the learners) are going to take (the action verb) blood samples indicating blood type and Rh factor (the contents). Performance or product learning goals are often more clear when demonstrated with examples, models, or films: a dance routine, a graphic design, or an experimental procedure—whatever it takes so that confusion does not detract from learners' expectation to succeed.

Dick and Carey (1990) suggest two more elements of specific learning objectives: conditions under which the learning is to be demonstrated and the criteria for acceptable performance. Examples of given conditions are

With the following problem . . .

Using this software . . .

When a patient declines assistance . . .

Some examples of criteria for acceptable performance are

... with 80 percent correct

... with three or fewer errors

... with completion in thirty minutes

2. *Problem-solving goals*. Much of what we aspire to and cherish as human beings is not amenable to uniform and specific description. How could one convincingly define integrity or describe how water tastes? As Eisner (1985, p. 115) states, "To expect all of our educational aspirations to be either verbally describable or measurable is to expect too little."

The problem-solving goal differs in a significant way from the conventional instructional objective (Schön, 1987). In working on a problem-solving goal, the learners formulate or are given a problem to solve. *Although the goal is clear (solve the problem), the learning is not definite or known beforehand.* For example, in a social science course, learners might be asked how to reduce crime in a particular area, or in a design seminar, learners might be asked to create a paper structure that will hold two bricks sixteen inches above a table. In both situations, there is a range of possible solutions and learning. Problem-solving goals place a premium on intellectual exploration and the higher mental processes while supporting different cultural perspectives and values. Students' alternative solutions offer explicit evidence of the benefit of diverse talents and viewpoints. Relevant and genuine problems are most likely to elicit learner motivation.

3. *Expressive outcomes*. Another type of educational goal identified by Eisner (1985) focuses on expressive outcomes, learning objectives that emerge as the result of an intentionally planned activity. In these instances, learning goals do not precede an educational activity; they occur in the process of the activity itself. They are what we and the learners construct after some form of

engagement. How many times have we read a book, seen a film, or had a conversation with learners the resonance of which affords so many questions and inspirations that to limit learners to our own educational intention is a confinement of imagination? Encouraging expressive outcomes allows us to share reciprocally with learners various media or experiences derived from our own lives, such as critical incidents (Brookfield, 1995). Afterwards, through dialogue, we can mutually decide what direction learning should take.

Problem-solving goals and expressive outcomes support the preeminence of adult self-determination and perspective in defining relevant learning goals. These forms of establishing a learning purpose are an excellent means to initiate transformative learning (Mezirow, 1997) and critical teaching (Freire, 1970). They more readily allow knowledge to be examined and constructed rather than prescribed. I once began a course in adolescent psychology by watching with the class a few excellent films in which adolescents were the main characters. After this viewing and through the compelling dialogue that evolved, we constructed the course topics, reading list, and projects to facilitate learning. The resulting course proved so powerfully informative that it was expanded the next semester to include two seniors from the local high school as coteachers.

STRATEGY 7: *Emphasize the human purpose of what is being learned and its relationship to the learners' personal lives and contemporary situations.*

Adults will feel a part of something that is relevant to them. They will want to belong to a group because it meets their personal needs. Finding a human purpose in what they are learning that is connected to their real world gives them something to care deeply about and to work in common to achieve. This purpose has the potential to be a shared vision, one that inspires cohesion, participation, and action.

This strategy is based on the assumption that *anything* that is taught somehow bears a relationship to a human need, feeling, or interest. Otherwise why else would we instruct or train for it? For us as instructors the question is, What are the human ramifications of what we are helping learners know or do? Once we have an answer to this question, the relevance of what we instruct will be clearer, and we can think of ideas to make this meaning part of the learning process. Whether we are teaching people how to wire a circuit, how to speak a foreign language, or how to write a complete sentence, there are human purposes that these skills and knowledge serve. If we can understand these qualities, especially as they may relate to the daily lives of our learners, we have some guidance in selecting those social aspects of the learning experience we may wish to emphasize.

Giving a human or social perspective to a learning experience infuses it with value beyond the technical requirements of the task and changes it from an expendable, isolated activity into a potentially valued source of personal satisfaction for the learner (Kitayama and Markus, 1994): for example, "We are not just studying how to use a new telecommunications system; we are learning a dynamically more effective and efficient way to communicate that benefits ourselves and our clients." If this viewpoint is sincerely portrayed by the instructor and embraced by the learner, the instructional activity has acquired a transcendent meaning. In plain words, this makes learning special. In fact, the structure of the previous quotation can be used to help glean the human ramifications for any specific learning objective: "We are not just studying [a specific topic or skill]; we are learning [human purpose]."

When human beings are in any way the topic of study, do their morals, values, decisions, problems, feelings, and behavior bear a relationship to similar qualities in our learners? If so, it may be worth the time to ask our learners to deal with these aspects of human existence through reflection, discussion, writing, or any other learning process. When our topics are in the realm of the physical and natural sciences, such as biology, chemistry, physics, and geology, showing how this knowledge relates to understanding challenges faced by humanity or how it can make life more sane and peaceful for everyone bonds learners in common cause. For skills from math to medicine, using human problems and concerns to illustrate and practice these useful tools can stimulate teamwork as well as emotional responsiveness in learners (Wilkerson and Gijselaers, 1996). In the technological fields, such as computer programming and database management, accentuating the contributions these processes make to human endeavors can diffuse their mechanistic isolation and humanize the learning process.

In the previous examples, we discussed emphasizing the human dimension of what is being learned so that learners can more easily identify with the topic at hand. Probably more emotionally relevant is any learning situation in which what is being learned has an immediate relationship to the *personal daily lives of adults* (Freire, 1970). If an instructor is conducting a seminar on alcoholism as a community problem, what are the implications of this information for the communities of those adults present and, more important, for their own families? In a similar vein, when an instructor is demonstrating a sales technique, why not demonstrate it with the type of client most often encountered by those sales personnel who are learning the technique? Consider a basic education instructor teaching the difference between a circle and a square. This may seem a highly abstract concept, but if, as a point of discussion, the instructor asks the learners to think of important circles and squares in their own lives, something abstract instantly becomes relevant. The closer we bring our topics and skills to the personal lives of our learners in the here and now, the more available their emotional involvement and sense of common purpose will be.

Creating a Climate of Respect Among Adults

Across most cultures, to be respected in a group means, at the minimum, that you have the freedom to express your own integrity without fear of threat or blame and that you know your opinion matters. When mutual respect is present in a learning environment, adults normally feel safe, capable, accepted, and able to influence the situation when appropriate or necessary. Among people with good intentions, misunderstanding is probably the most common enemy of respect. The first recommended strategy helps all members of a learning group avoid misapprehending their situation at the most vulnerable time in their tenure, the beginning.

STRATEGY 8: *Assess learners' current expectations and needs and their previous experience as it relates to your course or training.*

Although we may already have conducted a needs assessment of the learners, they may still have perspectives they haven't voiced or important interim experiences of which we are not aware. I vividly remember conducting a workshop on motivation for a group of teachers a few years ago. I did not know they were going to strike that same afternoon. Needless to say, things weren't going very splendidly, and I hadn't a clue why. Until I asked the participants what was going on, my enthusiastic self-admonition, "Carpe diem!" made no difference.

We can confirm or alter our prior expectations or assessments with information gathered face-to-face during the opening segment of the learning experience. We can do this as part of the introductions; we can simply say, "When you are introducing yourself, please include your expectations for the course." Asking learners to fill out a short questionnaire or to answer a few questions placed on the overhead projector is also a possibility. Giving learners the chance to describe areas of worry or concern can often provide insight into the perspectives and issues they may hold regarding the course or training.

For learning experiences during which there is likely to be controversy, we may want to provide a private way for learners to convey their expectations and needs. Maurianne Adams (Adams, Bell, and Griffin, 1997, p. 317), who teaches courses in social justice, offers a good example of this approach:

> At the end of the first class, I give students time to write to me, telling me whatever they want me to know about themselves, such as their background or preparation for the class, their goals for themselves in this class, any worries they may have about the class, or any physical or other disabilities they want me to know about so I can adjust assignments and activities. These are confidential. Then during the semester, I ask them to write again, telling me how they are doing, what they are struggling with, what questions or problems they have, what aspects of my teaching they find helpful, and what they wish I would change.

Adams's description emphasizes the importance of *checking in* with learners during a course or training. My experience has been that the more diverse the group, the more important it is to check in early and often to see how successfully the course and I are meeting expectations. For example, for a three-day workshop, I will check in every day no matter how well things seem to be going. When we are working with diverse learners, it is often easy to leave people out in terms of their goals and experiences without realizing it. Unless respectfully invited, people from cultures with high power distance usually are not forthcoming with this kind of information. Frequent checking in helps us adjust our instruction with minimum difficulty for learners and for us. My experience is that most adults see checking in as a caring and respectful thing to do.

STRATEGY 9: *Explicitly introduce important norms and participation guidelines.*

Every learning group is as unique as a fingerprint. It develops its own internal procedures, patterns of interaction, and limits. To some extent, it is as if imaginary lines guide and control the behavior of learners in a group. Norms are the group's common beliefs regarding appropriate behavior for its members (Johnson and Johnson, 1996). These *shared expectations* guide the perceptions, thinking, feeling, and behavior of group participants and help group interaction by specifying the kinds of responses that are expected and acceptable in particular situations. All learning groups have norms, set either formally or informally. For a group norm to influence members' behavior, members must recognize that it exists, be aware that other group members accept and follow the expectation, and feel some internal commitment to the norm.

Norms are the core constructs held in common that can ensure safety and build community among learners. Norms can create the kind of atmosphere that allows charged feelings and disagreements to be buffered as well as respectfully considered. The norms of collaboration, sharing the ownership of knowing, and a nonblameful view (see Chapter Two) are critical to fostering inclusion among diverse adult learners (Wlodkowski and Ginsberg, 1995). However, a norm can be confusing to people whose culture has not socialized them for it. People who are more oriented toward individualism, high power distance, or uncertainty avoidance may feel perplexed as well as distressed by the norms just mentioned. That's why these and all important norms should be made explicit. Knowing the boundaries in a group helps members immensely in guiding their behavior.

There are several ways to implement norms (and participation guidelines) in a group. One common method is simply to state them as the rules that govern the behavior of the group. Certainly, we want to offer a rationale for them and an opportunity for discussion, remaining flexible where appropriate. We can support norms through modeling. Our formal and informal behavior toward learners has a powerful effect on the norms of the learning group. Another method is to incorporate the institutional norms of group members into the learning group. This is a common method in business settings. Learners often assume that the norms that govern their behavior in a particular institution will transfer to learning events sponsored by that institution.

Norms can also be established through consensus. Learners might suggest which norms are needed or which need editing or specific discussion. The instructor can then lead the group through a decision-making process to gain the group's consent for acceptable recommendations. Two group skills extremely important for appropriately handling this process are conflict negotiation and consensual decision making (Johnson and Johnson, 1996). Generally, adults will more actively accept norms they have helped establish. Ownership gives them a sense of personal choice, an understanding that the norms reflect their values, and a better awareness of the need for their support to maintain the norms. Finally, the more clearly they see how a norm aids in the accomplishment of a salient goal to which they are committed, the more readily adults will accept and internalize the norm.

When course or training content is challenging and the learning process is experiential and interactive, adults appreciate *participation guidelines*. By clearly identifying the kinds of interactions and discussion that will be encouraged and discouraged, the instructor and learners create a climate of safety, ensuring that everyone will be respected.

The first meeting is an appropriate time to establish these guidelines and to request cooperation in implementing them. The following rules usually prove to be acceptable as well as extremely beneficial to establishing inclusion (Wlodkowski and Ginsberg, 1995; Griffin, 1997b):

- Listen carefully, especially to different perspectives.

- Keep personal information shared in the group confidential.

- Speak from your own experience, saying, for example, "I think . . . ," or, "In my experience I have found . . . ," rather than generalizing your experience to others by saying, for example, "People say . . . ," or, "We believe . . ."

- Do no blaming or scapegoating.

- Avoid generalizing about groups of people.

- Share airtime.

- Focus on your own learning.

I have found that instructors who use participation guidelines usually have a few that are nonnegotiable (Tatum, 1992). This makes sense because everyone is safer when we as instructors know what our professional limits are. Although the list is sometimes longer or shorter, most adults accept and generate these guidelines because these rules reduce feelings of fear, awkwardness, embarrassment, and shame. They also provide a safety net for critical discourse. Leaving participation guidelines open to further additions and referring to them when necessary keeps the boundaries of the learning environment clear and dynamic.

STRATEGY 10: *When issuing mandatory assignments or training requirements, give your rationale for these stipulations.*

Adults hate busywork. Many of them have had teachers who were simply authoritarian and handed out assignments without rhyme or reason. Because requirements demand time, energy, and responsibility, even the most motivated adult learner will feel cautious when the assignments are handed out. (Notice how quiet it gets!)

When we state the rationale for stipulations, learners will more likely know that we have carefully considered the matter; that we realize the obligations, benefits, and results of the requirements; and most important, that we respect learners and want to share this information. It is also no mean advantage to us that by revealing the rationale, we are more likely to ensure that learners won't misinterpret the motive or purpose of the assignment.

As in most matters of communication, difficult news is best received when it is delivered directly and concisely. Here are two examples. An instructor might say: "At the end of this unit, I will ask each of you to role-play a conflict management situation in a small-group setting. Each of you will be asked to resolve this problem by applying the suggestions for conflict management that are most relevant to a collectivist culture. This will give me the opportunity to give each of you guided practice and feedback so that you can refine your skills and have a chance to test this approach under simulated conditions." Or an instructor might say: "In addition to the readings in your textbook, I've assigned three outside articles and put them on reserve at the local library. I realize this may be somewhat of an inconvenience for you. However, each of these articles contains a case study that is far more realistic and comprehensive than any of those found in your text. These case studies will provide much better examples of the principles you are studying and give you a chance to explore the benefits of these theories in situations much closer to your own real-life experiences."

Even with the clearest rationale behind them, assignments are assignments, and usually no one applauds after they are given. This silence often simply reflects the realistic concern of adult learners who are accepting a new responsibility.

STRATEGY 11: *To the degree authentically possible, reflect the language, perspective, and attitudes of adult learners.*

Counselors call this practice *pacing and mirroring*. It is considered essential to establishing rapport with other people (Pedersen, 1994). In pacing and mirroring, the instructor matches the verbal and nonverbal behavior of adult learners—literally reflecting their speech, mannerisms, and perceptions. Specialists in intercultural communication refer to this process as *anticipatory communication* or *receiver centeredness*: the ability to capture and mirror the implicit meaning of other people, a sensitivity much valued by those from high-context cultures (Yum, 1997).

Friends mirror each other naturally. They "understand" each other, usually have something in common, and speak a similar language. Strangers striking up a relationship follow a similar pattern. They cast about for some common interest—the weather, sports, or current news. When they hit a common chord, they share perspectives that may lead to some shared viewpoint that further intensifies the relationship. Feeling connected with someone usually means finding mutual interests, values, and outlooks in that person. Friends who have not seen each other for a long time often talk about the "old days," using shared past experiences to renew their sense of rapport. People are sometimes accused of "talking shop" at parties, but this professional rapport is usually the true foundation for their relationship. It might be difficult for them to have a genuine conversation without referring to the workplace.

One of the easiest things we can do to gain the acceptance of adult learners is to fluently use their language and their perspective. People understand other people by their own definitions and their own attitudes. They not only have a difficult time understanding someone who speaks differently than they do but also have a more difficult time trusting that person. This is a universal, historical fact. Our assuming the language and perspective of our adult learners makes us more clearly understandable, more trustworthy, and more effective as models. This is why listening is so important. Until we really understand someone, it is difficult to accurately use his or her language. We are not talking down or up to anybody but being sensitively aware of the predicates, figures of speech, interests, and values that adult learners have in common with us. We use our awareness of these factors to construct a language and perspective that we use with integrity to communicate effectively. If a person uses the expression *bottom line* to mean "personal limit" and displays a very analytical approach to a political question, we are wise to use a similar expression and approach if we want to be well understood regarding the same political question. The goal is not to be a chameleon but to select wisely from among what we hold in common with learners and to be willing to learn new perspectives and expressions from them. This approach encourages the use of the voice of the learners and gives us access to the knowledge and realities both of their world and our own. When we approach communication this way, we create a language to transcend our own limits, moving us toward greater learning for all.

STRATEGY 12: *Introduce the concepts of comfort zones and learning edges to help learners accommodate more intense emotions during episodes of new learning.*

The concepts of comfort zones and learning edges can support adults as they struggle to understand and explore their reactions to challenging class activities and to other learners' perspectives (Griffin, 1997b). When we are dealing with topics or activities with which we are familiar, we usually feel comfortable and without serious tension or anxiety. This is learning *within our comfort zone*. When we are solidly in our comfort zone and not challenged, we are usually not learning anything very new. When we are dealing with unfamiliar topics and activities or seeing familiar topics in new ways, we are *outside our comfort zone* or on its edge. If we are too far outside our comfort zone, we usually try to withdraw or to strongly resist the new information or experiences; we keep ourselves safe.

When we are on the edge of our comfort zone, we are in a very good place to stretch our understanding, take in a different perspective, and expand our awareness. This is our *learning edge*. It is important to recognize our learning edge, because the time when we are on it is an optimum time for new learning but is often accompanied by feelings of annoyance, anxiety, surprise, confusion, defensiveness, and sometimes anger. These emotions frequently are signs that our way of seeing things is being challenged. As Griffin (1997b, p. 68) wisely cautions, "If we retreat to our comfort zone, by dismissing whatever we encounter that does not agree with our way of seeing the world, we lose an opportunity to expand our understanding. The challenge is to recognize when we are on a learning edge and then to stay there with the discomfort we are experiencing to see what we can learn."

Comfort zones and learning edges are important concepts for adults to acknowledge. We normally don't like to have our beliefs challenged, because they are the sources of stability in our lives. Some courses and training push the learning edge more than others. I have found that in those courses I teach that deal with diversity or social issues, offering learners a chance to become familiar with the concepts of comfort zones and learning edges gives them a language and a means of adjustment that offers real relief for some of their anxiety. Taking a couple of minutes to exchange stories with a partner about times he or she has been on a learning edge with new information or skills (especially those he or she is now glad of having) gives learners a chance to familiarize themselves with these concepts from their own experience. Usually the discussions are about things like sports, dancing, new relationships, social issues, and tough academic courses. It is also helpful to ask learners to identify the internal cues that alert them to their learning edge. Pounding hearts, dry mouths, and shaky stomachs are universal experiences accompanying the birth of important new learning.

STRATEGY 13: *Acknowledge different ways of knowing, different languages, and different levels of knowledge or skill to engender a safe learning environment.*

One of the myths perpetuated about adults is that if you're older you know more. This fiction doesn't account for all we have learned that was wrong, incorrect, unethical, or misleading. It also doesn't cover for what we have forgotten and confused, not to mention those vast stores of irrelevance attached to our dendrites. (Does anyone really care that I can name every movie Gilbert Roland played in?) We may certainly know more about some things, but we do have our limits. At best, aging and wisdom are dubious partners. Nonetheless, the myth is an intimidating one, and many adults feel uncomfortable when they realize they may know less than other participants in a course or training. Often it's more a case of knowing things differently or with a different language. In teaching about research, for example, with its buckets of jargon, I have found adults openly relieved to know *reliability* means something as straightforward as consistency.

To relax things a bit, we can acknowledge to learners that we would appreciate knowing when there's a different way they understand something or a different language they use. As an example, I often qualify research findings by noting they are a particular way of knowing something and, at best, they can only inform our experience. We can also ask how our experience can inform this research.

For many learning experiences, from child psychology classes to computer training, adults in attendance also may differ extensively from one another in their experience and knowledge, some people being novices and others having more experience than the instructor. After performing some form of assessment to understand these disparities and acknowledging that the disparities are OK, we need to find a way to move forward together. We may do this using special project work, grouping systems, cooperative learning, or panel discussions—whatever allows us to learn most effectively and remain a mutually respectful community.

As I close this chapter, it is probably a good time to say a few words about resistance in a learning group when it occurs in the beginning of a course or training. Resistance often comes up because the learning experience is required or because people believe they have been unfairly mandated to attend. The group feeling tends to be some version of "we don't need this" or "this is going to be a waste of time." In these circumstances, it is usually best to openly acknowledge the situation and the possible feelings that may be occurring in the group. If appropriate, we might pace and mirror the learners as we listen. Then we can plan or engage in learning that emphasizes immediate relevance and choice (discussed in Chapter Five) for them. These procedures have a good chance of moving the group forward.

The challenge of inclusion is to find ways to allow all adults to be respected as part of a learning community, without diminishing their spirit, their experience, their perspective, and their feeling. A mere strategy does not create such a milieu. Inclusion is the result of a determined living harmony, a constancy of practices blended with ideals from the beginning to the end of every lesson of every session of every course.

5

Helping Adults Develop
Positive Attitudes Toward Learning

*Exhortation is used more and accomplishes less than
almost any behavior-changing tool known.*

Robert F. Mager

W e all spend a great deal of our time trying to influence other
people's attitudes, especially the attitudes of those for whose
work or effort we have some responsibility. We talk, show evidence,
list logical reasons, and in some instances, actually give personal testimony to the positive results of this desired attitude. We are trying
to be persuasive. Intuitively, we know it is best for people to like
what they must do. Instructors want learners to feel positively toward
learning and the effort it takes to accomplish it. However, exhort-
ing, arguing, explaining, and cajoling are usually very inefficient
means of helping someone develop a positive attitude toward learning. All these methods have a glaring weakness: they are simply
words—"talk," if you will—that have nowhere near the impact of
the consequences, conditions, and people involved in the learning
task itself. When successful, the *process* and *outcomes* of learning are
what tell the story for the learner. When unsuccessful, persuasion
becomes a form of linguistic static, badgering, or nagging that under-
mines the development of a positive attitude in the adult learner.

In general, it is probably best not to try to talk adults into learning. There are far more powerful things we can do in the presentation

of the subject matter as well as in our treatment of adults to help them build positive attitudes toward their learning and themselves as learners. This chapter will examine a number of strategies that encourage adults to look forward to learning and, perhaps most important, feel eager to learn more.

Four Important Attitudinal Directions

As stated in Chapter Two, attitudes predispose adults to respond favorably or unfavorably toward particular people, groups, ideas, events, or objects. From a sociocultural view, relevance and choice are two of the qualities that most determine a positive attitude among adult learners. When relevance and choice are present, most adults initially perceive the learning as appealing, as an activity they would freely endorse as something they want to do. From a more analytic, individualistic view, we can say that adult attitudes usually move in one or more of four directions, which together determine how appealing learning is for adults: (1) toward the instructor, (2) toward the subject, 3) toward the adults themselves as learners, and (4) toward the adults' expectancy for success.

This more cognitive-behavioral understanding is limited in its sensitivity to culture (Okun, 1990) but offers a well-researched, useful interpretation of attitude as a combination of a perception with a judgment that often results in an emotion that influences behavior (Ellis, 1989). The examples in Table 5.1 illustrate the influence that attitudes can have on behavior and performance in learning tasks.

Whenever we instruct, we want to establish a learning environment in which these four important attitudinal directions are positive and unified for the learner. We want adults *to like and respect us and the subject matter and to feel confident as learners who realistically believe they can succeed in the learning task at hand.*

If any one of these four attitudinal directions becomes seriously negative for the adult, his or her motivation to learn can be impaired. A person could respect the instructor, feel confident as a

Table 5.1. Attitudinal Directions.

Perception	+	Judgment	→	Emotion	→	Behavior
I see my instructor.		He seems helpful.		I feel appreciative.		I will cooperate.
The instructor announces the beginning of a new unit on family relations. (subject matter)		Learning more about being an effective parent is helpful to me.		I feel interested.		I will pay close attention.
It is my turn to present my project to the seminar. (self as learner)		I am knowledgeable and well prepared for this.		I feel confident.		I will do a good job and give a smooth and articulate presentation.
The instructor is giving a surprise quiz. (expectancy for success)		I have not studied this material and will probably flunk this quiz.		I feel very anxious.		I can't think straight and won't be able to answer the questions.

learner, and objectively expect to do well but still intensely dislike the subject area. This sometimes happens with required courses or training; competent instructors find capable adults disinterested and apathetic. In a similar vein, an adult could like the instructor and the subject and be confident as a learner but realize there is not enough time or proper materials to prepare and be successful in the learning task. It is quite likely that this person's overall motivation to learn will be significantly reduced, and his trying hard will probably lead only to frustration. This situation often arises when someone has to compete against someone else whose preparation and material advantages seem far superior to his own.

In most instances, adults experience their attitudes immediately, without premeditation or serious reflection. They hear or see something, and the attitude begins to run its course. The instructor introduces the topic, and the learner's attitude toward that topic emerges. The instructor assigns homework, and the learner quickly has an attitude toward the assignment. "Wait and see" makes a great deal of sense, but that is not how attitudes work. We use this self-administered advice in an appeal for caution because we understand how instantly attitudes (including erroneous ones) influence us. "Wait and maybe I can change this attitude" is probably a more accurate self-admonition. Once a person has had an experience, the attitude will occur, like it or not. It may be only a vague feeling, but it is still an influence on behavior. That is why we as instructors have to be aware of what can be done to influence learner attitudes positively at the beginning of any learning experience. The attitudes will be there from the very start. Having them *work for* learners and us gives the best chance for motivated learning to occur. Although most of the following strategies can be implemented throughout the learning experience, the discussion here will stress their use at the beginning of learning and training activities.

Creating a Positive Attitude Toward the Instructor

Even in the case of distance education, learning is significantly associated with the instructor (Dillon and Smith, 1992). We want that association to be positive. It is more difficult for adults to accept what they are offered when the person who is giving it to them is someone they do not like or respect. A learner's negative attitude toward an instructor makes that instructor a barrier between the material to be learned and the learner. Instead of feeling consonant and at ease because a respected instructor is offering an attractive lesson, the learner may feel dissonant and psychologically tense because a disliked instructor is offering an attractive lesson. The same principle occurs in everyday behavior. We feel uneasy purchasing a car from a salesperson we don't like or accepting a gift from someone we disrespect. In most instances, it seems better for us not to buy the car or not to accept the gift, because then our actions are consistent with how we feel toward the person. In learning situations, adults will be more open, accepting, and responsive to materials and tasks they receive from an instructor they like and respect. They will be quite the opposite with an instructor they don't like or respect. Optimal motivation for learning will probably decrease.

As discussed in Chapter Two, the core characteristics of expertise, empathy, and cultural responsiveness will be major influences in establishing a positive attitude toward the instructor. Because the learners' relationship to the instructor bears so strongly on learners' sense of inclusion, the strategies directed toward creating a positive attitude toward the instructor appeared in Chapter Four (which discusses strategies that establish inclusion). They are summarized here:

- Allow for introductions. (Strategy 1)

- Concretely indicate your cooperative intentions to help adults learn. (Strategy 3)

- Share something of value with your adult learners. (Strategy 4)

- When issuing mandatory assignments or training requirements, give your rationale for these stipulations. (Strategy 10)

- To the degree authentically possible, reflect the language, perspective, and attitudes of adult learners. (Strategy 11)

- Acknowledge different ways of knowing, different languages, and different levels of knowledge or skill to engender a safe learning environment. (Strategy 13)

Building a Positive Attitude Toward the Subject

Please read the following words out loud:

English	Grammar	History
Computers	Math	Reading
Biology	Music	Spelling
Writing	Algebra	Chemistry

Which word evoked the strongest emotional reaction in you? Was it a positive or a negative feeling? Most of the listed subject areas are common to the educational experience of adults. Adults have taken such courses, and they usually have distinct attitudes toward them. Any new learning that involves elements from these former subjects will cause immediate attitudinal reactions on the part of adults. That is why adults so often ask questions like these at the beginning of new courses and training sessions: How much reading will I have to do? What kind of math does this training require? What will I have to write? Adults have strong opinions about both their capabilities and their feelings toward such requirements. They carry attitudes toward them that often are decades old and very entrenched (Smith, 1982). New learning often causes mixed reactions in adults. They might want to learn about innovative uses of computers but honestly have real fears if any math is involved in the training.

To some extent, new learning goes against the grain of the personal autonomy and security of adults. Older adults have usually found a way to cope with life and have formulated a set of convictions (Schaie and Willis, 1996). New learning often asks them to become temporarily dependent, to open their minds to new ideas, to rethink certain beliefs, and to try different ways of doing things. This may be threatening to them, and their attitudes can easily lock in to support their resistance.

It has also been documented that adults may react with apprehension to specific areas of content, such as math and foreign languages (Smith, 1982). For some, speaking in front of the group is a real ordeal. Others find specific learning techniques, such as role playing and videotaping of themselves, to be quite anxiety producing.

Whatever we can do as instructors to minimize adults' negative attitudes and to foster the development of their positive attitudes toward the subject and the instructional process will improve their motivation for learning. Invigorated by our enthusiasm, the following strategies are a means to this end.

STRATEGY 14: *Eliminate or minimize any negative conditions that surround the subject.*

Mager (1968) once wrote that people learn to avoid the things they are hit with. It is a common fact of learning that when a person is presented with an item or subject and is at the same time in the presence of negative (unpleasant) conditions, that item or subject becomes a stimulus for avoidance behavior. Things or subjects that frighten adults are often associated with antagonists and situations that make them uncomfortable, tense, or scared. Therefore, it is best not to associate the subject with any of the following conditions. These tend to support negative learner attitudes and repel adult interest:

- *Pain:* acute physical and psychological discomfort, such as continuous failure (where learner effort makes no difference), poorly fitting equipment, or uncomfortable room temperature

- *Fear and anxiety:* distress and tension resulting from anticipation of the unpleasant or dangerous, such as threat of failure or punishment, public exposure of ignorance, or unpredictability of potential negative consequences

- *Frustration:* an emotional reaction to the blockage or defeat of purposeful behavior, such as occurs when information is presented too quickly or too slowly or when the learner receives unannounced tests or inadequate feedback on performance

- *Humiliation:* an emotional reaction to being shamed, disrespected, or degraded, such as occurs when a person receives sarcasm, insult, sexist comment, or public comparison of inadequate learning

- *Boredom:* a cognitive and emotional reaction to a situation in which stimuli impinging on a learner are weak, repetitive, or infrequent, as occurs when learning situations lack variety, cover material already known, or contain excessively predictable discussion respondents (the same people talking over and over again)

This list is quite dismal. However, just as a slate must be wiped clean before clear and lucid new writing can be set down, learning environments must have these negative conditions removed before positive conditions can effectively occur. Otherwise, the best efforts of motivating instructors can be contaminated and diffused by the mere presence of such oppressive elements.

STRATEGY 15: *Ensure successful learning with mastery learning conditions.*

It is difficult for anyone to dislike a subject in which they are successful. Conversely, it is rare to find anyone who really likes a subject in which they are unsuccessful. Competent learning in a subject is probably one of the surest ways to sustain a positive attitude toward that subject. According to Bloom (1981), most learners (perhaps more than 90 percent) can master what is generally taught. The important qualification is that some learners take a great deal more time to learn something than others do. In general,

Bloom's studies indicated that slow learners may take six times longer to learn the same material as faster learners do. With effective instruction and efficient use of learner time, he estimated this ratio could be cut down to three to one.

Some adults may be discouraged when they realize how much extra time and effort they will need to expend to master what we are teaching. However, we can positively influence their attitudes as well as those of our faster learners when we guarantee the following three conditions: (1) quality instruction that will help them learn if they try to learn, (2) concrete evidence that their effort makes a difference, and (3) continual feedback regarding the progress of their learning.

In addition, it helps us as instructors to realize that few adults know for certain how much time and effort it will take to master a particular subject. When the three conditions just cited are present from the very beginning of a course, learners have a much better chance to experience success. Here are Bloom's *guidelines* (1981) for establishing these conditions:

- In addition to your main instructional techniques (laboratory and discussion, textbook, and so forth), have a number of alternative instructional processes available to meet the needs of individual learners. The following are some alternatives:

    Group study procedures might be available to learners as they need them. Small groups of learners (two or three) could meet regularly to go over points of difficulty in the learning process. If you use group study, avoid competitive forms of evaluation, so that everyone feels able to gain from cooperating with the others.

    Other suggested textbooks might offer a clearer or better-exemplified discussion of material the learner is having difficulty grasping in the adopted textbook.

Workshops, programmed instruction units, and computer-assisted instruction might provide the drill and specific tasks that regular instruction cannot. Some learners need small steps and frequent reinforcement to overcome particular learning difficulties.

Media, films, and the Internet might sometimes provide the illustrations and vivid explanations not found in regular learning procedures.

Tutorial help is often a last resort but is certainly a legitimate and helpful one for many learners.

- Set clear (that is, understandable) standards of mastery and excellence. When adults know the criteria by which their learning will be evaluated, they know better what to do in order to do well in a particular subject.

- Avoid competition for scores and grades. When adults do not have to fear each other's progress to protect their self-esteem, an extra and valuable corps of instructional assistants becomes available in the learning environment.

- Break down courses or training into smaller units of learning. Such a learning unit may correspond to a chapter in a book, a well-defined content portion of a training seminar, or a particular time unit. Segmenting instruction into smaller increments allows the learner to perceive progress more easily, just as gauging a minute on a clock is easier to do than gauging an hour. Every time we can help our learners say that they have concretely learned something, we have helped them feel a sense of progress. This also helps them maintain their concentration.

- Frequently use *formative evaluation*. These are exams
  and tests, written, oral, or performance, that are used
  only to diagnose progress (meaning they are *not graded*).
  They are meant to assess learner progress and to indicate points of learner difficulty or instructional in-
  adequacy; they are tailored to the particular unit of
  learning. For those learners who have mastered the
  unit, formative evaluation will give them positive feedback. They can honestly say, "With that instructor, I
  really know how well I'm doing." For those learners
  who lack mastery of a unit, formative evaluation will
  point out the particular ideas, skills, and processes they
  still need to work on and the instructional delivery the
  instructor may need to alter. Bloom found that learners
  respond best when the instructor refers them to particular instructional materials or processes intended to
  help them correct their difficulties. They can at least
  say, "I know where I am, and I know what I have to do
  to help myself."

Ensuring successful learning is a powerful strategy. Success breeds
interest and motivation for further learning. Research indicates that
using this approach can enhance learner attitudes and achievement,
particularly for those who have difficulty in conventional college
learning environments (Kulik, Kulik, and Bangert-Drowns, 1990).

STRATEGY 16: *Positively confront the erroneous beliefs, expectations,
and assumptions that may underlie a negative learner attitude.*

Some learners have mistaken beliefs that support their negative
attitudes. For example, learners may think, "If I have to do any
math in this course, I won't do well in it," or, "Communications
training has never helped anyone I know," or, "If I make a mistake,

I'll really look bad." Assumptions of this sort can cause learners to fear and resist a subject (Ellis, 1989). People maintain their negative attitudes by repeating such beliefs to themselves. If you think an individual or a group is holding such beliefs, you can engage in an appropriate discussion along the following guidelines to help reduce the negative attitude:

1. Tactfully find out what the learner might be telling herself that leads to the negative attitude. ("You seem somewhat discouraged. Could you tell me what might be happening or what you might be thinking that's leading to such feelings?")

2. If the learner appears to have a self-defeating belief, point out how negative feelings would naturally follow from such a belief. ("If you believe making a mistake will really make you look foolish in front of your peers, you probably feel fearful and anxious about trying some of the group exercises.")

3. Suggest other assumptions that might be more helpful to the learner. ("You might tell yourself that this is guided practice, where everyone including your instructor expects some mistakes, and that the purpose of the exercises is to refine skills, not to demonstrate them at a level of perfection.")

4. Encourage the learner to develop beliefs, based on present reality, that promote well-being. ("When you start to feel discouraged or negative, check out what you are telling yourself and see if it really helps you. Consider whether there might be some other beliefs or expectancies that would do you more good. You might want to discuss this with me so that I can give you feedback and other possible ways of looking at the situation that might be more helpful.")

Sometimes it's useful to ask the learner "what might have to happen" for her to believe she could do well or to change her attitude in a positive direction. This question may help the learner describe relevant examples of evidence that will fit her perspective and produce a shift in attitude. At a workshop, I once asked this question of a group of reluctant college faculty. They anonymously wrote their answers on cards, which I read back to them. Midway through the deck I found myself reading one that stated, "A public hanging of the dean." Fortunately, she graciously laughed. Her sense of humor and compassion took us to another level of discourse, and the workshop progressed with much more effectiveness.

STRATEGY 17: *Use assisted learning to scaffold complex learning.*

Assisted learning is a pragmatic blend of individualistic and socioconstructivist thinking. Vygotsky (1978) realized there were certain problems and skills that a person could solve or master when given appropriate help and support. Such learning, often called assisted learning, provides *scaffolding*—giving clues, information, prompts, reminders, and encouragement at the appropriate time and in the appropriate amounts and then gradually allowing the learner to do more and more independently. Most of us naturally scaffold when we teach someone to drive a car or play a card game. The *zone of proximal development* is the phase in a learning task when a learner can benefit from assistance (Wertsch, 1991). The upper limit of the zone is the place at which the learner can perform the task independently; the lower limit is the place where the learner can perform the task but needs assistance. Most of us learned to drive a car with someone in the seat next to us who prompted and reminded us of what to do and when to do it as we navigated a road. In the beginning, this "coach" usually had to scaffold pretty intensely: "Check your speedometer"; "I think you're speeding"; "Watch out for that car"; "If you don't stop, we are going to have an accident." We were obviously in the lower limit of our zone of proximal development for driving. But eventually most of us required less coaching; we reached the upper limit and began to drive independently.

Myriad other learning tasks strongly benefit from scaffolding. Whether adults are learning to solve math problems, conduct experiments, or use a personal computer, our assessing their zone of proximal development and structuring the appropriate scaffold can lead to success. Adults deeply appreciate the support assisted learning offers because it tends to be concrete, immediate, and tailored to their obvious needs. The following are some of the methods specific to assisted learning that can be used to scaffold more complex learning (Association for Supervision and Curriculum Development, 1990). The description of each method includes an example in which I model assisting students to learn to write a research report.

- *Modeling:* the instructor carries out the skill while the learners observe, or the instructor offers actual examples of learning outcomes, such as finished papers or solved problems. (I ask the learners to read two previously completed reports. One is excellent, the other is satisfactory.)

- *Thinking out loud:* the instructor states actual thought processes in carrying out the learning task. (I talk about some of the goals and criteria I would consider before writing the report. I ask the learners why one report was considered excellent and the other only satisfactory. I supplement the learners' perceptions with my own.)

- *Anticipating difficulties:* as the learning proceeds, the instructor and learners discuss areas where support is needed and mistakes are more likely to occur. (Because the sections of the report that discuss findings and statistical analyses seem most challenging to learners, we discuss how these sections were done in the two reports and arrange for prompt feedback on the learners' initial drafts of these sections in their own reports.)

- *Providing prompts and cues:* the instructor highlights, emphasizes, or structures procedural steps and important responses to help learners clearly recognize their place and their importance to the learning task. (I provide an outline for writing a research report with exemplars from previous reports.)

- *Regulating the difficulty:* the instructor introduces a more complex task with simpler tasks and may offer some practice with these. (I give the learners a basic research scenario, a hypothesis, data, and an analysis scheme and ask them to write a brief research report with this information.)

- *Using reciprocal teaching:* the instructor and the learners rotate the role of instructor; in that role, each learner provides guidance and suggestions to others. (While I monitor, each learner presents his or her brief research report to a learning partner who acts as the instructor and gives supportive feedback. Then they reverse roles. The same process is carried out with the first draft of their actual research report.)

- *Providing a checklist:* learners use self-checking procedures to monitor the quality of their learning. (I give the learners a checklist of questions and quality criteria to consider as they write their reports.)

Consider the possible metaphors for the provider of assisted learning: sensitive tutor, seasoned coach, wise parent—all people who tell us just enough, what we need to know when we need to know it, trusting us to chart the rest of our journey to learning. Assisted learning conveys an underlying message: "You may stray, but you will not be lost. In this endeavor, you are not alone." The image is not one of the rugged individualist or the solitary explorer.

Rather, assisted learning embraces a vision of remarkable possibility nurtured by a caring community.

Developing a Positive Self-Concept for Learning

Goethe believed that the greatest evil that can befall a person is that he should come to think ill of himself. Some learners may not have a negative attitude toward their instructor or the subject, but they may have a negative attitude toward themselves. They may believe their capabilities to perform a task and succeed at it are inadequate. A person holding such negative beliefs is often said to have a "poor self-concept." His or her motivation to learn is often diminished.

Among adults, self-concept tends to be situation-specific (Pintrich and Schunk, 1996). A person might feel quite physically adept but very incompetent in academic situations. This kind of breakdown exists within the academic self-concept as well. A learner might feel quite superior in English and very inferior in math. Adults constantly modify their self-concepts in specific areas of learning, which means that during our instructional or training session we have a chance to positively affect a person's self-estimation.

There are some cautions. The adult has a firmer and more fully formed self-concept than does the child (Brundage and MacKeracher, 1980). It is not uncommon for adults to harbor doubts about their personal learning ability. They often underestimate and underuse their capacities (Knox, 1977). Their own family members may reinforce their self-doubts by questioning their abilities or need for certain learning. Later adulthood and old age are periods when many learners are more prone to this source of anxiety.

Regardless of the state of the adult's self-concept on entering our learning situation, we can provide the experiences from which each adult can derive self-confidence as a learner. Before we move to particular strategies, it is important to emphasize again the strategies of *ensuring successful learning* and *scaffolding* (Strategies 15 and 17, respectively). These strategies powerfully affect both the learner's attitude toward the subject and the learner's attitude toward the self as learner. In fact, we should consider them prerequisites for all the strategies that follow. The fundamental basis for acquiring a positive self-concept for learning in any area is realistically seeing oneself as a *successful* learner from one's own perspective.

STRATEGY 18: *Encourage the learner.*

We can use this strategy with a group or an individual. Encouragement is any behavior on our part by which we show the learner (1) that we respect the learner as a person, no matter what is learned, (2) that we trust and believe in the learner's effort to learn, and (3) that the learner *can* learn. An adult who perceives that the instructor's respect is contingent only on learning performance will feel dehumanized. Such a criterion for acceptance by the instructor denies the adult's other worthy qualities and makes the person into a "thing" that learns without feelings or dignity. The primary foundation for encouragement is our caring about and acceptance of the learner. This caring and acceptance creates the context in which we choose ways to show confidence and personal regard for the learner's effort and achievement. These ways include the following:

Giving recognition for effort. Any time a person seriously attempts to learn something, that individual is taking a risk. Intentional learning is a courageous act. No one learns 100 percent of the time. Some risk is usually involved. We can help by acknowledging learners' effort and by respecting their perseverance. Any comment that says, "I like the way you try," can help learners understand that we value their effort. When insecure learners know that we honestly esteem their effort during the time preceding eventual achievement, it does a great deal to reduce their performance anxiety and its debilitating effects.

Minimizing mistakes while the learner is struggling. Sometimes learning is like a battle. The critical edge between advancement and withdrawal or between hope and despair is fragile at best. Our emphasis on a learner's mistakes at such a critical moment will accentuate whatever pessimistic emotions the learner is already feeling and is a sure way to encourage self-defeat.

Emphasizing learning from mistakes. Help adults see a mistake as a way to improve future learning. When we actually help them learn from a mistake, we directly show them how thinking and trying are in their best interest and that we have confidence they will learn.

For each learning task, demonstrating a confident and realistic expectancy that the learner will learn. Essentially we are conveying the message, "You can do it," but without implying that the task is easy or simple. Whenever we tell a person that something is easy, we have placed that person in a lose-lose dilemma. If the person successfully does the task, she feels no pride, because the task was easy in the first place. If the person fails, she feels shame, because the task was implied to be simple.

Showing faith in the adult's capacity as a learner. This faith translates into "sometimes it may be difficult, but I believe you can learn, and I will work with you toward that goal." Whenever we give up on a learner, we also give up on ourselves as instructors. Realistically, some of our learners actually may prefer that we give up. It makes it easier for them to stop trying. By showing consistent trust in the learner's capacity to achieve, we maintain our responsibility as instructors, and we emphasize the learner's responsibility for continued effort.

Working with the learner at the beginning of difficult tasks. It's amazing what can be lifted and moved with just a little help. Sometimes a learner might be momentarily confused or not know what to do next. As a form of early scaffolding, our proximity and minimal assistance can be just enough for the learner to find the right direction, continue involvement, and gain the initial confidence to proceed with learning.

Affirming the process of learning. This means acknowledging all parts of the learning endeavor—the information seeking, the studying, the practicing, the cooperating, and so forth. If we wait for the final product—the test results, project, or whatever the final goal is—we may be too late. Some learners may have given up by this time. Our delay also implies that the learner should wait until the end of learning to feel good about learning. Even waiting for some minimal progress can sometimes be a mistake. Learning does not follow a linear progression; there are often wide spaces, deep holes, dead ends, and regressions. Real encouragement says the task of learning is itself important and emphasizes the intrinsic value of the entire process of learning.

STRATEGY 19: *Promote the learner's personal control of the context of learning.*

It is very important for learners to be successful and to feel encouraged, but for people to build confidence as learners, they usually need to realize that their own behavior is most responsible for their learning. This is especially the case for those with individualistic values; they are more compelled to feel a sense of personal causation in the process of learning—that they mainly *control* how, what, and when they learn (Deci and Ryan, 1991). At first, this may seem obvious: if a person pays attention, studies, and practices, of course the person will feel responsible for any successful achievement. However, when we remember that instructors usually establish requirements, issue assignments, give tests, generally set the standards for achievement, often control the learning environment, and sometimes pressure learner involvement, it is not too difficult to understand how a learner could come to believe it is the instructor who is most responsible for achievement. Even when a person is successful, he or she may feel very dependent as a learner and consequently bound to the demands and directions of the instructor for future learning. In this way, a person can feel like a pawn while learning and not develop self-confidence as a learner.

Adults are inclined toward autonomy in many aspects of their daily lives; the following methods to increase their sense of personal causation while learning should effectively complement this tendency.

The learner plans and sets goals for learning. Planning validates the individual as the originator and guide of the process.

To the extent appropriate, the learner makes choices about what, how, with whom, where, and when to learn something. Choice is the essence of responsibility. It permits the learner to feel ownership of the learning experience. The learner can choose topics, assignments, with whom to learn, when to be evaluated, how to be evaluated, and so forth.

The learner uses self-assessment procedures. When a learner can appraise mistakes and successes while learning, she experiences a concrete sense of participation in the learning act. Sometimes learners can get the feeling that mistakes are created by the instructor more than committed by the learner. Self-assessment procedures can prevent this misperception and give the learner a sense of control from the beginning to the end of the learning experience. When a person can determine for herself whether she is really learning something, she feels more responsible for that learning.

The instructor helps the learner identify personal strengths while learning. For example, "You have a number of assignments to choose from, but it seems to me you have a real talent for explaining things well and could probably give a very interesting oral presentation. What do you think?" A learner who knows and takes advantage of personal assets while learning feels a real sense of power and confidence.

The learner logs personal progress while learning. This allows the learner to feel personal growth and learning concretely, as they take place.

The learner participates in analyzing potential blocks to progress in learning. For example, the instructor might ask, "What do you think the difficulty might be?" or, "In your estimation, where do you think the confusion begins?" By participating in solving the learning problem, the learner feels more commitment to its resolution and is more aware of her role in the learning process. An added plus for instructors—adult learners frequently know better than we do where problems in learning are occurring.

When advisable, the learner makes a commitment to the learning task. This accentuates the learner's personal choice. It prevents denial or withdrawal of personal responsibility for learning. When we ask a learner, "Are you sure you're going to do it?" or, "Can I feel certain that you're going to try?" and we receive a sincere affirmative answer, we are helping to amplify the learner's sense of self-determination. However, use this technique sparingly and with careful forethought. If it lacks integrity, it becomes a mere manipulation and an insult to the learner.

The learner has access to prompt feedback. Prompt feedback during learning leads to stronger feelings of personal control and responsibility. This is one of the main reasons computer-assisted instruction can be fantastic for increasing motivation. The computer has the mechanical ability to give immediate feedback. The learner has moment-to-moment awareness of progress in learning. This constant back-and-forth *dialogue* between computer and learner gives the learner a strong sense of control in the learning process. In so many ways, the computer tells the learner it will not respond until the learner responds first. The learner's personal control is undeniable.

In contrast, the longer it takes for a person to know if a response has had an effect, the more difficult it can become to know whether that response had any effect at all. Imagine having a conversation with someone who waited at least a minute or longer to answer any question you asked. It is likely that you would wonder if you were actually being heard. Anything an instructor can do to ensure the best possible pace of accurate feedback will concretely help emphasize learner responsibility. See Chapter Seven for a more comprehensive discussion of the appropriate use of feedback.

The purpose of these methods is to emphasize that the *majority* of responsibility for learning is under the control of the learner. For an adult to feel "I can do it" when it comes to future learning, he or she has to have felt "I did it" during previous experiences in learning.

STRATEGY 20: *Help learners accurately attribute their success to their capability, effort, and knowledge.*

Whereas the last strategy dealt with the *context* of learning, this strategy focuses on the *outcome* of learning. That outcome is *success*, and I use the term here in its broadest sense. Success can mean passing a test, receiving an excellent grade, completing a fine project, satisfactorily demonstrating a new skill, correctly answering a problem—any achievement that turns out well in the eyes of the learner.

Adults frequently think about the consequences of their behavior. *If they have a success, they will often reflect on a reason or a cause for that success.* Some cognitive psychologists call these inferred causes *attributions* and have created a theory and body of research to demonstrate their significant effects on human behavior (Weiner, 1992). For instructors, the important understanding is this: when people have had a learning success, it will probably best enhance their self-concept and their motivation to believe that the major causes for that success are their capability, effort, and knowledge. We might suppose that if learners had a good deal of personal control over the learning context and were successful, at least they would take credit for their effort. Certainly this is probable, but some learners find such attributions as luck, easiness, and fear just as plausible. There is no way to guarantee what a person will think. Because of this unpredictability, it is vital that we do whatever we can to directly help learners see their capability, effort, and knowledge as the causes of their learning success.

There are a number of reasons why the adult learner benefits from believing capability, effort, and knowledge are the causes of personal academic success. Belief in these causes is *realistic* self-understanding. It usually is some combination of capability, effort, and knowledge that makes learning success possible. Because the learner internally controls those causes, he or she can feel genuine pride. Capability also has a stable quality to it (it lasts), and the adult can feel more confident when similar learning tasks arise. Effort and knowledge are less stable (sometimes it's difficult to persevere or remember), but it is probably these aspects of behavior over which the learner feels the most control. Knowing that knowledge or skill can be gained through study and practice and that effort is often a matter of will reduces the learner's feelings of helplessness and increases persistence. Attributions to effort and knowledge provide realistic hope.

Here are some ways to help learners attribute their success to capability, effort, and knowledge.

- Provide learners with learning tasks suitable to their capabilities. "Just within reach" is a good rule of thumb. These kinds of tasks challenge learners' capabilities and require knowledge and moderate effort for success.

- Before initiating a learning task, stress the importance of learners' effort and knowledge for success. This should be a reminder and not a threat: for example, "Considering the challenge of this task, we'll have to practice and become proficient before we apply what we know." This alerts the learners to their responsibility and increases the likelihood that learners will attribute their success to effort and knowledge.

- Send verbal and written messages to accentuate learners' perceptions of capability, effort, and knowledge in relation to their success. Here are a few examples: "Great to see your hard work pay off." "Your skills made a real difference." "That's a talented performance." "Your knowledge is apparent in your writing." "I know a lot of perseverance went into this project." *Knowledge can also mean skill or strategy.* The great thing about such statements is that they can be distributed all the time.

Certain subjects, such as math, writing, and art, are conventionally understood to be *aptitude-driven* when in reality they greatly benefit from effort and strategy. For example, knowing there are five interesting ways to begin an essay (with a statistic, quotation, question, anecdote, or revelation) is a strategy that can make starting a new paper an enjoyable challenge rather than an oppressive frustration. When we attribute effective learning to an attainable skill or strategy, we can build learners' confidence as well as contribute relevant knowledge.

Strategy 21: *When learning tasks are suitable to learners' capability, help learners understand that effort and knowledge can overcome their failures.*

The term *failure* is used here in its broadest sense—mistakes, errors, lack of completion, poor test results, low grades, unskilled performance, or any lack of achievement that turns out poorly in the eyes of the learner. If a learner experiences an unsuccessful learning outcome, there is very little he can do to improve unless he believes further personal effort or knowledge can make a difference. To paraphrase Seligman (1975), intelligence, no matter how high, cannot manifest itself if the person believes that his own actions will have no effect. If a person believes failure is due to lack of aptitude, then more effort will seem to make little difference, because ability, in the eyes of most people, is very difficult to change. The result will be discouragement. Bad luck, too difficult a task, and poor materials are all attributions learners might make that indicate personal effort will only have a small impact on their future performance. Sometimes these attributions are correct, but sometimes they are rationalizations that ease learners' guilt and frustration.

If we have honest reasons to believe greater effort will improve performance, we need to let the learner know. Strategic knowledge can also be extremely encouraging. The idea of "working smarter" rather than just harder has its appeal. Whether they are following an outline or using the Internet, adults can see how these strategies make learning easier as well as more informative. Attributions of effort and knowledge evoke real hope for future performance. The ability to tactfully reveal them to the learner is an immeasurable asset: for example, "I realize you might be feeling quite bad about how this assignment turned out, but my honest estimation of your performance is that with continued effort you can definitely improve. Here are the units that seem to need further review. . . ." So often what seems like defeat can actually lead to a higher level of creativity and learning.

Establishing Expectancy for Success

It is possible that a learner could initially like a subject, feel positively toward the instructor, have a good academic self-concept, and still not expect to succeed. The person simply might decide there is not enough time to study for the training or course. For adults, time is a critical issue because of their many other roles and responsibilities. The decision to invest time in a learning activity may be as important as the decision to invest money or effort (Lowe, 1996). Sometimes learners do not understand what is necessary to do well in a course, and this confusion leads to discouragement. Sometimes the materials and training are so new and different to the learners that many of them actually have difficulty seeing themselves as potential performers in the necessary learning tasks.

There are many different reasons why adult learners might not expect to succeed. And when they don't have this expectation, they probably consider it in their best interest not to get enthusiastic. If they do, they will experience greater pain and disappointment if they fail. In fact, for people to try at something they do not believe they can do is usually not very intelligent behavior and is often a waste of time. When expectancy for success is low, learners tend to protect their well-being by remaining withdrawn or negative. Instructors often interpret this as apathy or resistance, but for the learners it is usually self-protection, more to do with realistic doubt than with being ornery. In such instances, our demonstrating clearly that the learning task is concretely possible to achieve is a significant positive influence on learners' attitudes.

STRATEGY 22: *Make the criteria of assessment as fair and clear as possible.*

Assessment is thoroughly discussed in Chapter Seven. However, because learning goals and assessment procedures go hand in hand in the beginning of most adult education courses and training, we need to pay some attention to assessment as an attitudinal issue. In the view of most adults, how they are assessed will play a crucial role in determining their expectation for success. The outcomes of assessment in the form of grades and quantitative scores can powerfully influence their self-determination, sense of self-worth, and access to careers, further education, and financial aid (for example, scholarships and grants). Therefore, assessment criteria are extremely relevant to developing or inhibiting a positive attitude toward learning. Whenever we formulate learning goals, we should simultaneously address assessment procedures and criteria.

If learners understand the criteria and agree to them as fair, they know which elements of performance are essential. They can more easily self-assess and self-determine their learning as they proceed (Wiggins, 1993). This should enhance their motivation, because they can anticipate the results of their learning and regulate how they learn (for example, studying, writing, practicing, and so on) with more certainty.

In general, we ought to demonstrate how we or the learners can go about assessing the quality of their learning: what is being looked for in the assessment, how it is valued, and how this value will be indicated. This discussion of evaluation usually entails clarifying terms, standards, and calibration of measurement, so that all of us come to a common understanding and agreement about how these indicators of learning are applied, scored, and integrated.

The less mystery there is surrounding evaluation criteria, the more likely learners are to direct their own learning. We are wise to allow for questions and suggestions about assessment. It is very beneficial to make available some examples of concrete learning outcomes—past tests, papers, projects, and media—that you have already evaluated using the same criteria, thus giving learners realistic illustrations of how you have applied them. Exemplary models of other learners' accomplishments often hold the power to inspire adults. When I look back on my teaching, it is clear that demystifying the criteria of assessment and providing exemplars of past student learning have been among the most powerful strategies I have ever learned for enhancing adult motivation and performance.

STRATEGY 23: *Use relevant models to demonstrate expected learning.*

Because many adults often find learning new as well as abstract, they honestly wonder if they can do it. Any time we can provide examples of people who are similar to the learners enthusiastically and successfully performing the expected learning activity, we have taken a significant step toward enhancing learners' expectancy for success (Pintrich and Schunk, 1996). This strategy is derived from the research of Bandura (1982, pp. 126–127): "Seeing similar others perform successfully can raise efficacy expectations in observers who then judge that they too possess the capabilities to master comparable activities. . . . Vicariously derived information alters perceived self-efficacy through ways other than social comparison. . . . Modeling displays convey information about the nature and predictability of environmental events. Competent models also teach observers effective strategies for dealing with challenging or threatening situations."

With film and video technology, we have wonderful ways to organize and demonstrate what we want our learners to achieve. Former students and trainees are another source for live modeling sessions. If something can be learned and demonstrated, be it a skill, technique, or discussion, today's technology enables us to bring it to our learners and to raise in a concrete way their expectations for success.

STRATEGY 24: *Announce the expected amount of time needed for study and practice for successful learning.*

As we have discussed, time is precious to adults. It is often very difficult for adult learners to estimate the amount of time a given course, assignment, or practice regimen might take. Some will overestimate. Some will underestimate. Others will procrastinate, as busy people often do. If a learning activity will require a significant amount of time, it is best for learners to know this so that they can plan more effectively, realize their responsibility, avoid procrastination, and attribute their success to effort.

STRATEGY 25: *Use goal-setting methods.*

This is a more individualized approach to increasing learners' expectancy for success and their self-efficacy. Bandura (1986, p. 391) defines *self-efficacy* as "people's judgements of their capabilities to organize and execute courses of action required to attain designated types of performances." Adults who perceive low self-efficacy for a task tend to avoid that task, whereas those who believe they are capable are likely to get involved. Efficacious learners persist longer, especially when they encounter difficulties.

The advantage of goal setting is that it brings the future into the present and allows the learner to become aware of what he needs to do to have a successful learning experience. Goal setting not only prevents the learner from making an unrealistic expectation but also gives him a chance to evaluate and plan specifically for those obstacles that prevent success. Using the goal-setting model, the learner feels more control and can calculate what to do to avoid wasting time or experiencing self-defeat. Thus, before even beginning the learning task, the learner knows that the effort he expends will be worthwhile and that there is a good probability for success. As postsecondary education evolves into a greater number of alternative forms and as learning more frequently involves projects and complex tasks, goal setting is a real asset to the instructor and the adult learner.

There are many different methods of goal setting (Locke and Latham, 1990). The one that follows is an eclectic adaptation of various models in the literature. If the learner is to have a good chance of reaching the learning goal (and therefore of initiating the learning experience), instructor and learner should consider the following criteria together. In order to take these criteria beyond abstract suggestions, I present an actual case from my experience to exemplify how the criteria can be applied.

Yolanda Scott-Machado, whose tribal affiliation is Makah, is an adult learner in a research course. To learn more about a variety of skills and concepts including research design, validity, reliability, sampling procedures, statistical analysis, and operationalization, Yolanda wants to design, conduct, and report a research study in an area of personal interest. She has questions about the concept of learning styles, especially as it is applied to American Indians. She wants to carry out a study to determine if urban Indian high school students, when compared to urban European American high school students, score significantly higher in the field-sensitive mode as measured by Witkin's Group Embedded Figures Test. This is an ambitious study for a beginning research student. We launch the goal-setting process by examining the criterion of achievability.

1. Discuss whether the goal is achievable.

Can the learner reach the learning goal with the skills and knowledge at hand? If not, is there any assistance available, and how dependable is that assistance?

Yolanda feels confident, and her competent completion of exercises in class substantiates that confidence. She is also a member of a class cooperative learning group and values her peers as knowledgeable resources. We work out a plan that includes a preliminary conference with peers to garner their support, and a follow-up call to me.

Is there enough time to reach the goal? If not, can more time be found, or should the goal be divided into smaller goals?

This question is a bit tricky. Yolanda will need at least fifty students in each of her comparison groups. At the minimum, she will need to involve two high schools. Can she get the necessary permission? Who will do the testing, and when? The bureaucratic maneuvering and testing could drag on and complicate the study.

2. Determine how progress will be measured.

In what specific ways will the learner be able to gauge progress toward the achievement of the goal? In many circumstances, this measure can be something as simple as problems completed, pages read, or exercises finished. To respect learners' different ideas of how to accomplish their long-range goals, you should schedule meetings to talk about their evolving experience.

We decide that the most important "next step" is for Yolanda to write
a research proposal and bring it in for a meeting with me. Then we
might work out a schedule for her completion of the study.

3. Determine how much the learner desires the goal.

Why is the goal important? Is the goal something the learner
wants to do? The learner may have to do it or perhaps should do it,
but is the goal wanted as well? If it isn't, then the learner's satisfaction level and sense of self-determination will be less. Goal setting
can be used for "must" situations, but it is best handled if you are
clear about it and admit to the learner the reality of the situation
to avoid any sense of manipulation. When possible, aligning the
goal with other, desired goals is helpful. This alignment can increase
a learner's motivation, much as a railroad engine gains power by
hooking up with another moving engine.

Yolanda wants to do this study. She believes that certain teaching
practices derived from learning styles research may not apply to
some Northwest Indian tribes or urban Indians. Because educators
so often advocate these methods for teaching Indians, Yolanda
believes more caution about their use may be necessary. In addition,
she is considering advanced graduate study in psychology and views
research skills as an important addition to her résumé.

4. Create a consistent way to focus on the goal (optional).

Some learners feel the need for a daily plan that keeps the goal
in their awareness; the plan helps them avoid forgetting or pro-
crastinating. For others, such an idea may seem oppressive. Possible
reminders are outlines, chalkboard messages, and daily logs.

Yolanda finds this option unnecessary.

5. Preplan to consider and remove potential obstacles.

The question for the learner is, "What do you think might interfere with reaching your goal?" Obstacles may include anything from

other obligations to lack of a quiet place to study. Planning ahead to reduce these barriers should decrease their obstructive force and give the learner added leverage to contend with them.

> When I ask Yolanda about potential obstacles, she remarks that her "plate is pretty full," and probably the biggest obstacle would be to take on something else while she is conducting the research project. We joke about practicing to say no and eventually decide to leave this possibility to her best judgment.

6. Identify resources and learning processes with the learner.

Engaging the learner in a dialogue about how she would like to reach the learning goal can be a very creative process. This is the time to consider the learner's various talents and preferred ways of knowing. Will accomplishing the learning goal involve media, art, writing, or some other possibility? What form should it take—a story, a research project, or a multimedia presentation? Identifying outside resources—such as library materials, local experts, exemplary models, or films—aids and sometimes inspires the entire learning process.

> Yolanda decides to review the literature on learning styles, especially as it refers to American Indians and other native people. She also chooses to interview a professor at another university and an Indian administrator at a local school district. She decides that her format for reporting her study will be the conventional research thesis outline.

7. The learner makes a commitment.

This is a formal or informal gesture that indicates the learner's acceptance of the learning goal. It can range from a shared copy of notes taken at the meeting to a contract. This affirms the learner's self-determination and acknowledges the mutual agreement between the learner and the teacher, building trust, motivation, and cooperation for further work together.

Yolanda composes a contract, which we agree on at our next meeting. (Her contract appears as an example in the discussion of Strategy 26.)

8. Arrange a goal review schedule.

To maintain progress and refine learning procedures, the learner
and the instructor may need to stay in contact. Because of the way
time varies in its meaning and feeling to different people, contact
can occur at regular or irregular intervals. The main idea is that trust
and support continue. If progress has deteriorated, reexamine the
criteria. Asking, for example, "What did you do instead?" may help
uncover hidden distractions or competing goals.

We have three meetings at irregular intervals prior to Yolanda's completion of an excellent study. To find a large enough sample for her
research, she eventually involves five high schools. Her research indicates that urban Indian high school students are more field-independent
than European American high school students, suggesting the possibility that previous research conducted on American Indian learning
styles is far from conclusive across tribes and regions.

STRATEGY 26: *Use contracting methods.*

Learning contracts often complement goal setting. They are
considered by practitioners in adult education to be a significant
means for fostering self-direction and expectancy for success
(Knowles, 1986). They are effective for assisting adults in understanding their learning interests, planning learning activities, identifying relevant resources, and becoming skilled at self-assessment
(Brookfield, 1986). The ability to write contracts is a learned skill,
and teachers may have to spend considerable time helping learners
focus on realistic as well as manageable activities. My experience as
a teacher supports Brookfield's observation (pp. 82–83): "Particularly in institutions where other departments and program areas

conform to a more traditional mode, learners will often find it unsettling, inconvenient, and annoying to be asked to work as self-directed learning partners in some kind of negotiated learning project. Notwithstanding the fact that learners may ultimately express satisfaction with this experience, initially, at least, there may be substantial resistance. It is crucial, then, that learners be eased into this mode . . . and faculty must make explicit from the outset the rationale behind the adoption of these techniques."

Learning contracts can individualize the learning process and provide maximum flexibility for content, pace, process, and outcome. They usually detail in writing what will be learned, how the learning will be accomplished, the period of time involved, and frequently the criteria to be used in assessing the learning. Learners can construct all, most, or part of the contract depending on the learner's and teacher's knowledge of the subject matter, the resources available, the restrictions of the program, and so on. For example, what is learned (the objective) may not be negotiable, but how it is learned may be wide open to individual discretion.

The contract document often follows the outline of categories shown here (O'Donnell and Caffarella, 1990):

1. Learning goal or objective. (What are you going to learn?)

2. Choice of resources, strategies, and activities for learning. (How are you going to learn it?)

3. Target date for completion.

4. Evidence of accomplishment. (How are you going to demonstrate that you have learned it?)

5. Assessment of the learning. (What are the criteria by which you will judge the learning, and who will be involved in the judging process?)

The following are two examples of learning contracts. The first covers a specific skill to be accomplished in a short period of time in an undergraduate communication skills course. The second is the contract submitted by Yolanda Scott-Machado.

Sample Contract: Paraphrasing Skills

Learning goal: To apply paraphrasing skills to actual communication situations.

Learning resources and activities: View videotapes of paraphrasing scenarios. One hour of role playing paraphrasing situations with peers.

Target date: End of one week (date specified).

Evidence of accomplishment: Participate in paraphrasing exercise under teacher's supervision.

Assessment of learning: Can contribute appropriate paraphrasing responses to 80 percent of the communicated messages, to be validated by teacher.

Sample Contract: Research Project of Yolanda Scott-Machado

Learning goal: To conduct a research study to determine if urban Indian high school students when compared to urban European American high school students have a significant perceptual difference as measured by Witkin's Group Embedded Figures Test.

Learning resources and activities: Conduct a review of the literature on learning styles, especially as this concept relates to American Indians. Interview a professor at the University of Washington who specializes in the relation of learning styles to people of color. Also, interview a local American Indian school administrator who has responsibility for a number of projects involving American Indian students. Carry out the research, remaining in communication with my cooperative learning group and our teacher.

Target date: Two weeks before the end of the semester, to allow for revisions.

Evidence of accomplishment: Completed research study according to the design agreed on by me and my teacher.

Evaluation of learning: A self-evaluation indicating what I learned and why it was important to me. Validation by the teacher regarding the quality of my research design and analysis and the soundness of my discussion and conclusion as drawn from the research evidence.

O'Donnell and Caffarella (1990) have some helpful ideas about the use of learning contracts with learners who are inexperienced or unfamiliar with them.

- Enlist the aid of those learners more familiar with designing learning contracts to help those beginning this process.

- Give those with less experience more time to develop their plans.

- Allow the less experienced learners to develop a mini-learning plan first and then complete a more in-depth one.

- Give learners clear guidelines for developing contracts. Supply a number of diverse samples to encourage a variety of learning processes and outcomes.

In general, the use of learning contracts is, like good writing, often a process of revision and refinement. Using collaborative groups and remaining open to feedback from learners about contracts and their formats are ways to ensure their effective use.

Creating Relevant Learning Experiences

The last section of this chapter emphasizes relevance and choice. The strategies described here could have been placed along with those aligned with *attitude toward the subject* (Strategies 14 through 17). However, these strategies originate more from literature and research related to a sociocultural perspective. Each is an approach to creating learning activities that respect the learner's perspective and unique talents. Also embedded in these strategies is a concern for maintaining a connection between what is learned and the ongoing use of that learning by the learner in the real world (Wiske, 1998).

To be truly relevant, instruction has to go beyond adult interests; it must ensure that learning is accessible through the person's ways of knowing. It requires us to teach to a range of profiles of intelligences (see Gardner, 1993, chap. 1) and learning styles. The following strategy helps us be responsive to the learning preferences and differences we will encounter in a group of diverse adults.

STRATEGY 27: *Use the five entry points suggested by multiple intelligences research as ways of learning about a topic or concept.*

When we offer adults only a single way of knowing a concept or problem, they are forced to understand it in a most limited and rigid fashion. By encouraging learners to develop multiple representations and having them relate these representations to one another, we can move away from the tyranny of the "correct answer" so often dominant in education and arrive at a fuller understanding of our world. Most knowledgeable and innovative practitioners of any discipline are characterized precisely by their capacity to access critical concepts through a variety of routes and apply them to a diversity of situations. In addition, this overall approach makes us colearners with our students and more likely to take their views and ideas seriously; all of us can thus develop a more comprehensive understanding.

Gardner (1993) proposes that any concept worth teaching can be approached in at least five different ways that, roughly speaking, map onto the multiple intelligences and allow all learners relevant access. He advocates thinking of any topic as a room with at least five doors or entry points. Awareness of these entry points can help us introduce the topic with materials and formats that accommodate the wide range of cultural backgrounds and profiles of intelligences found among a group of diverse adults.

Let us look at these five entry points one by one, using an example from the natural sciences (photosynthesis) and one from the social sciences (democracy) to show how each entry point might be used in approaching topics or concepts.

Using the *narrational* entry point, we present a story or narrative account about the concept in question. In the case of photosynthesis, we might describe with appropriate vocabulary this process as it occurs in several plants or trees living in our environment, describing differences as they are noted. In the case of democracy, we could trace its beginnings in ancient history and make comparisons with the early development of constitutional government in a selected nation.

Using the *logical-quantitative* entry point, we approach the concept with numerical considerations or deductive and inductive reasoning processes. We could approach photosynthesis by creating a time line of the steps of photosynthesis and a chemical analysis of the process. In the case of democracy, we could create a time line of presidential mandates, congressional bills, constitutional amendments, and Supreme Court decisions that broadened democratic principles among people in the United States or analyze the arguments used for and against democracy by relevant political leaders throughout history.

The *foundational* entry point explores the philosophical and terminological facets of a concept. This approach is appropriate for people who like to pose fundamental questions, of the sort that we often associate with young children and with philosophers. A foundational corridor to photosynthesis might examine a transformative experience of our own or of a relevant individual, family, or institution and compare it with the process of photosynthesis, assigning parallel roles as they fit (for example, source of energy, catalyst, and so on). A foundational means of access to democracy could ponder the root meaning of the word, the relationship of democracy to other relevant forms of decision making and government, and the reasons one might prefer or not prefer a democratic rather than a social political philosophy.

Using the *esthetic* entry point, we emphasize sensory or surface features that will appeal to learners who favor an artistic stance toward the experience of living. In the case of photosynthesis we could look for visual, musical, or literary transformations that imitate or parallel photosynthesis, and represent them in artistic formats that might include painting, dance, mime, video, cartooning, or a dramatic sketch. With reference to democracy, we could experience and consider the variations of artistic performance that are characterized by group control as opposed to individual control: an orchestra as compared to a string quartet, ballet compared to experimental modern dance, a stage play compared to improvisational acting, and so on.

The last entry point is the *experiential* approach. Some people learn best with a hands-on approach, dealing directly with the materials that embody or convey the concept. In studying photosynthesis, such individuals might carry out a series of experiments involving photosynthesis. Those learners dealing with democracy might consider a relevant news issue and "enact" a democratic procedure, whether a legislative, judicial, or executive process. Then they could enact another approach to the same issue, replicating a less democratic system from another country, and compare their experience of the two diverse processes.

As instructors, we can open a number of doors on the same concept. Rather than presenting photosynthesis only by example, or only in terms of quantitative considerations, we can make available several entry points at the beginning or over time. In this way, we improve the chances that diverse learners with different ways of knowing and differing intelligence profiles can find relevant and engaging ways of learning. Learners may also suggest entry points of their own design. The use of technology, such as films, microcomputers, and interactive video, further enhances these efforts. Exhibit 5.1 presents a planning format and another example of a concept with five entry points.

Although Gardner's scheme of multiple intelligences is acknowledged in adult education, it has not been widely applied (Torff and Sternberg, 1998). However, this theory is very promising. Its integration of multiple intelligences and culture provides a substantive, unified, and generally applicable way to understand many of the findings of learning styles research regarding how people prefer to perceive, organize, and process information.

STRATEGY 28: *Make the learning activity an irresistible invitation to learn.*

The first time people experience anything that is new or that occurs in a different setting, they form an impression that will have a lasting impact (Scott, 1969). It is essential that we make the first learning experience for a new instructional unit or workshop an irresistible invitation to learn. We achieve such an effect when the learning activity meets the following five criteria.

1. *Safe:* there is little risk of the learners suffering any form of personal embarrassment from lack of knowledge, personal self-disclosure, or a hostile or arrogant social environment.

2. *Successful:* there is some form of acknowledgment, consequence, or product that shows that the learners are effective or, at the very least, that their effort is worthwhile.

Exhibit 5.1. Learning Activities Based on the Five Entry Points from Multiple Intelligences Theory.

Concept: All living things are systemically related.

Related principle: All human behaviors affect the earth's land, water, and air.

Entry Point	*Example*
Narrational	Report incidents that reflect one's understanding of the effects of human behavior on other countries and on distant places. Identify behaviors according to whether they harm or benefit the planet. Based on interests generated, select relevant reading materials.
Logical-quantitative	Choose a harmful but controversial human systemic influence, such as overpopulation. After finding data that quantify various (population) trends and the effects that result from this systemic influence, search for cultural, economic, and political factors (possibly from a country of interest) that inhibit or exacerbate this influence.
Foundational	Reflect on one's personal influence on the local environment. Consider those behaviors that improve the environment and those that pollute it. Examine the beliefs, assumptions, and values that appear critical to each set of behaviors. Create a personal environmental philosophy. Sharing it in small groups is optional.
Esthetic	Choose from the following options: create a sketch, a photo journal, a video, or poetry to depict relevant systemic relationships in one's own environment.
Experiential	Create mini-environments in local yards, in terrariums, or both. Experiment according to relevant influences (for example, temperature, water, pollutants, pets, traffic, and so forth). Observe and report effects on various life forms.

3. *Interesting:* the learning activity has some parts that are novel, engaging, challenging, or stimulating.

4. *Self-determined:* learners are encouraged to make choices that significantly affect the learning experience (for example, what they share, how they learn, what they learn, when they learn, with whom they learn, where they learn, or how they are assessed), basing those choices on their values, needs, concerns, or feelings. At the very least, learners have an opportunity to voice their perspectives.

5. *Personally relevant:* the instructor uses learners' concerns, interests, or prior experiences to create elements of the learning activity or develops the activity in concert with the learners. At the very least, a resource-rich learning environment is available to encourage learners' selections based on personal interest (for example, the library, the Internet, or a community setting).

I vividly remember experiencing this strategy in a workshop on adapting to the culture of another country. The initial learning activity focused on learning important expressions in the language of that country. The instructor began by asking the participants which expressions they most wanted to learn and recorded them on a flip chart ("Hello," "Good-bye," "Where is the bathroom?" "How much does this cost?" and the like). The instructor thus met the criteria of *personally relevant* and *self-determined.* After she taught us the expressions, she asked us to pick a partner and practice until we felt proficient. We could then move on to another partner for further practice. The instructor maintained *safety* by keeping the groups small (dyads). *Success* was immediate, and it was *interesting* (and fun) to practice with two different people. From that moment forward, participants used these expressions during breaks and free time.

I have found this strategy so useful that I have made it a mainstay in all my motivational planning. Every learning activity I create has to meet these five criteria. When an activity does not go well, I use the criteria to critique, refine, and improve the experience. A prototypical example of this strategy is brainstorming a relevant topic, because such brainstorming is

Safe	All answers are initially acceptable.
Successful	A list is created and acknowledged.
Interesting	Creative answers usually occur.
Self-determined	Answers are voluntary and self-chosen.
Personally relevant	The topic was selected because it was relevant.

STRATEGY 29: *Use the K-W-L strategy to introduce new topics and concepts.*

Originated by Donna Ogle (1986), the K-W-L strategy is an elegant way to construct meaning for a new topic or concept based on the prior knowledge of the learners. Adults have a storehouse of experiences that can give extraordinary meaning to novel ideas. The K-W-L strategy offers a simple and direct way to creatively probe adults' vast reservoir of knowledge.

During the first phase of the strategy, the learners identify what they think they Know about the topic. Whether the topic is black holes, the gross domestic product, phobias, or acid rain, this is a nonthreatening way to list some of the unique and varied ways adults understand something. It allows for multiple perspectives and numerous historical contexts. Just think of what the possibilities might be for a diverse group of adults initiating a unit on immigration law. The discussion of what adults Know about a topic can involve drawing, storytelling, critical incidents, and predictions.

In the second phase, the learners suggest what they Want to know about the topic. This information may be listed as questions or subtopics for exploration and research. For example, if the topic were immigration law, some questions might be as follows: Where do most immigrants come from today? Ten years ago? Fifty years ago? What was the last significant immigration law enacted by Congress? Is there evidence that immigrants deny work opportunities to established citizens of the United States? What are some noteworthy contributions of recent immigrants? These questions can serve as ideas for using the five entry points discussed under the multiple intelligences strategy (for example, a narrational entry point could be used to look at immigration history and an experiential and logical-quantitative entry point could be used to conduct research on recent immigration patterns). The K-W-L strategy also meets the five criteria for irresistible learning.

In the last phase, the learners identify what they have *Learned*, which may be the answers to their questions, important related information, and perhaps new information that counters some inaccuracies they may have held prior to this learning.

STRATEGY 30: *Use brainstorming webs to develop and link new information.*

A brainstorming web is a visual tool: symbols graphically linked by mental associations to create a pattern of information and a form of knowledge about an idea (Clarke, 1991). Brainstorming webs can be linear or nonlinear and individually or collaboratively constructed on paper, board, or a computer screen. (Figure 5.1 shows an example.) They allow adults, especially those more visually oriented, to construct mental models that reflect the unique set of relationships an idea can generate in their minds.

Brainstorming webs are the most idiosyncratic of visual tools, allowing adults the freedom to create the form of graphics and the associations themselves (Hyerle, 1996). There are a number of webbing techniques; I will emphasize the *mindmapping* techniques of Tony Buzan (1979). His approach (as shown in Figure 5.1) begins with a key word or image in the center of the page (in this case, *economics*), followed by extensions expanding outward.

Figure 5.1. A Learner Example of Mindmapping.

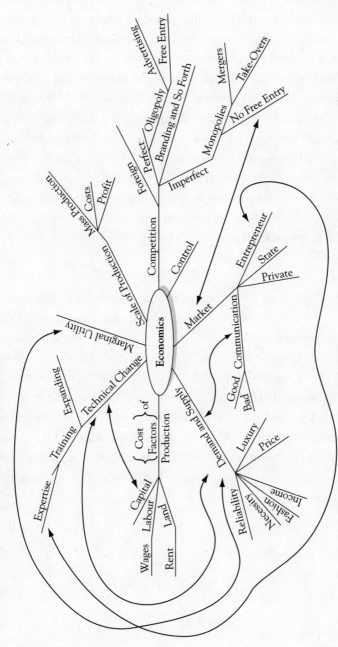

Source: From USE BOTH SIDES OF YOUR BRAIN by Tony Buzan. Copyright © 1974, 1983 by Tony Buzan. Used by permission of Dutton, a division of Penguin Putnam Inc.

Arrows and lines in other areas of the map connect secondary ideas to each other; the more important concepts are drawn nearer to the center. All words are printed in capitals, and single words are suggested for each line. Brainstorming webs can be made more holographic through the use of such highlights as arrows, asterisks, question marks, geometric shapes, three-dimensional drawings, and personal images. Multiple colors can enhance the web as a mnemonic tool. These techniques can make recall easier and information more accessible, encouraging learners to create relevant, comprehensive views of connected information. We therefore should not overly prescribe the techniques and uses of brainstorming webs. For additional information about other visual tools and their uses, see *Visual Tools for Constructing Knowledge* (Hyerle, 1996).

In this chapter, we have looked at numerous ways to build more positive attitudes toward learning. Which strategies you select will be based on your sensitive awareness of yourself, your adult learners, and the learning situation. When your material is relevant and all four of the important attitudinal directions are positive—toward you, the subject, the learner's self-concept, and the learner's expectancy for success—you have motivational force to support any instructional endeavor. Also, because attitudes seem most consequential at the beginning of any human contact, executing these strategies early in your instructional design creates an advantage for both the learner and you.

6

Enhancing Meaning
in Learning Activities

Against boredom even the gods themselves struggle in
vain.

Friedrich Nietzsche

For centuries, boredom has been a nemesis to the quality of life almost everywhere. Rare is the individual who seems able to continuously escape its oppressive grasp. Work and learning appear to be two areas in which people are especially vulnerable to the spontaneous emergence of this vague but powerful emotion. Unlike so many other predicaments of human existence, boredom threatens us not so much with something bad that may happen but with the realization that *nothing* may happen.

At first glance, boredom seems simple to define and easy to explain. It is often considered to be an individual's emotional response to an environment that is perceived to be monotonous (Davies, Shackleton, and Parasuraman, 1983). However, when adults are interviewed, the reasons they give for feelings of boredom include constraint, meaninglessness, lack of interest and challenge, repetitiveness, and the never-ending nature of a task or job.

Although conventional wisdom would support the idea that boredom directly interferes with learning and performance, the research is far from conclusive on this issue (Hockey and Hamilton, 1983; Renninger, Hidi, and Krapp, 1992). There is a reduction in alertness, but performance and memory do not appear to readily diminish even in prolonged work situations. Through means of personal will and self-regulation, people seem amazingly capable of continued effort to concentrate when they want to (Tobias, 1994). When we consider how much we have learned while in a state of boredom, this is not so surprising. Who has not passed a course, read a book, endured a class, or completed a homework assignment that was an exercise in tedium? Some successful adults would say that most of their formal learning experiences have been and continue to be a series of boring events. What personal experience and the research do seem to support is the finding that a host of negative influences on human performance appear to follow or accompany boredom—irritability, fatigue, strain, distractibility, and carelessness (Hockey, 1983).

Boredom may not in and of itself decrease learning, but it is a fertile ground for those vexations that disrupt and diminish a person's ability to maintain effort and attention. At best, under conditions of continual boredom a person will learn while in a state of distress. It does not require a great leap in logic to understand that such classical conditioning can erode the motivation of many adults to learn. In such situations, the instructor's quest for optimal performance from cooperative learners is a lost cause. Also, when adults work and learn in circumstances that are continually boring, their motivators tend to be fear, pressure, and extrinsic goals (paychecks, grades, job status, and so on). Obviously, these motivators work for many people. However, their long-term human consequences—such as stress (Hockey, 1983), minimal competence, and negative attitudes (Deci and Ryan, 1991)—are formidable. In many ways, motivation while learning acts like a timed-release capsule. Its negative or positive consequences discharge into our psychological systems long after the learning tasks have been completed.

So what can we as instructors do about boredom? How do we prevent the common decay that this viral influence so potently exerts on learner motivation? The opposite of boring is interesting,

and interest is the bridge to *meaning*, the most transcendent anti-
dote to boredom.

Interest, Meaning, and Learner Involvement

In recent years, research based on the concept of interest has dramatically increased (Pintrich and Schunk, 1996). The distinction
between interest and meaning often blurs. What is interesting usually has meaning for us, but not always. Novelty is often interesting
but initially may carry very little meaning. For example, a rapidly
moving object in the distance evokes my interest, and I follow it for
a period of time, but I do so with little understanding or construction of what it means.

Interest may be defined as a person's desire or preference for
interaction with something. We realize the person is interested by
his or her continuing attention and sense of delight during the
interaction (Deci, 1992). Interest stems from curiosity and is a common phenomenon. When interest becomes emotionally potent and
more passionate, it may be experienced as fascination, a less common occurrence. I might be interested in a good book, but it is a
rare book that I find fascinating (gripping and spellbinding). However, I am attentive and do enjoy reading a good book. Krapp, Hidi,
and Renninger (1992) have identified three types of interest to
make sense of this diverse and growing body of research: situational
interest, personal interest, and interest as a psychological state.

Situational Interest

Situational interest has been defined as interest generated mainly
by environmental conditions, such as novelty, surprise, complexity,
ambiguity, and universal themes (birth, death, and so on). Most of
the research is of the cognitive, individualistic sort and has been
tied to features of the environment, including media, computers,
and books. From a sociocultural, constructive perspective, I would
add the myriad things teachers can do to question, provoke, and
stimulate learner interest.

Adults are oceans of curiosity. Every day we are challenged to bring order out of chaos and meaning from paradox. What is puzzling, bizarre, and surprising compels our attention not so much through its relevance but through intrigue. The same wonder that makes a beach a miracle of small astonishments for a child elicits amazement from an adult in the presence of a gifted magician. To some extent our capacity for beguilement is beyond relevance, anchored in our need to remain alive. We anticipate in order to survive, whether to take a step or to enter traffic on a high-speed freeway. We human beings make countless predictions as we live our lives. When the reality turns out to be something unexpected, our reactions can range from a reflexive startle to an enduring fascination.

Personal Interest

Personal interest is often defined as a trait or characteristic of the adult that is relatively stable and enduring (Krapp, Hidi, and Renninger, 1992). We may have an interest in the arts, sciences, or sports that has been quite constant for many years. This kind of personal interest has for decades been a staple component of the task of matching adults to educational and occupational activities (Campbell and Hansen, 1981). Personal interest can also occur because of the importance or personal significance of a topic. It is this latter meaning that has more of a sociocultural bent to it and encompasses the learner's values and concerns. Personal significance is often a bridge to deeper meaning. For example, a relevant problem usually draws out our concerns and experiences. If an instructor asks the question, "Why is psychology important?" we might be initially interested in an abstract sort of way. But if that same instructor asks, "How has psychology helped or hindered people in our families?" we now have a personal interest of much deeper meaning.

Personal interests evolve out of our experience and socialization. Our families, our friends, and our opportunities develop these interests in us. We have only to look at our own families and lives to see the deep prints of these past stories.

However, academic interests are often shaped by personal capacity (intelligence profiles) and personal history of success (Deci, 1992). As instructors of adults, we may often have learners who have little initial experience with what we are teaching and therefore little personal interest—technological innovations come to mind. Initial success will be a significant contributor to learners' interest no matter how we connect the academic content to learners' concerns or experiences.

Interest as a Psychological State: Enhancing Meaning Through Engagement and Challenge

Interest as a psychological state unites interest and meaning. In terms of psychological research, it is the point at which the more cognitive, individualistic theory melds with the sociocultural understanding of motivation and learning. Interest as a psychological state is an interactive and relational understanding of interest: the individual's personal interest engages with environmental features to produce a psychological state of interest (Krapp, Hidi, and Renninger, 1992). Here is a basic example: a learner who possesses a personal interest in science has the opportunity to read a book about science and finds her interest in science as well as her motivation to learn more about science deepened by this experience. The sociocultural aspects of this scenario are the social and cultural features of the text, the possible scaffolding that led to the selection and reading level of the book, and the interaction between the learner and the book.

From this point forward, I will use the motivational condition of *enhancing meaning* and the qualities of *engagement and challenge* to describe strategies that elicit and heighten adult motivation. The sociocultural constructive literature is richer and broader in its possibilities for more active involvement between the learner and the environment. Such strategies as posing problems, conducting authentic research, and using case study methods engage and challenge learners with culturally relevant and, therefore, interesting content. For these activities, learners have to clarify distinctions, construct explanations, and create complex understandings. Often there needs to be a dialogue from multiple perspectives among learners that results in a collective understanding. In a way, through these processes, learners cannot help but heighten their own meaning and be involved. The learners are searching, evaluating, constructing, creating, and organizing the learning material into new or better ideas, memories, skills, understandings, solutions, or decisions. They may create a product or reach a goal. This may be a novel insight they have applied, a new skill learned, a problem solved, or a case completed. In the opinion of many scholars, engaging and challenging learning activities are the best and most productive way to learn (Lambert and McCombs, 1998). However, before we explore those activities, we just might need a few strategies to get the learners' attention.

How to Maintain Learners' Attention

"Pay attention or you won't learn anything!" The words have an unsettling effect. They conjure up disquieting, distant images of former teachers, harsh faces, and shrill voices. And whether we liked it or not, they were right. No attention, no learning. As instructors we know this dictum only too well. But demanding attention from adults is one of the least effective ways to get it. In fact, pressuring people to watch or listen to us will probably only diminish their willingness to cooperate.

When we want to maintain learners' attention we are looking for ways to evoke more alertness among learners, to help them be more ready to follow the learning material, acquire information, and participate in the learning activity (Anderson, 1995). Our effort usually involves an arousal of their energy and a refocusing toward the event at hand. Attention is not the same as interest. Attention is of shorter duration and may not be infused with desire or emotion, but it should, at least, open the way for or restore interest.

Although paying attention is the first step in learning, it is a very limited resource for an instructor. Due to distraction, attention can dissipate in a moment. For adults, who have many responsibilities, mental distraction is a palpable reality in any learning situation. The following strategies can be most helpful to maintain their attention.

STRATEGY 31: *Provide frequent response opportunities to all learners on an equitable basis.*

Whenever people are in a learning situation, the amount they will publicly interact with their instructor or peers will have an important effect on the attention they give to the learning activity (Kerman, 1979). If learners know they are not going to respond or perform in a given learning session, these incentives for paying attention are absent, with predictable results. Learners can afford not to be alert because lack of alertness has no immediate consequences. If taking notes, monitoring information, or listening to other learners has no imminent effect on their relationship to their instructor or peers, they will lose an important reason for concentrating on the task at hand. Also, if they see the same few people dominating the response opportunities in a given activity, learners may become discouraged and resentful of the entire process.

Response opportunities are any chances we or the learning activity provide for learners to participate or perform publicly. These include answering questions, giving opinions, demonstrating skills, and reacting to feedback. Our goal as instructors is to instill within our learners a constant awareness that they will be receiving opportunities to respond or perform during the learning activity.

When using this strategy for larger group discussions, there are four guidelines for maintaining an atmosphere that is humane and respectful. First, announce to the learning group that you would like to have as many people participating as possible but that it is always OK to "pass." This gives everyone a choice, keeps the discussion safe, and particularly respects those adults who have not been socialized to respond in front of groups. It also creates an expectancy everyone can use to make sure they are prepared and alert. People do not like to be caught off guard, and many adults have had years of conditioning in situations where if they did not volunteer to respond, they were given no opportunity to do so.

Second, make sure everyone does get an equitable chance to respond or perform. Seating charts can be invaluable for this process (and some minor record keeping may be necessary). We may gently revisit those who have passed.

Third, random selection is best on a moment-to-moment basis. This form of unpredictability gives everyone the feeling that they may be next. However, if the skill or response demands some degree of advance preparation on the learner's part, a more orderly process of selection may be beneficial. Also, calling only on volunteers can be hazardous unless everyone tends to volunteer. We have all had the experience of seeing the same few people in a group responding or performing over and over again because no one else seems to volunteer. You may find it necessary to call a moratorium on voluntary responding (a few sessions may be all that it takes) so as to give everyone a chance.

Fourth, always dignify the learner's response. For most adults, the real fear in public responding is embarrassment. They must know they will be treated respectfully for their efforts. By consistently giving learners some degree of credit for their response and by using their responses to move toward further learning, we model this respect for everyone. A helpful mental attitude that enables us to carry on this process is to remember that even the wrong answer is the right answer to another question. For example, if I ask who the president was during World War I and someone responds, "Abraham Lincoln," I can say, "Yes, he was president during a very important war—the Civil War. Now let's find out who was president during World War I." I move on, smoothly and respectfully. Most mistakes are not random (Gage and Berliner, 1998). They are usually logical and have a pattern. By giving learners the most credit possible for their participation and by helping them learn from their errors while still respecting their integrity, we can reduce their fears. Our guiding frame of mind is to let learners know what they can competently do and then, as fluidly as possible, help them take the next possible step. In some cases, this might mean probing further, giving a hint or a second chance, waiting a while longer, or soliciting help from another learner. As long as we avoid assuming a right-or-wrong attitude toward our learners, so much is possible.

The following are some specific techniques for enhancing learners' reaction to response opportunities:

- When asking a question or announcing an opportunity to perform a task, wait three seconds or more before selecting a respondent (Tobin, 1987). This technique allows everyone to consider the possible answer or skill to be demonstrated. It gives learners a chance to organize themselves mentally and emotionally for their response. It also helps focus everyone else's attention on the forthcoming answer or demonstration.

- When you are looking for a volunteer, ask for a show of hands in response to your question or activity and wait three to five seconds after the first indication of a volunteer before selecting a respondent. This technique has the same advantages as the first point, and it increases the number of possible respondents from which to choose. When we tend to call on the first few volunteers, we often unwittingly "teach" the rest of the learners not to volunteer.

- While pausing before selecting a respondent, look over the entire group. This will tend to increase everyone's attentiveness because your survey encompasses the learners as a unified body.

- For responses and demonstrations of some duration, alert the rest of the learning community that they will be asked to respond in some fashion to what they have observed. For example: "After Zachary has presented his case study, I'd like to ask a few of you to give him your evaluation of which sales techniques were critical to his success with his client." This method invests the entire learning community in the task at hand and affirms their responsibility to their peers.

- Sometimes use light, humorous, unpredictable methods of selecting a respondent. For example: "The next people to get a chance are all those with birthdays in February," or, "Well, let's see who had toast for breakfast. OK, we've got three volunteers." Or try asking someone, "What's your favorite color? Blue; that's great. Now check in your group to see who is wearing the most blue, because that's who's going to try the next problem for us."

- During any task where learners are working on their own or in small groups, move among them as an available resource and observer. Depending on the situation, you can comment, question, react, advise, or simply quietly observe. Under such conditions, learners are no longer isolated in their work, and you have provided numerous response opportunities for them.

STRATEGY 32: *Help learners realize their accountability for what they are learning.*

People tend to take more seriously learning for which they are held accountable (Good and Brophy, 1994). There are times when paying attention takes real effort and determined resolve. Even under conditions that are normally stimulating, fatigue, satiation, and life's everyday problems can take their toll on adults' ability to concentrate. They are more likely to find the willpower to remain attentive when they clearly know that the knowledge and skills they will have to demonstrate are directly dependent on their learning experiences.

One sees an almost automatic focusing of attention among learners when any instructor announces, "What we will cover next will be on the final exam." Although many accountability schemes rely on testing, there are many other possibilities, such as job performance, projects, target behaviors, and skill demonstrations. Whatever the form of accountability, adults will usually intensify their concentration on those aspects of their learning experience that directly bear on what they or someone else holds them responsible for knowing. However, adults can construe accountability as a coercive force for paying attention. When we mention exams and final projects as being related to their learning tasks, they may feel threatened. Their anxiety is real. We have all felt it. Therefore, we must use accountability to enlist learners' attention only when necessary and in an empathic manner, not as a menacing manipulation.

One of the best ways to ensure that accountability is used in an appropriate manner is to be certain that all components of the curriculum or instructional design are imperative for the achievement of the learning goal and for the means by which it is assessed. In this way the learners know that *all* the learning activities are valuable and build toward the competencies they must exhibit. There is no busywork or learning experience that does not vitally contribute to the end result. A good analogy for this approach is a recipe for a fine soufflé. Every ingredient and every process that mixes and prepares the ingredients is necessary to the final outcome. Once we are certain the learning activities are a concise and efficient body of requisite experiences geared to achievement of the learning goal, the following methods may help to encourage learners' attentiveness.

• Where appropriate, demonstrate how your learning program is efficiently designed to build the requisite skills and knowledge for which the learners will be held accountable. Use syllabi, outlines, models, or diagrams to briefly but lucidly show the integrated plan of your program and related learning goals. Indicate how you will assess learners (tests, projects, job performance, and so forth) and how assessment is functionally dependent on the learning process and content. This will help learners understand that their concentration is necessary every step of the way.

• Selectively use *manding stimuli*. Mands are verbal statements that have a highly probable consequence associated with them (Skinner, 1957). When a person yells, "Watch out!" people usually stop what they are doing and quickly check their surroundings for immediate information or action. Instructors have available to them many mands that can focus learners' attention and cue their concentration. Here are some examples: "Please note this"; "Now listen closely"; "It is critical to realize that . . ."; "It will help a great deal in understanding this if you remember that . . ."; "The point that brings this all together is . . ." Wise use of such mands can be a continual instructional resource for directing learners' attention to material that does make a difference in their training or education.

• Selectively employ handouts. These can be outlines, models, diagrams, advance organizers (Woolfolk, 1998), key concepts, definitions, and any combination of these. They help learners follow and focus on your lecture, presentation, or demonstration. Learners are more likely to pay attention to what is important when what is important is concretely noted, well organized, and literally within their grasp.

• Intersperse lectures and demonstrations with the *think-pair-share* process. This is a short processing method to increase attention and involvement in a relevant manner. The instructor asks learners to *think briefly about* what has been stated or observed and then to *pair up* with someone to *share* their reflections for a few minutes. It's a wonderful way to intersperse any passive learning experience with a thoughtful procedure that invites the learners' per-spectives and dialogue. The directions can be specifically focused or more general, as the following example illustrates. "Please take a minute to think about how this material relates to your own life. Then turn to a partner and have a brief conversation about your reflections." After completion of this procedure, the instructor can begin a whole-group discussion, solicit comments, list insights, take questions, or move on to the next segment of the lecture or demon-stration.

STRATEGY 33: *Provide variety in personal presentation style, modes of instruction, and learning materials.*

Variety has motivational effects (Gage and Berliner, 1998). It is stimulating and draws learners' attention toward its source. People tend to pay more attention to things that are changing than to things that are unchanging. However, to use variety simply for the sake of variety is not a good idea, because concentration and learn-ing often demand that a stimulus be held constant for further under-standing and retention. That is why microscopes, photographs, and slides are so valuable to people in the pursuit of knowledge. When-ever we as instructors can change some element of the process of instruction without making that variance so extreme that it distracts learners from the subject at hand, we will probably help them pay attention. Timing variety so that it can serve as a cue to important information or skills is probably one of the best ways to use it to the advantage of motivation and learning.

First, there is *variety in personal presentation style*. At the physical level, every instructor is an instrument of stimulation. How instruc-tors use their bodies and voices can be a constant source of variety for their learners. The following is a checklist of those categories of human characteristics that instructors can vary to stimulate their learners. Each category contains a series of related questions that you can use to assess your presentation style during instruction.

- Body movement. How often do you move? In what direction? Are you ever among your learners? Are you predictable in your movements? Some movement during instruction is desirable. Across the room as well as along the sides of the room are possible directions. Now and then "going in" among your learners is another variation. Such movement brings you temporarily closer to all learners and makes them more likely to pay attention to where you will be next.

- Gestures and facial expressions. Do you use gestures? If so, what kind? When? How animated is your face? How often do you smile? How does your body language change in relationship to learners' questions, responses, and behavior? Considering the significant intercultural differences in the meaning of gestures and facial expressions (see Chapter Four), it is difficult to make generalizations about how an instructor should act. Being energetic and friendly is appealing to most adult learners, however.

- Voice. What is the tone and pitch of your voice? How often and when do these change? How is your voice used for emphasis, emotion, and support of your topic? If someone could not see you but only hear you, would your voice alone provide sufficient stimulation and variety? Of all the aspects of personal presentation style, the voice is probably the most important yet one of the least studied (Andersen, 1997). Voice is a constant *metacommunication:* communication about communication. It influences everything learners hear their instructors say. Adults tend to accept the vocal quality of a message as the correct cue when a person's words seem in conflict with the way they are spoken (Hurt, Scott, and McCroskey, 1978). For example: "*That* is a good job?" would not be a compliment to adults. Because so much of instruction is talking, creative use and variation of your voice is a major asset to gaining learners' attention. With appropriate pauses, the voice can be doubly effective.

- Pauses. When and how often do you pause? How long do you remain silent? For what purposes do you use pauses? Like variations in color, pauses are orienting stimuli that arouse our attention (Gage and Berliner, 1998). Pauses can greatly enhance verbal instruction.

You can use them to break informational segments into smaller pieces for better understanding, capture attention by contrasting sound with silence, signal learners to listen, emphasize an important point, provide time for reflection, and create suspense or expectation.

Second, there is *variety in modes of instruction and learning materials*. Modes of instruction are the ways in which instructors interact with learners and the activities in which learners can participate while they are learning. Lecturing, discussing, showing a video, and playing a simulation game are four different modes of instruction. Learning materials are the physical resources used to instruct, such as films, books, compact discs, and chalkboards. Variety in either of these areas will usually stimulate adults. Some specific guidelines for this approach are as follows:

• Vary the modality of learning (usually between auditory, visual, and tactile modes). For example, when you switch the channel of communication from auditory to visual, even momentarily, learners usually become more alert to adjust their attention. By selectively using interactive video, graphs, storyboards, overhead transparencies, computer programs, and other media, learners stimulate their own attention. Although substantial research has been conducted over the years to determine which media are best for achieving particular learning goals, there are no firm conclusions (Rothwell and Kazanas, 1992). When it comes to visual media, it seems that the clearer and simpler the text or diagram, the more effective it is. Parsimoniously using visual aids to draw attention to new or critical information increases their effectiveness (Smith and Delahaye, 1983). Varying the intensity of any stimuli (size, shape, color, loudness, and complexity) has been found to attract learners' attention (Day, 1981).

• Diversify the process of learning, designing interaction so that learners think or act differently from one activity to another. For example, they move from listening to a recording to solving a problem, or they watch a film and then discuss its contents, or they work alone and then work in small groups. In each of these cases, different forms of thinking, acting, and communicating are involved. Every time adults alter the process of learning, they use different mental and physical resources, which prevents fatigue and maintains energy. As the old adage goes, a change is as good as a rest.

STRATEGY 34: *Introduce, connect, and end learning activities attractively and clearly.*

Each instructional session usually comprises a number of learning activities. During this time, learners might see a video, engage in a dialogue, work on a case study, and complete a self-assessment. A class session is analogous to a sporting event during which each team receives clearly delineated opportunities to exercise its skills. Baseball gives a team three outs to score; football allows four downs to go ten yards. In sports, these units of participation have obvious beginnings and endings to simplify transitions, to focus spectators' and players' attention, and to keep the game running clearly and smoothly. In a similar manner, a learning activity is significantly enhanced when it is distinctly introduced and evidently connected to previous and future learning activities.

Just as a kickoff tells the crowd, "Pay attention, the action is about to begin," an attractive introduction gives learners the same message. Some stimulating methods aside from the use of media and shifts in personal presentation style are as follows:

- *Asking provocative questions:* "How many of you have ever . . . ?" "When was the last time . . . ?" "Did you imagine before you took this training that you were going to . . . ?" "What do you think would happen if . . . ?"

- *Calling on learners to become active:* ask them to help, to move, to observe, to assess, and so on.

- *Creating anticipation:* "I have been looking forward to doing this activity with you since your training session began." "This film will show the concrete advantages of applying the skills you have been learning." "This next set of problems is really tricky; let's see how we do."

- *Relating the learning activity to pop culture and current events:* "You might say the next person we are going to discuss is the Michael Jordan of the computer world." "This case study could provide lyrics for a country western ballad." "What we are going to take a look at next has been organized like an Olympic sporting event."

Connecting learning activities is a real art. Instructors make numerous transitions in any learning session. To segue automatically and fluidly helps maintain learners' attention and maximize instructional impact. The following are some helpful techniques:

- *Using organizational aids:* such as handouts, outlines, models, and graphs that interrelate concepts, topics, key points, and essential information.

- *Indicating what the new activity relates to:* such as how it continues the building of a skill or how it further demonstrates a concept or how it may contribute to a future learning goal.

- *Making directions and instructions for the next learning activity as clear as possible:* this technique applies to introducing as well as connecting learning activities. People often stop paying attention simply because they are confused about what they are supposed to do. By giving accurate directions, we can avoid unnecessary distractions.

- *Checking for understanding:* any time we provide important information, whether it is a concept or a procedure, and especially if what comes next is dependent on this information, we should take a few moments to see if everyone understands. Checking for understanding can run the gamut from a simple question ("Are these directions clear enough?") to formal assessment. *Not* checking for understanding is one of the most common omissions I see in training and teaching. (Fact is, *I still* have to remind myself to check for understanding.)

Closure refers to how we end a learning activity and help learners feel a sense of completion. Closure not only focuses their attention but also gives them the feeling of satisfaction that naturally arises from their awareness that they have accomplished a learning task. Some helpful means to this end are as follows:

- *Reviewing the basic concepts or skills achieved during the learning activity:* "Before we move on, let us review the main ideas we have discussed thus far."

- *Allowing for clarification at the end of the learning activity:* "Now that we have finished this section, are there any questions about what we have done?"

- *Requesting feedback, opinions, or evaluation:* "Perhaps the best way to end this exercise would be to share with one another what we have learned from cooperating in this task."

- *Being sensitive to the possibilities of spontaneous closure that can arise within any group of learners:* for example, after the training group has just voluntarily applauded the response of a colleague, saying, "I can't think of a better way to end this discussion. Let's take a break."

STRATEGY 35: *Selectively use breaks, physical exercises, and energizers.*

Most learning requires effort, and prolonged expenditure of effort usually produces fatigue. Also, adults often come to learning activities having already expended large amounts of their energy in their family and workplace. It is highly probable that adults will become tired, even in an interesting environment. Once adults become fatigued, their ability to pay attention can readily decline, and the meaning of any activity may diminish. To avoid this problem, selectively give breaks or incorporate physical exercise and energizers into your instructional plan. A ten-minute respite can make a world of difference. When breaks are not possible or are too inconvenient, learners can stand up and stretch or participate in small sets of physical exercises. Also consider the possibility of energizers (Weinstein and Goodman, 1980), which are very short adult games (ten to fifteen minutes) that can add enjoyment and social contact to the process of renewing energy. A final suggestion: please do not let the clock solely determine when breaks are taken. Fatigue is not chronological. Our flexibility about such matters can greatly enhance the amount of attention learners can give. By investing ten minutes of time on a break *when it is needed*, we may gain as much as sixty minutes of alertness.

How to Invite and Evoke Learners' Interest

When learning activities invite or evoke interest, adults willingly participate. They may not always expend a great deal of effort, but they are open and responsible learners who want to concentrate on, understand, and retain what they are learning.

At this point, we need to remember that the motivational purposes of *attention, interest,* and *engagement and challenge* (covered in the last section of this chapter) may overlap. What is attention-getting may become interesting, and what is interesting could naturally be a part of an engaging and challenging learning activity. All three motivational purposes contribute to the motivational condition of *meaning*. What categorically separates interest strategies from engagement and challenge strategies is that the latter—case studies and authentic research, for example—are entire methodologies. By their very nature they offer considerable challenge, requiring complex and substantive interactions that usually result in a learning product. For example, one strategy to evoke interest is to use humor (Strategy 38), but it doesn't require a learning product or the extensive, prolonged effort that research does. However, we might use humor to make research more interesting. And that's another distinction: we can often use the strategies for attention and interest to deepen engagement and challenge. This section describes strategies that elicit adult interest so as to make learning more compelling. We begin with those more likely to invite personal interest from adult learners.

STRATEGY 36: *Relate learning to adult interests, concerns, and values.*

By embedding the learning activity and what we say and do in current adult interests, concerns, and values, we provide learners a constant stream of *relevant* material. In this manner, we are exposing them to experiences that will naturally connect to their desire for understanding. Interest surveys for adults (Smith, 1982) do exist and can be informative. In general, the most stirring examples, analogies, supporting evidence, and current events are those that vividly touch on what people already find interesting.

One of the developmental dimensions of maturation during adulthood is a fuller awareness of deep concerns (Knowles, 1980). *Concerns* are especially provocative of adults' emotions. They are more profound and more persistent than are interests because they contain an inner uneasiness. They usually represent a gap between some ideal and reality. They often indicate some fear or worry about people's aspirations. Parents are not only *interested* in their children's health; they are frequently *concerned* about their children's health. In like manner, business owners are not only *interested* in profits but also frequently *concerned* about profits. If learning is related to adults' concerns, their emotions will be elicited quickly. The question for instructors here is, Does anything about this topic or skill relate to adults' concerns, and if so, can I constructively deal with it? For example, a seminar on human relations would very likely bring out learners' concerns if the issue of sexual harassment were used as a basis for skill development. However, the instructor has to be able to deal constructively with this issue if optimal motivation is to be maintained.

Concerns often relate to human values. *Values* represent the important and stable ideas, beliefs, and assumptions that consistently affect a person's behavior (Fuhrmann and Grasha, 1983). Someone who values politics does not merely vote. That person probably also joins a political organization, donates some amount of money to political causes, writes to political representatives about selected issues, reads about political matters, acts on behalf of political candidates, and frequently talks about politics with friends. Every adult has some strong values. When these are integrated with a learning experience, the adult's interest and other emotions will surface.

When learning events correspond to people's values, people will usually feel reassured. People are pleased to hear their political beliefs supported and to know they are rearing their children soundly and appropriately. But when the instructional content or other learners' perspectives do not mesh with adults' values, there is a good chance that learners will feel tense, threatened, frustrated, or sometimes angry; they are out of their comfort zone. The following topics are areas with which many adults associate firmly held values (Loden and Rosener, 1991):

Politics	Friends	War, peace
Ethnicity	Money	Authority
Work	Age	Gender
Leisure	Death	Sex
Education	Health	Love
Family	Race	Material possessions
Sexual orientation (clothes, hairstyle, manners)	Religion, spirituality	Culture (art, music, literature)
		Personal tastes

When these topics become any part of the learning experience, adults' emotional responsiveness is likely to increase. On some occasions there may be disagreement or controversy. Please remember: the degree to which learners generally feel the motivational condition of inclusion does a great deal to maintain mutual respect, as does their understanding of the participation guidelines (see Chapter Four). However, this is an appropriate place to discuss leadership tasks and effective communication.

Let's begin by saying that beyond the instructor's careful attention to the discussion at hand and his or her exercising the core characteristic of cultural responsiveness (see Chapter Two), the communication roles described here require some experience for proficient use. Please consider practice, feedback, and coaching to improve their effectiveness. The following paragraphs are an adaptation of Pat Griffin's suggestions (1997a, pp. 286–291) regarding communication roles instructors can consider using during value-laden discussions.

• Giving information. At times, offering factual information in the form of statistics or documented facts is useful. This is often an important way to address misconceptions.

Example. A learner states that gay men are child molesters. The instructor responds, "That's a frequently held notion that's received a lot of attention over the years. However, police records show that well over 90 percent of child sexual abuse involves heterosexual men molesting female children. (Notice that the first statement tends to deflect any listener reaction that this idea belongs only to the learner making the remark. This helps to diminish defensiveness.)

• Conceptualizing. Feelings can overwhelm people and cause them to shut down or lose focus. The introduction of a conceptual model or a recourse to useful questions can give people a way to understand their feelings and a means to proceed more productively.

Example. Several learners are arguing back and forth about the degree of racism that continues to exist in the United States. The instructor says, "I think some of us might be on a learning edge here. Please check and see if this might be true for you. Any suggestions for what we might do to expand our comfort zone?" Or, "We have some differences of opinion here. What questions might provide insights or clarify the differences between these viewpoints?" (Learners could break into small groups to generate questions, and the instructor could list their questions.)

• Reflecting. Sometimes one of the best ways to encourage adults to reconsider their position is to reflect back what they say so that they understand the impact of their words or can begin to identify underlying assumptions.

Example. The instructor repeats a learner's statement: "So what you're saying is that the Arab population in this city is not really discriminated against because they're financially secure."

• Working with silence. Sometimes silence reflects fear or discomfort. Silences can actually provide a powerful learning opportunity and deepen dialogue. On such occasions, we have a number of options. We can ask learners to write down their feelings at that moment or turn to a partner and share their thoughts. Both options give learners a chance to acknowledge and clarify their reactions.

Sometimes something as simple as commenting on the silence opens the discussion at a deeper level.

Example. Two adults begin to argue vigorously about the role of the federal government in municipal affairs. As their confrontation tails off, silence envelopes the learning group. The instructor says, "I'm not sure what this silence means. Can anyone say what you're thinking or feeling right now?" Or, "Why don't we each take a few minutes to write down what we are thinking or feeling right now. Then, to the degree that you're comfortable, talk about it with a partner before we come back to the entire group."

• Redistributing. At times, we need to make space for other adults to participate in a discussion.

Example. "Before we hear from you again, Pat, I'd like to see if some of the people who haven't had a chance to speak would like to say something." Or, "This is great! Everyone wants to talk. Let's try it this way. I'll call three people, and after they've had their turn, I'll call three more, until everyone's had a chance. OK? Let's go."

• Accepting the expression of feelings. For some instructors and adult learners, the expression of intense feelings in a learning environment is an unusual experience. At times like this, how we react as instructors will strongly influence the feelings of security and respect for all learners present. There is no formula. Usually, our reaction is spontaneous. When I look back on my own behavior, it tends to include an acknowledgment and validation of the feeling. Sometimes appreciation is appropriate. Ultimately, we need to guide learners to the next phase of learning.

Example. A learner begins to cry as he tells about the difficulties his mother endured at school because of a severe disability. The instructor says, "Seems like that's still a painful memory for you (*acknowledgment*). It's difficult to see those we love suffer (*validation*). Thanks for giving us a chance to learn from your own experience (*appreciation*). Now let's take a look at how we might influence a situation like this as administrators (*learning connection*)." (It's never this tidy!)

- Disclosing personal information. When we disclose personal information, we need to be clear about the purpose of the disclosure. I agree with Griffin (p. 290), who states, "It is never appropriate for facilitators to work out their own issues during a class." If we tell too many personal stories, adults may begin to discount the course as our own "agenda." Personal stories should help learners arrive at a better understanding of a topic or idea.

Example. The instructor says, "I'd like to tell you about something I learned about silence from a Japanese friend. I don't think I could have learned this otherwise." In this case, the personal disclosure is to help learners realize, and recount from their own experience, that different cultural perspectives sometimes give us insights that we cannot gain through our own culture.

- Addressing conflict. There are times when we need to encourage the expression of conflicting ideas. (I discuss this further in the section dealing with critical incidents.) Learner dialogue related to conflicting ideas is an important part of transformative learning. In productive conflict, all learners have a voice, their right to express differing perspectives is assured, respect is maintained, and the participation guidelines (see Chapter Four) are in effect.

STRATEGY 37: *When possible, clearly state or demonstrate the benefits that will result from the learning activity.*

People usually want to know more about anything that benefits them. They often want to be better, quicker, and more creative in doing what they value. There are many things they want to save and gain, such as time and money. Most adults want to overcome their limitations in health, endurance, and speed. Any learning that offers the possibility of acquiring a significant advantage is not only interesting but also can, indeed, be fascinating.

Following is a list of general items (McLagan, 1978), some quite simple and some quite profound, that many adults want to gain:

Health	Security	Advancement
Time	Efficiency	Money
Comfort	Popularity	Leisure
Enjoyment	Freedom	Competence
Self-confidence	Respect	Praise (vocational or social)
Improved appearance	Personal prestige	

If anything we offer adults to learn can help them acquire any of these items, adults will probably consider that learning to be beneficial. This is not an exhaustive list. The most important questions for us are, What are the real benefits to adults that this learning experience offers? and, How can I make the benefits apparent and available to these learners? If we can answer these questions clearly, we have a vital opportunity to increase adults' interest. For example, what technician could easily remain indifferent to a trainer who introduced a new tool with the statement, "This instrument can repair 90 percent of all malfunctions in this system."

The remaining strategies in this section offer ways to evoke situational interest. They are probably most applicable to direct instruction, such as presentations and demonstrations, but the first—humor—seems welcome at any time.

STRATEGY 38: *While instructing, use humor liberally and frequently.*

Humor has many qualities—being *interesting* is one of them. People love to laugh. They will be a little more interested in anyone or anything that provides this possibility. Humor offers enjoyment, a unique perspective, and unpredictability. All these qualities are attractive and stimulating to most human beings. I have yet to hear an adult come out of a training session and say, "*I'm not going back. It's too funny in there. All we ever do is laugh.*"

But how does one develop a sense of humor? It still seems to be a bit of a mystery. I've heard Neil Simon say that some words are funny and some are not. For example, *chicken* is funny; *computer* is not. So for years I've challenged technologists to tell me a good computer joke. This is the best so far: Who had the first computer? Adam and Eve. It was an Apple with two megabytes. Maybe Mr. Simon was right.

Well then, how does an instructor successfully incorporate humor into learning activities? There is no guaranteed formula. However, Goodman (1981) has some helpful suggestions:

- Remember that people are more humorous when they feel safe and accepted.

- Laugh *with* people (which includes), not *at* them (which excludes).

- Humor is an attitude. Be open to the unexpected, insane, silly, and ridiculous that life daily offers.

- Do not take yourself too seriously. How easily can you laugh at yourself?

- Be spontaneous.

- Don't be a perfectionist with humor. It will intimidate you. No one can be witty or funny 100 percent of the time. (Talk shows are a living testament to this.)

- Have comic vision. If you look for humor, humor will find you.

STRATEGY 39: *Selectively induce parapathic emotions.*

Parapathic emotions (Apter, 1982) are strong feelings (anger, delight, affection, sorrow) people undergo as they experience something essentially make-believe. For example, parapathic emotions are the intense feelings we may have from watching a movie or a play. People tend to become interested in anything that can induce such emotions. Excellent speakers often use stories, anecdotes, and quotations to elicit parapathic emotions in their audiences. In colloquial terms, these *grabbers* act as magnets to attract high levels of audience interest. They are often used in the beginning of speeches and presentations for this very purpose. Adults cannot easily turn their attention away from anything that has made them feel deeply. Whenever we can use such devices within the context of our learning activities, we will have an excellent means to arouse and sustain learner interest. Any medium that can induce powerful emotions, such as literature, drama, and music, is a fertile field to consider as a possible resource.

STRATEGY 40: *Selectively use examples, analogies, metaphors, and stories.*

This strategy may seem redundant. This book is filled with examples, and many of its motivational strategies discuss how to use examples effectively. However, I have such respect for the impact of appropriate exemplification that I have included an explicit discussion of its merits here.

Examples are the bread and butter of any good instructional effort. They not only stimulate but also, perhaps more than anything else an instructor might easily do, tell learners how well they really comprehend what has preceded those examples (Gage and Berliner, 1998). For learners, examples are the "moment of truth" for personal meaning—when the information, concept, or demonstration is clarified, applied, or accentuated. Good examples give learners a way to focus new learning so that it is concretely illustrated in their own minds. A fine example nurtures learners, enhancing their concentration and mental effort. Most important, it is difficult for learners to remain interested in anything they cannot understand. Examples are the refueling stations in any learner's journey to new knowledge. Choose them carefully, make them vivid, and use them generously. We must also realize that when learners construct their own good examples, they create meaning that reflects language and imagery more firmly anchored in their world than what we as instructors usually have to offer. In the long run, this is deeper learning.

Analogies and metaphors are examples that enhance interest by colorfully showing new ideas and information in forms and contexts that learners already understand. Because adults are experientially rich learners with considerable mental powers of abstraction and deduction, they readily create, use, and appreciate analogies and metaphors (Deshler, 1990). Metaphors allow us to reach meanings not possible with more academic language. For example, to say being the mayor of a large city is enormously challenging is logically clear, but to say being the mayor of a large city sometimes gives you the feeling you might be steering the *Titanic* adds insight and expands meaning to a much deeper and more emotional level. Deshler's method of metaphor analysis (1990) offers rich possibilities for critically reflecting on the values of personal, popular, and organizational cultures.

Stories, especially when they are well told, imaginative, and unpredictable, are extremely interesting. Used wisely and relevantly, they can captivate a group of learners. They are also the way people give meaning to their own lives. Ask anyone to tell their favorite family story or how they celebrated their birthday as a child or an important dream from their past, and you have opened doors to personal understanding beyond most psychology textbooks. Sometimes it's great fun to have a workshop or course *storyteller*, someone who summarizes the story of the learning group at significant intervals, such as the end of the day or week.

STRATEGY 41: *Use uncertainty, anticipation, and prediction to the degree that learners enjoy them with a sense of security.*

We don't want to act too weird, but we do want how we instruct to have some quality of the unexpected to it. Unpredictability is very stimulating. In fact, the more unexpected the event, the greater the arousal people feel (Apter, 1982). Every form of entertainment, including sports, art, fiction, and humor, makes use of such properties as uncertainty and surprise in secure contexts. When our learners do not know exactly what is going to happen next or when it is going to happen, we have usually captured their interest and anticipation. This is the way learning can become an adventure. When adults feel safe and capable, unpredictability breeds a sense of enjoyable excitement. Being in a course or training session where anything might happen but no one will be hurt is exhilarating. The following are some of the ways we can make instruction unpredictable yet secure:

• We can *plan the unexpected,* diagnosing our materials and methods for patterns of predictability and inserting the unpredictable. For example, in a situation where textual or modular materials have dominated learning, we can choose to depart from them, switching to real-life situations and more personalized learner interests. Moment to moment, we might make a mistake on purpose, lecture from a seat among our learners, act a bit out of character, tell a self-deprecating story, or put a great cartoon on the overhead simply because it's a great cartoon. In the context of good taste and proper timing, there are myriad possibilities.

• We can *attempt instructional experiments.* In these instances, we do things that we have carefully considered and that seem effective to us but that we have no certainty about until we actually do them. Every creative instructor does this now and then because new methods and materials often can only be tested on the job. We may even tell our learners that what we are about to do is something quite new and enlist their support and feedback.

• We can *stay aware of the moment and trust our intuition.* Every learning situation is unique, and our next important instructional moment may be entirely dependent on circumstances we could not predict. A question, a cultural or political event, a learner's problem, or the mood of a group can create a learning opportunity only our spontaneity and flexibility can affirm. Adults appreciate relevance and an instructor who can adjust instruction to the important matters that unexpectedly evolve in a human situation, whether it's a headline in the morning paper or the fact that one of our learners has just found a job.

- We can *invite learners to anticipate and predict*. Because of our need to survive, we constantly anticipate and predict. Whether we are attending to the direction another car will take, the number of steps as we go down a stairway, a line continuing on to the next page of a book, or the last glass of milk out of a carton, we regularly assess our environments for what we think will happen next. When what we predict doesn't go as expected, we pay close attention. Take the example of a car or person moving near to us in a direction we did not anticipate. We promptly become interested because when something happens that we didn't anticipate, the situation can get risky very quickly. Our lives are full of possible falls, crashes, and faux pas.

The upside of this phenomenon is that whenever individuals predict or estimate something, they become interested—hooked, you might say—in finding out how it will turn out. For example, there are five capitals in the United States that begin with the letter A. One of them is Atlanta. What are the rest? If you've even thought of a city that begins with the letter A, you're into this. You want to know what the other four capitals are and may even put this book aside to find out. This sort of question is the stuff of many trivia games but also the stuff of good novels, films, and plays. So when we build anticipation or ask learners to predict an outcome in any subject from accounting to marriage counseling, we have encouraged their interest. Not only that, sometimes it is a delight.

For all four of these suggestions, the guiding rule of thumb is learner security. We may take a chance. We may even make a mistake, but as long as we have maintained the integrity of our learners, we can continue to learn from the process, acting as professionals who know that creativity demands some degree of risk with consequences that are not totally predictable.

How to Develop Engagement and Challenge with Adult Learners

As we consider the strategies for engagement and challenge, we have to remember that the content of learning is only as important as the learners' interaction with that content. These strategies offer ways to learn that respect the multiple perspectives and differing profiles of intelligences found among diverse adults. All are highly interactive processes. Most result in a concrete product created by the learner and use learners' reflection and dialogue to construct knowledge. In a way, these strategies create a life of their own, a learning narrative to follow. They are composed of procedures that engage the learner with challenging questions, thoughts, and actions to propel learning toward deeper meaning and accomplishment. For example, a case study strategy usually starts with an analysis of the case, which naturally leads to reflection and discussion, followed by an attempt at resolution. The sequence for a research strategy is often to observe, analyze, predict, test, and reflect on results. When the strategies in this section are carried out optimally, learners experience *flow*, the joy of complete engagement.

According to Csikszentmihalyi (1997, p. 32), when we're in flow, "living becomes its own justification." I agree. I love the feeling of flow—the deeply satisfying experience of an intrinsically motivating activity. We have all had *flow experiences* outside an educational context: the feeling and concentration that sometimes emerge in a closely contested athletic contest, in a challenging board game such as chess, or more simply, in reading a book that seems as if it were written just for us or in the spontaneous exhilaration that accompanies a long, deep conversation with an old friend. In such activities, we feel totally absorbed, with no time to worry about what might happen next and with a sense that we are fully participating with all the skills necessary at the moment. There is often a loss of self-awareness that sometimes results in a feeling of transcendence or a merging with the activity and the environment (Csikszentmihalyi, 1997). Writers, dancers, therapists, surgeons, pilots, and instructors report feelings of flow during engrossing tasks in their repertoire of activities. In fact, when interviewed, they report that flow experiences are among the major reasons why they enjoy and continue to do the work they do.

Learners can have flow experiences as well. If we think of our best courses and finest instructors, we often can remember being captivated by the learning events we shared with them—challenging and creative activities in which we participated at a level where a new depth and extension of our capabilities emerged. Time passed quickly during such experiences, and our desire to return to them was self-evident. They were also not trivial. Effort and concentration on our part was necessary to gain what we did accomplish.

Because flow can be found across cultures, it may be a sense that humans have developed in order to recognize patterns of action that are worth preserving (Massimini, Csikszentmihalyi, and Delle Fave, 1988). Whether we are inspired in a course or in ecstasy in a spiritual ritual, our flow experiences have remarkably similar characteristics:

Goals are clear and compatible. That's why playing games like chess, tennis, and poker induce flow, but so can playing a musical piece or writing a computer program. As long as our intentions are clear and our emotions support them, we can concentrate even when the task is difficult. We absorb ourselves in those vivid dreams to which we commit. In such matters, cultural relevance is an inescapable necessity.

Feedback is immediate and relevant. We are clear about how well we are doing. Each move of a game usually tells us whether we are advancing or retreating from our goal; as we read we *flow* across lines and paragraphs and pages. In a good conversation, words, facial expressions, and gestures give immediate feedback. In learning situations, there should be distinct information or signals that let us assess our work.

The challenge is in balance with our skills or knowledge. In other words, the challenge is just about manageable. Flow experiences usually occur when our ability to act and the available opportunity for action correspond (see Figure 6.1). If challenges get beyond our skills, we usually begin to worry; and if they get too far away from what we're capable of doing, real anxiety or fear can emerge. To use a cliché, we're in over our heads, whether it's a project, a job, or a sport. Conversely, when the challenge is minimal, even if we have

Figure 6.1. Flow Experience.

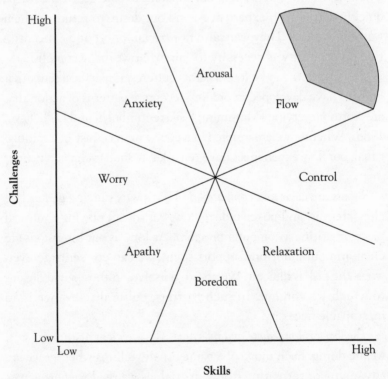

Source: Csikszentmihalyi, 1997, p. 31. Used by permission.

the skills we'll feel apathetic. (Busywork comes to mind.) When the challenge is reasonable but our skills still exceed it, we become bored. However, when desired challenges and personal skills approach harmony, we become energized and stop worrying about control. We're acting instinctively with full concentration, and deep involvement and exhilaration lie ahead. For example, just think of the last time you've had a great match in any game, sport, project, or job-related activity. When I'm with a class and we're really "cooking," I still get goose bumps when it's over and need to find a quiet place afterwards just to resonate with the feelings I have. Remarkable.

Experientially, flow is one of the pinnacles of what learning can be. When the aforementioned characteristics are present, any learning activity can approximate or become a flow experience. This deep involvement is much more possible than many instructors realize. One in five people have this experience often, as frequently as several times a day (Csikszentmihalyi, 1997). Generally, it happens when they're with friends or doing their favorite activities.

The goal of this book is to make learning a favorite activity for all of us. However, the learning activities we devise with diverse adults will need to have a range of challenges broad and flexible enough to accommodate learners' various backgrounds and profiles of intelligences. The following strategies are ideal for this purpose.

STRATEGY 42: *Use critical questions to stimulate learner engagement and challenge.*

Dewey (1933) wrote that thinking itself is questioning. Leaders in adult education and culturally responsive teaching (Mezirow and Associates, 1990; Wlodkowski and Ginsberg, 1995) advocate critical thinking and, therefore, critical questioning. We should distinguish between a *make-sense orientation* and a *critical orientation*. In the former, the criteria for the validity of a statement are that the statement seems to hang together and fit with one's prior beliefs. If something appears self-evident and makes sense, there is no need to think any more about it (Perkins, Allen, and Hafner, 1983). With a critical orientation, there is still a need to examine the data and reasoning for inconsistencies, to take alternative perspectives, and to look for bias and overgeneralization. This is a socioculturally constructive process that allows us to include a wider human panorama and to realize from different perspectives the social implications of any idea. Beyer (1987) discerns ten critical thinking skills:

1. Distinguishing between verifiable facts and value claims
2. Distinguishing relevant from irrelevant information, claims, or reasons
3. Determining the factual accuracy of a statement
4. Determining the credibility of a source
5. Identifying ambiguous claims or arguments
6. Identifying unstated assumptions
7. Detecting bias
8. Identifying logical fallacies
9. Recognizing logical inconsistencies in a line of reasoning
10. Determining the strength of an argument or claim

Motivationally speaking, thought-provoking questions make instructors and adults colearners, prompting everyone to make connections between what he or she already knows and what is presented. We all can use our own information and experience to become involved, deepen learning, and transform knowledge into new meanings.

Critical questioning stimulates people to analyze, infer, synthesize, apply, evaluate, compare, contrast, verify, substantiate, explain, and hypothesize. However, many adults are not experienced in using mindful questions. Research shows that fewer than 5 percent of questions posed by teachers request complex thinking, and the number of student-generated questions of any sort is infinitesimally low (Dillon, 1988). King (1994) has developed and extensively tested an instructional procedure for teaching postsecondary learners to pose their own thought-provoking questions. I have found this approach to be a thinking strategy adult learners can use either on their own or in groups.

Using this procedure, the teacher gives the learners a written set of question starters such as, "What do we already know about . . . ?" and, "How do you think . . . would see the issue of . . . ?" These questions encourage knowledge construction because they serve as prompts to induce more critical thinking on the part of learners and of the instructor as well. Learners use these question starters to guide them in formulating their own specific questions pertaining to the material to be discussed. Exhibit 6.1 includes a list of these thoughtful question stems, which can be adapted to any subject by being completed with information relevant to that subject. The critical thinking processes these questions elicit are also listed in Exhibit 6.1. When the instructor offers these question stems to learners for their conversations and dialogue, learners can use their own information and examples to deepen the content of what is to be studied.

In addition to King's list, I like to use the five types of questions Paul (1990) associates with a Socratic dialogue:

Clarification	"What do you mean by . . . ?"
	"Could you give me an example?"
Probing for assumptions	"What are you assuming when you say . . . ?"
	"What is underlying what you say?"
Probing for reasons and evidence	"How do you know that . . . ?"
	"What are your reasons for saying . . . ?"

Exhibit 6.1. Guiding Critical Questioning.

Question Starters	Specific Thinking Skills
What is a new example of . . . ?	Application
How could . . . be used to . . . ?	Application
What would happen if . . . ?	Prediction/hypothesizing
What are the implications of . . . ?	Analysis/inference
What are the strengths and weaknesses of . . . ?	Analysis/inference
What is . . . analogous to?	Identification and creation of analogies and metaphors
What do we already know about . . . ?	Activation of prior knowledge
How does . . . affect . . . ?	Analysis of relationship (cause-effect)
How does . . . tie in with what we learned before?	Activation of prior knowledge
Explain why . . .	Analysis
Explain how . . .	Analysis
What is the meaning of . . . ?	Analysis
Why is . . . important?	Analysis of significance
What is the difference between . . . and . . . ?	Comparison-contrast
How are . . . and . . . similar?	Comparison-contrast
How does . . . apply to everyday life?	Application—to the real world
What is the counterargument for . . . ?	Rebuttal argument
What is the best . . . , and why?	Evaluation and provision of evidence
What are some possible solutions to the problem of . . . ?	Synthesis of ideas
Compare . . . and . . . with regard to . . .	Comparison-contrast
What do you think causes . . . ? Why?	Analysis of relationship (cause-effect)
Do you agree or disagree with this statement: . . . ? What evidence is there to support your answer?	Evaluation and provision of evidence
How do you think . . . would see the issue of . . . ?	Taking other perspectives

Source: King, 1994, p. 24. Used by permission.

Other perspectives	"What might someone say who believed that . . . ?"
	"What is an alternative for . . . ?"
Probing for implications and consequences	"What are you implying by . . . ?"
	"Because of . . . , what might happen?"

Learners can use these question stems to guide them in generating their own critical questions following a presentation, a class, or a reading.

Let us say we have read *Invisible Man,* by Ralph Ellison. We have agreed that we will each bring along two questions, based on the list in Exhibit 6.1, regarding any aspect of the book that we find significant to our lives. We break into dyads, and my partner and I each place our two questions before us. They read as follows:

1. How does the last line of the book, "Who knows but that, on the lower frequencies, I speak for you?" apply to our everyday lives?

2. What is the *Brotherhood* analogous to in our own contemporary society?

3. The book has many strengths. It has been heralded as one of the greatest American novels of the second half of the twentieth century. From your perspective, what were its weaknesses?

4. What are examples of invisibility at this institution?

With these queries, we have an opportunity to relate ideas from this novel to our own knowledge and experience. We can have an extensive discussion that may clarify some inadequacies in our comprehension, and each of us has a chance to guide, to some extent, the thinking that will occur. There is opportunity to infer, compare, evaluate, and explain, all of which can lead to better understanding, fuller awareness of social issues, and the possibility of modifying our own thinking.

No matter what kinds of questions we as instructors ask, there are a number of questioning practices that can increase learners' responsiveness. The following are suggestions for improving questioning during instruction:

- Avoid instructor echo, that is, repeating portions of learners' responses to a question. This echoing tends to arbitrarily conclude what the learner has said and dulls further reflection.

- Avoid pressuring learners to "think" about what has been asked. Adults usually resent this form of indirect intimidation, which implies they are not motivated or capable in the first place. The question itself should stimulate engagement.

- Avoid frequent evaluative comments, such as, "That's good," "Excellent," "Fine answer," and the like. Even though these may be positive, they make you the judge and jury, deciding what is better or worse. Acknowledgment, appreciation, and transition responses, such as, "Now I see how you understand it," or, "Thank you," or, "Well, that might mean . . ." (followed by a new question), tend to have greater chances of continuing discussion, interest, and thinking.

- Avoid a "yes . . . but" reaction to a learner's answer. Essentially, this is a rejection of the learner's response. The "but" cancels out what precedes it and affirms what follows it (for example: "Yes, I think that might work, but here is another way").

- Probe answers to stimulate more thinking and dialogue. Probes are questions or comments that require learners to provide more support, to be clearer or more accurate, and to offer greater specificity or originality. Some examples: "How did you arrive at that conclusion?" "I don't quite understand." "Please, explain a bit more." Many of the questions found in Exhibit 6.1 can be used as probes.

STRATEGY 43: *Use relevant problems to facilitate learning.*

A problem can be very broadly characterized as any situation in which a person wants to achieve a goal for which an obstacle exists (Voss, 1989). If relevant, and within the range of an adult's capacity, problems by definition are engaging and challenging. Some of the processes for solving problems can be culture-bound to a significant extent (Hofstede, 1986). Differences in perspective and social and ethical codes may influence how people conceive and approach a problem, from building a home to settling a divorce. The variance across the world is extraordinary; however, this remarkable variety among diverse adults in terms of how a problem is perceived and resolved can make for a wonderful learning experience.

Adult education has enjoyed a long history in the use of problems as a procedure for learning. Freire's problem-posing (Shor, 1992) is a distinguished and influential pedagogy throughout the world. Ill-structured problems (that is, those not solvable with certainty) have been advocated for transformative learning for over a decade (Mezirow and Associates, 1990). Today, *problem-based learning* is ascending as a general and international approach to learning across multiple disciplines (Wilkerson and Gijselaers, 1996).

Although the basic steps used in problem-based learning may vary, they generally constitute a practical model for designing instruction in which learning is a self-directed, constructive process and social context an important factor (Albanese and Mitchell, 1993). Problem-based learning is characterized by the use of real-world problems as a means for people to learn critical thinking, problem-solving skills, and the essential concepts of a particular discipline. According to Eisner (1985), any course has two types of objectives, *instructional* and *expressive*. The instructional objectives are the informational elements or the skills the learner is expected to acquire. The expressive objectives are those that are evoked rather than prescribed. They are usually based on learners' interests and concerns. Expressive objectives can elicit generative themes: substantial, relevant issues affecting the collective good of society, such as health, pollution, or economics.

To explore the possible steps for problem-based learning, I have adapted an example from an inquiry course in arts and sciences at McMaster University taught by P. K. Rangachari (1996). In this unit, learners are exploring the dimensions of health and illness in the modern world, in particular the interaction between providers and recipients of health care.

1. *Brainstorming.* In order to evoke expressive objectives, the first meeting is a brainstorming session during which learners discuss what they believe to be critical issues in health care. Distilled from this effort are such topics as medical ethics, alternative medicine, appropriate technology in medicine, and funding for health care.

2. *The problems.* Working with the learners' list, the instructor writes the problems, such as the one that follows. This problem is based on the learners' expressed desire to discuss the appropriateness of technological procedures in medicine, specifically surgical rates.

An article titled "Study Finds Region Surgeons Scalpel-Happy" has appeared in the local tabloid. Naming names, the article identifies the hospital and notes that patients there are twice as likely to undergo cholecystectomy, three times as likely to have a mastectomy, and five times as likely to have a hysterectomy compared to other regions in Ontario. The findings implicate the hospital surgeons to be an incompetent, money-grubbing, and misogynistic lot. The president of the hospital has demanded an explanation from the chief of surgery and the chief is livid.

Possible learning issues include (1) a study of variability in the rates of cesarean sections, (2) a profile of a surgeon, (3) an assessment of the surgery and technology identified in the problem, and (4) an examination of how to handle scandal. (Note the variety of entry points for multiple intelligences.)

3. *Definition of learning issues and formation of study groups.* Learners receive the problem. They organize their ideas and previous knowledge related to the problem. They pose questions on aspects of the problem they do not understand or know and wish to learn. These are usually called learning issues, and they are often the basis for the learning activities carried out by the students. (In some cases, a problem is so constructed that the essential concepts of the skills of a discipline become intrinsic to the students' learning issues). Learners rank the learning issues they generate in order of importance. Through dialogue and by personal preference, they decide which issues to assign to small groups and which to individuals. In two weeks, learners will teach the findings related to these issues to the rest of the group. The instructor guides the learners toward resources and necessary research.

4. *Preparation for presentations.* During the two weeks prior to their presentations, learners meet, discuss, find and evaluate information, write their reports, and prepare for their presentations. To preserve continuity, the instructor holds an intervening session to discuss any issues that require clarification. Learners also share information and act as resources for one another.

5. *Presentations and assessment.* Learners present the information they have gathered related to their learning issues. The rest of

the learners and the instructor grade the presentations and give comments. The instructor provides guidelines for the assessment. In this case, high marks are given "for clear statements of objectives, clear and concise presentations, logical sequencing of individual sections, concepts supported by good examples, enjoyable format, precise answers to questions, and provision of new and useful information" (Rangachari, 1996, p. 69). Along with the marks, each learner receives a typed sheet with the other learners' collated comments. Each presenter (or group) is also required to submit a thousand-word written report of the presentation that the instructor alone grades and comments on.

This example is just one of a number of possible approaches to problem-based learning (Engel, 1991). Aside from problem-based learning, problems may be used to initiate other motivational strategies that are highly engaging and challenging. Among those too lengthy to include in this book are problem posing (Shor, 1992), critical incidents (Brookfield, 1990), the Critical Incident Questionnaire (Brookfield, 1995), and decision making and authentic research (Wlodkowski and Ginsberg, 1995).

STRATEGY 44: *Use an intriguing problem to make instructional material meaningful.*

Sometimes we have to teach material that is initially irrelevant to learners. Science and technology are rife with concepts and tools with which people may have had little or no previous experience. At one time, for some of us who are older adults, laser discs, cell phones, and e-mail had more the sound of science fiction than of everyday necessities. When adults have few links between new information and their existing knowledge base, we can use intriguing problems to make this material meaningful.

As these problems engage adults in concrete experience or discourse, they create disequilibrium in adults' thinking. Things don't quite make sense. This modest cognitive conflict stimulates intense interest. The fascinating nature of these problems evokes our perspectives, hypotheses, and predictions. They make us wonder and imagine. Once that happens, the problems become relevant to us because we cannot easily push aside what we find intriguing. The following example (see Figure 6.2) adapted from the work of Jacqueline Grennon Brooks and Martin Brooks (1993) invites learners to better understand the concepts of momentum and energy.

The instructor presents a set of five hanging pendula, metal balls of equal size all touching each other in a resting position. The instructor raises one ball and releases it; the learners note that one ball swings out on the other side. The instructor then raises and releases two balls, and the learners observe that two balls swing out on the other side. Raising three balls, the instructor asks the group to predict what will happen when the three balls are let go.

Figure 6.2. A Set of Five Hanging Pendula.

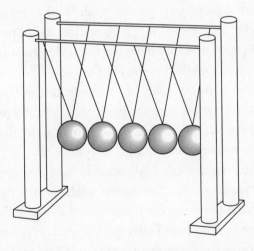

Learners usually respond with some or all of the following predictions: (1) one ball will go out, but higher; (2) two balls will go out, but higher; (3) three balls will go out; (4) the balls will "go crazy"; (5) the balls will stop; and (6) the balls will swing together. The learners explain their responses, react to others' responses, and indicate whether they have changed their minds upon hearing others' predictions. Meaning develops through dialogue. Of course, immediate feedback by the apparatus itself will enlighten all possible ideas, and in fact, within about half an hour most groups *demand* the release of the three balls in order to test their theories. Further activities are developed based on the learners' emerging interests and understandings.

Presenting learners with discrepant events and contradictory information is a corollary to this strategy. For example, learners may become more interested in the principles of heat transference when they have a chance to think about why the bottom of a paper cup does not burn from the flame of a lighter when the cup is filled with water. Social contradictions can also stimulate learners' interest with this sort of perplexity. For example: "The world can produce enough food to feed everyone, yet starvation and hunger run rampant even in countries that have the highest standards of living." Or: "This training method is the most criticized but also the most widely used in business today." In these instances there must be respect for the learners' contributions and a socially relevant discussion. Otherwise, this method remains little more than an expedient trick to enliven conventional learning.

Most of the strategies that follow could be characterized as problem-solving processes. Yet they possess sufficient structure and popular use to merit their own classification—the case study method is a good example. Although I offer guidelines, I do not present prescriptive steps for the use of these strategies. There are just too many creative ways for instructors and learners to improvise and to incorporate these methods into their own best ways of learning.

STRATEGY 45: *Use case study methods to enhance meaning.*

A case study portrays provocative questions and undercurrents in a narrative of real events. It requires learners to analyze, deliberate, and advance informed judgments from an array of perspectives and concepts (Christensen and Hansen, 1987). The hallmark of cases is their authenticity. With lifelike, concrete details and characters expressing a personal voice, they put flesh and blood on otherwise abstract concepts.

Because cases present a dilemma and are open ended, they tend to stimulate different reactions among members of a group. Yet they permit learners and instructors to be more open and less defensive because the situation is someone else's (Hutchings, 1993). We can share our uncertainty as well as our knowledge and experience because a case presents a knotty problem, not one given to glib resolution. Dialogue therefore is not limited to the mere exchange of opinions but rather is imaginative and open to many ideas.

Having a thorough understanding of the case and its nuances before teaching it is very important. By reading the case a few times over, you can begin to see if it meets such criteria as relevance, authenticity, narrative strength, and complexity to merit its selection for use. Here are some useful questions to reflect on as you read a case:

What is your first impression?

What are the different ways to interpret this case?

What are the teaching and learning issues?

What is culturally relevant in this case?

Can people construct principles and applications from this case?

Please keep these questions in mind as you read the following scenario, a case composed to stimulate the discussion and application of ideas in this book.

Issues of Instruction and Diversity

Beverly Hallman is a recently hired instructor at Central College, a large urban community college. She is twenty-six years old and has just completed her master's degree in educational psychology. As a European American woman from a middle-class suburban community, Beverly has grown up with very little experience with Latino and immigrant populations. She regards herself as a conscientious instructor with a very challenging job.

Beverly teaches introductory psychology. One-third of her students are learners whose language of origin is Spanish. She is concerned that these students do not participate enough in class but is at a loss as to what to do about it. She also has a significant number of students who were born in Central and Eastern Europe. Although she would not care to admit it, she finds the male students among this group to be too often overly aggressive in class discussions. The rest of the students are African American and European American. At least a third of the students in her course are over thirty-five years of age.

Beverly's general approach is to be fair to everyone and to try to interest everyone in psychology. The best way she knows to be fair is to treat all students the same way and to try to ignore cultural and ethnic differences as much as possible. There seems to be a tension in the class and no visible attempts to form intercultural friendships.

There are thirty students in Beverly's class. Her teaching approach is to use short lectures followed by short general discussions. Usually the same few students dominate the discussion. Most of them are male and over forty years of age, and none of them are Hispanic. When these students talk about their experiences, the younger students in the class are visibly disengaged and some seem resentful. Beverly administers a weekly quiz that is graded and returned to students. This structure keeps the students focused on note taking and makes the classroom climate tolerable.

As a new teacher, Beverly feels this is too early to be in a rut. She'd like to spark the class but is afraid of controversy. She believes a psychology course should be more than vocabulary enhancement but is at a loss as to what to do beyond showing a few films. She intuitively knows that some of what she is teaching, especially about social relations, personality theory, and motivation, is for cultural reasons not realistic or relevant to a good number of her students. But again, she doesn't quite know how to address this issue with her students. Also, for Beverly to admit that cultural differences can make some aspects of psychological theory less relevant might make the past quizzes and tests seem unfair.

The worst part is that her students are generally doing poorly. This is most obvious on the summative test she gave at midsemester. Beverly feels responsible. She has half a semester left to go and decides she will ask a more experienced teacher in her department for assistance.

It is a good first step to be sure learners comprehend the goals of a particular case study. For the case study in this example, some possible goals might be the following:

To increase understanding of how to improve instruction with particular attention to inclusion, motivation, and learning among diverse students

To improve understanding of diversity issues—age, ethnicity, bias, fear of conflict, and the like—as they relate to instruction

To analyze and explore multiple perspectives on the issues found in the case

To consider ideas found in this book as they might assist Beverly in the improvement of her instruction

Depending on such factors as the kind of material covered in the case and the experience, trust, and sense of community among the learners, cases can be processed in small groups or as a whole group. It is very important to open the discussion of the case in a manner that invites wide participation and relevant and interested commentary. Here are some suggestions with which to experiment (Hutchings, 1993):

- Ask learners to "free write" (put pencil to paper in a flow of consciousness) for a couple of minutes after reading the case so that they have some reflections to offer.

- Ask each learner to talk with a partner for a few minutes about key issues in the case before you request individual responses.

- Ask a couple of learners to summarize the case before asking others to join in.

- Ask each learner to remark about one element she felt was important in the case and record these comments publicly. This lets everyone know there are a range of interpretations before discussion begins.

During the discussion, the kinds of questions we ask can serve different purposes—for example, to encourage further analysis, challenge an idea, mediate between conflicting views, and guide learners to generate principles and concepts and to apply them. Creating a discussion outline for the case study and being open to addressing questions the learners may have to offer keep the case study process flowing and relevant.

A Possible Discussion Outline

1. Which items in this case stand out as significant teaching and learning issues?

   Probes   Which of these issues are you familiar with from your own teaching?

Which of these issues have you had some success in resolving?

Which of these issues arouse apprehension, and why?

2. What could Beverly do to improve the sense of community among her students?

Probes   What attitudes does Beverly have and what actions has she taken that may increase tension and separation among her students?

What can Beverly do to increase participation and collaboration among the students?

What do we know about adult learners that we could apply to make their participation more equitable? More relevant to the rest of the students?

3. How could Beverly be more motivating as an instructor?

Probes   How does Beverly's teaching suppress motivation to learn?

If you were to transform Beverly's approach to teaching, where would you start? What would you have her learn?

What in particular have you learned in this book that might be of genuine assistance to Beverly?

At times, it may be very effective to role-play aspects of the case ("What would be your remarks to Beverly if she were to ask you to observe her? Let's hear them, and one of us can react as she might.") Other times, it may be beneficial to record key information on the board or a chart. Direct quotes from the case can serve to focus the group. In general, after students have read the case, the pattern of learning moves from reflection and analysis to the surfacing of concepts and principles to the development of possible solutions and their related hypotheses and to the application of action strategies to individuals' own practices and purposes.

How you close the case discussion is critical. Most cases do not result in "the answer" or in a confident resolution of the problem. Nevertheless, there should be some opportunity for learners to reflect on what they have learned, to synthesize and identify new understandings, to air unresolved conflicts or questions, and to make plans for making changes or taking action. Some suggested approaches to closing the case study activity (Hutchings, 1993) are as follows:

- Ask learners to spend some time writing answers to such questions as, What new insights did you gain from this case study and its discussion? What are your lingering questions? What new ideas do you want to try out?

- Ask learners to brainstorm insights, personal changes in thinking or action, or new areas to explore as a result of the case study.

- Go around the group and ask each learner to provide one insight, question, lesson, change, or intuition that has emerged as a result of this process.

Using case studies in technical fields, such as chemistry, may require a more structured approach, but not to the extent that the structure would suppress the free flow of learners' ideas and perspectives. A final note: individually and collaboratively, adults are a great resource for constructing cases.

STRATEGY 46: *Use simulations and role playing to enhance meaning with a more realistic context.*

Simulations and role playing allow learners to practice and apply their learning in realistic contexts. When adults can sincerely experience perspectives, ideas, skills, and situations approximating authentic instances of life, they have a real opportunity both to enhance the meaning of what they are learning and to become more proficient.

Role playing is acting out a possible situation by personifying another individual or by imagining another scene or set of circumstances or by doing both. *Simulation exercises* are situations in which a whole group is involved, with learners assuming different roles as they act out a prescribed scenario. These scenarios allow learners to acquire or put into practice particular concepts or skills. Simulations often immerse learners in another social reality, allowing them to experience what might remain abstract in textual materials—for example, power, conflict, and discrimination. *Simulation games* are very similar to simulation exercises, but they are usually very structured and have a competitive, win-lose quality. (For further information on simulation design, see Alley, 1979.)

Because role playing has broad applicability across subject areas and accommodates flexible and learner-centered perspectives, it is a very useful strategy with diverse adult learners. Role playing gives learners a chance to try out ideas, skills, and perspectives that have been introduced formally by learning materials as well as more informally by instructors and peers. Depending on the degree of prescriptiveness and formality of the given scenario, role playing can blend into a simulation exercise. The main goal with either procedure is that the learner is genuinely involved with intellect, feeling, and bodily senses so that his experience is a deep and realistic one.

Role playing gives learners the opportunity to think in the moment, question their own perspectives, respond to novel or unexpected circumstances, and consider different ways of knowing (Meyers and Jones, 1993). Role playing can be used to practice a specific skill, such as critical questioning (see Strategy 42); a collaborative skill, such as collective bargaining; a problem-solving skill, such as a procedure for a biochemistry experiment; or a synthesizing skill, such as how to organize an instructional plan using motivational strategies from this book.

Role playing is also excellent for developing empathy and the skill to validate another person. It gives learners and instructors a chance to take on the viewpoints and rationales of people with different perspectives, as occurs, for example, when a lesbian couple and a heterosexual couple discuss the merits of a proposed law concerning domestic partnerships. When there is a chance to reverse roles so that learners act out roles that conflict with their own perspective (for example, when a union member takes on the role of management), learners have the opportunity to think and feel from a position they may never have been in. Role playing is an excellent procedure for shifting perspectives, adding insights, and starting conversations that are at times unimaginable before the introduction of this strategy.

The following are some guidelines adapted from the work of Meyers and Jones (1993) for conducting effective simulations and role playing:

- *Know where and how the simulation conforms to your instructional situation.* Is it a good fit given who your learners are, where the learning is heading, and what learners expect to do? Nothing is worse than a simulation that feels contrived or trivializes an important issue.

- *Plan well ahead.* You need to have some degree of confidence that your learners are familiar and proficient enough with the concepts or skills that will be practiced during the activity. Have they seen models or read cases that acquaint them with what they are expected to do? Do they have a fair knowledge of the cultural roles they may assume? If they are uncomfortable, can they excuse themselves or observe until they are more at ease about playing a role?

- *Be relatively sure everyone clearly understands the roles before you begin the role play.* Allow for questions and clarifications. Often it is helpful to write a script with learners describing the role's attitudes, experiences, and beliefs. The learners then study and use the script to deepen their familiarity with the role. For example, an excerpt from a script for a parent may include such statements as, "I am a single parent. I work nights in a service job. I often feel exhausted." And so on.

- *Set aside enough time for the simulation and the discussion that follows.* The discussion and analysis are as important as the simulation itself. What are the different perspectives, reactions, and insights? What are the learners' concerns? What has not been dealt with that still needs attention? Has the desired learning been accomplished? How? What about the process itself? How can it be improved? This is a good time to raise issues of critical consciousness (see Chapter Two), when impressions are fresh and resonant.

- *When role playing seems potentially embarrassing or threatening, it is often helpful for the instructor to model the first role play and discuss it.* This may alleviate some initial hesitation and allow learners to see our own comfort (we hope) with our imperfections and mistakes.

Freezing the action during a role play can serve many purposes: to critique a perspective, explore learners' reactions to a poignant comment, allow learners to make beneficial suggestions to the actors, and relieve tension. The follow-up activities for simulations are extremely important. Often they can connect what is learned to greater academic and social consequences. For example, a compelling next step after a role play could be to create action plans to use what has been practiced and discussed.

For many learners and instructors, simulations may be the only way to enter worlds apparently too distant or to try out actions initially too uncomfortable. In some instances, this procedure not only enhances meaning but also nurtures courage, the willingness to step beyond our self-conscious misgivings to encompass other realities and to act with new understanding.

STRATEGY 47: *Use invention, artistry, imagination, and enactment to render meaning and emotion in learning.*

Invention and artistry are ways of creating something with which to express oneself; respond to a need or desire; react to an experience; and make connections between the known and the unknown, the concrete and the abstract, and the worldly and the spiritual and among different people, places, and things. Through art and invention, adults attempt to answer such questions as, What do I want to express? What would I like to create? What is another way? What is a better way? What do I imagine? What do I wish to render?

I discuss invention and artistry together because the conceptual and subjective differences between them are difficult to discern and because both ought to be integral to learning and not, as is so often the case with art, separate entities in education. We can consider artistry as an embedding of art in learning rather than as a separate and frequently disenfranchised experience ("Now we are going to do art"). As Jamake Highwater (1994) has said, "Knowledge is barren without the capacity for feeling and imagination." Art is a vivid sensibility within life and learning across all cultures throughout the world. I believe the lack of meaning so frequently attributed to academic learning and professional training may be due to their indirect but nonetheless thorough separation of learning from artistry.

Although invention is more frequently associated with a specific product and technology, it is very difficult to tell the difference internally between when we are being inventive and when we are being artistic. Both processes can be used in every subject area. Both processes are open ended and entail kindling an awareness of creative possibility while considering educational or training goals. For example, one of my colleagues, Michele Naylor, teaching a course titled Foundations of Education, approached her learners with the question, "What are the things we, as educators in our communities, most deeply want to contribute and accomplish?" The learners were then given about an hour to reflect, write, and sketch their reactions to this question. Afterwards they met in small groups to share their responses. This led to the mutual agreement to post their sketches and conduct a large-group dialogue. From this activity the group decided to compose a mural depicting the theme of community and learning. Using poster paints, a large roll of paper, and masking tape, the participants collaborated with their ideas and sketches to create a mural that covered the entire bottom six feet of the circumference of the classroom. This took about six hours of their time. During the creation of the mural, one of the learners took photographs of the process and created a collage. Each learner also wrote a reflective paper discussing the process of creating the mural and the ideas represented. At the next class session, encircled by the mural they created, the learners summarized their reactions and made connections between this process and the work they do or intend to do in the community.

To exemplify invention, I recall a small cadre of adult learners who were struggling to comprehend systems theory and decided to invent a game, played according to systems theory, which could teach the fundamental concepts and principles of this theory to others in a pleasurable way. The game board was a narrow roll of cloth with simulated steps that when extended created a serpentine figure across the width of a small room. Along its path were several stations where players (other learners in the course) were to be interviewed or asked to complete activities and draw graphic models of systemic processes. The game became so popular as a teaching device that the university library acquired it as a resource.

My experience has been that learners across many cultures welcome the invitation to infuse their academic work with artwork, such as sketches and poetry. I have also found that projects that include works of fiction, playwriting, visual art, musical composition, songwriting, and performance art as essential components offer access to some of the most profound understandings adults gain from their learning.

When learners imagine or enact the physical and emotional properties of an idea, the concept becomes more salient and engaging (Sheik, 1983). Using images and the physical senses to experience ideas makes them more directly compelling and enhances their emotional associations. For example, it's one thing to say chemotherapy can be devastating. It's quite another to remember accompanying a friend during his sequence of treatments. In quite another direction, suppose the concept under discussion is excellence. Having adults remember what they did and how they felt reaching a previous excellent achievement in their lives can enrich and increase the vividness of what this concept really means.

If we can assist learners to see, hear, or feel an idea, we substantially increase their engagement. One of the best ways to do this is to create a situation in which learners can *enact a concept*. They become a representation of an idea and carry out a desired, challenging task. For example, when we learn about feedback, learners and I create a game analogous to "hot and cold": one of us has to find an object, and the rest of us use tapping as the only signal. We become feedback! Afterwards we are well prepared to discuss feedback conceptually and able to address its nuances concretely. Adventure education and Outward Bound courses do this to the maximum and make a lasting difference, especially with adults (Hattie, Marsh, Neill, and Richards, 1997). If you want to explore the meaning of challenge, crossing raging river rapids attached to a single rope with a $2 pulley gives you a memorable opportunity. Or, in a more tranquil manner, as an adult basic education instructor conducting a course in geography, you could have your learners physically represent the planets and their movements in order to understand the solar system. There are myriad possibilities with this approach. And it's great for experiencing flow.

———————

When it comes to enhancing meaning with adult learners, it seems important to have a criterion, one measured by feedback, by which we can estimate the motivational quality of our instruction. It's also important to remember that motivation ebbs and flows. Learners are not going to be as active when they are reflecting and contemplating. Sometimes, no matter how much we care, energy drains and dissipates. We also need to keep cultural differences in mind: the person silent and calm may be as intensely motivated as the person with the most bright-eyed expression in the group.

As an instructor, I have found paying attention to alertness in all its manifestations in a learning group is important. Boredom itself is not always easy to perceive, but sleepiness and what I call the presomnolent stare (eyes glazing over) seem to translate pretty consistently across cultures. If I see more than a few people showing these signs, I find it helpful to assess the learning activity for its qualities of engagement, value, and challenge.

I want to be sensitive to learners' self-determination, and I also want the best learning atmosphere possible. Adult learners are responsible for their learning climate as well. However, as their guide, I want this climate to be optimal. My role is to observe and respectfully orchestrate. If the energy in the group is declining, I may need to do something as simple as suggesting a break or refining the learning activity. The important point is that my observation of the group acts as a motivational altimeter that increases my awareness of learners' responsiveness, so when that responsiveness is falling to a level at which learning is less effective, I can select from among the best motivational strategies I know to stimulate the conditions that evoke motivation. This process is analogous to stoking a fire.

Nurturing an optimal climate for a community of adult learners is a constant challenge, and successfully meeting that challenge increases my feelings of competence and flow. Working in an optimal learning climate is like being in a remarkable conversation. The learning and the relationships are the "gravy" beyond the experience itself. Yet the years have taught me that there is a craft to facilitating these experiences. They are seldom serendipitous. We have to want and plan for an optimal learning climate. But this atmosphere happens only when we are fully present and keenly aware just about 100 percent of the time. It's worth it. Knowing we have helped create a group of vitally active and friendly adults who are enjoying learning can be quite a feeling.

7

Engendering Competence
Among Adult Learners

Only when we break the mirror and
climb into our vision,
only when we are the wind together
streaming and singing,
only in the dream we become with
our bones for spears,
we are real at last
and wake.

Marge Piercy

Being effective at what we value resonates with something beyond feeling competent. At some level, competence connects with our dreams, with that part of us that yearns for unity with something greater than ourselves. We want to matter. There are many ways to make this so: caring for someone we love, nurturing beauty, living with purpose, finding good in our work, and learning. Although we may do these things day in and day out, we need to believe we do them fairly well. If we do not, we must vaguely realize we are diminishing what makes life worth living and hope a constant in our midst. To be ineffective at what we value is a spiritual dilemma. By being competent we build the bridge that reconciles spiritual satisfaction, a moral life, and altruistic passion. The quest for competence starts with something as simple as a baby looking for a toy behind a pillow and ends in later life with what Erik Erikson called generativity, our desire to leave an enduring and beneficent legacy.

Competence is the most powerful of all the motivational conditions for adults. Competence is our reality check: it tells us what is possible by our own will. As adults we have a deep desire to be competent and often seek learning as a means to this end. *Across cultures, this human need for competence is not one to be acquired but one that already exists and can be strengthened or weakened through learning experiences.* Many people understand competence as individual proficiency, but others may conceive of it as a collective responsibility, carried out with regard for what is best for others— for future human and environmental well-being. Individual effectiveness is important, yet it is to be achieved with consideration of our interdependence with all things and our impact on the generations to come. This quest for a balanced sense of competence is found not only in many native cultures (Michelson, 1997) but also among many workers and employers who actively pursue social and environmental responsibility as an ethical commitment. The emphasis in this book is on finding ways to support adult competence while illuminating the socially redeemable aspects of the individual's increased effectiveness.

Supporting Self-Determined Competence

Self-determination and building competence go hand in hand. The norm of individual freedom and responsibility is very strong in this society; therefore, when *most* adults see themselves as the locus of causality for their learning—as self-determined learners—they are much more likely to be intrinsically and positively motivated. Adults are experienced self-directed learners, especially when solving their own problems (Caffarella, 1993). Today's world of work increasingly requires people who can capably self-direct in their jobs.

However, sometimes instructors encounter adults who seem dependent, lacking in self-confidence, or reluctant to take responsibility for their learning. There are a number of possible reasons for this. Three of the most common are that (1) these adults have not been socialized to see themselves as in control of their own learning, (2) their experience in school or in the particular domain of learning has been generally negative or unsuccessful, and (3) they do not believe they have a free choice as to whether or not they engage in the learning or training experience. This last reason, very common among adults, is a *personal security* issue. In many instances, adult learners need courses and training not so much because they want them but because they need the jobs, the promotions, and the money for which these learning experiences are basic requirements. This is the reality for many adults, and it may be one about which they feel they have little choice. "Just tell me what to do," is their common refrain.

Strategies to support adults in taking ownership of their learning have been discussed in the previous three chapters. Those strategies that relate to the motivational purposes of respect, self-concept, expectancy for success, and engagement and challenge are most effective in this regard. When combined with the following strategies to engender competence, they create a holistic system in which the competence and self-determination of adult learners mutually enhance each other. Proficiently applied, the strategies enable those adults who feel minimal control of their learning to grow in the realization that they do have a voice and can determine learning they value.

Permeating every competence strategy is the understanding that *informational* communication about a learner's effectiveness has the best chance to cultivate self-determination. According to the seminal work of Deci and Ryan (1991), when instructors tell adults about the quality of their work, these transactions can be either *informational* or *controlling*. Informational transactions tell learners something about their effectiveness and support their sense of self-determination for learning. Controlling transactions tend to undermine self-determination by making a learner's behavior appear to be dependent on implicit or explicit forces that demand, coerce, or seduce the learner's compliance. They encourage the learner to believe that the reason for learning is some condition outside the learner or the learning activity itself, such as a reward or pressure from the instructor. When verbally communicated, controlling transactions often contain imperative locutions such as *should* and *must*. For example, an instructor might say to an adult learner, "Your performance was excellent. As soon as you received concrete feedback, you were really able to apply your skill" (informational). Or the same instructor might say, "Your performance was excellent. As soon as I made the feedback concrete, you did exactly as you should do" (controlling). The difference between these two statements may seem subtle but is nonetheless very important. The former encourages self-determination, whereas the latter places much more of the emphasis on the instructor's control. The following competence strategies will always emphasize the informational approach, which not only nurtures self-determination but also promotes self-direction and is more likely to increase intrinsic motivation.

Relating Authenticity and Effectiveness to Assessment

In training and more formal learning experiences, assessment exerts a powerful motivational influence on adults because it is the educational procedure to communicate about their competence in a socially sanctioned way. Historically, more than any other action, assessment by the instructor has validated learners' competence. Our comments, scores, grades, and reports affect learners in the present and the future. Assessment often leaves a legacy for adults, directly or indirectly, by having an impact on their careers, vocational opportunities, professional advancement, and acceptance into various schools and programs.

Adults tend to undergo more stress in testing situations than do youths (Smith, 1982). They often feel awkward and anxious taking exams. Test anxiety is a widespread problem among adults (Sarason, 1980). There are many reasons for this uneasiness. Among them are fears of revelation of ignorance, of negative comparison with peers, and of inability to meet personal standards and goals. (Robert Smith, 1982, has written some helpful suggestions for training adults to cope with exams.)

For assessment to be intrinsically motivating for adults it has to be *authentic*—connected to adults' life circumstances, frames of reference, and values. For example, if a case study were used as an authentic assessment, it would ask learners to respond to a situation that mirrors their work or community life with the resources and conditions normally there. A real-life context for demonstrating learning enhances its relevance for adults, appeals to their pragmatism, and affirms their rich background of experiences (Kasworm and Marienau, 1997). In contrast, one can easily see how an impersonal multiple-choice exam might seem tedious and irrelevant to most adults.

Effectiveness is the learners' awareness of their command or accomplishment of something they find to be important in the *process* of learning or as an *outcome* of learning. Therefore, both the processes and the results of learning are significant information for adults. How well am I doing? and How well did this turn out? are a critical duet for adult learning activities. In the example of the case study, to judge the quality of their thinking as they *process* the case, the adults would likely want feedback about how well their responses relate to the issues found in the case study. In addition, when they finally resolve the case, they would want to assess the quality of this *outcome* for its merits as well. Motivation is elicited when adults realize they have competently performed an activity that leads to a valued goal. Awareness of competence affirms the need of adults, across all cultures, to relate adequately to their environment in areas they value.

If we take an institutional perspective, the first aim of assessment is usually to audit adult learning. However, the first edition of this book and, more recently, other scholars (Wiggins, 1998) have asserted that assessment should primarily be used to enhance learning and motivation. With respect to this assertion, let's begin with feedback as a motivational strategy, because self-adjustment based on feedback is central to learning. Adults change or maintain *how* they learn and *how* they perform based on the feedback they receive. Through feedback they *become* more competent, as well as realize they *are* competent.

STRATEGY 48: *Provide effective feedback.*

Feedback is information that learners receive about the quality of their work. Knowledge about the learning process and its results, comments about emerging skills, notes on a written assignment, and graphic records are forms of feedback that instructors and learners use. Feedback appears to enhance the motivation of learners because learners are able to evaluate their progress, locate their performance within a framework of understanding, maintain their efforts toward realistic goals, self-assess, correct their errors efficiently, self-adjust, and receive encouragement from their instructors and other learners.

Some writers (Wiggins, 1998) distinguish feedback from the way the instructor might evaluate and guide the learners' performance. In their opinion, feedback is information about what exactly resulted from the learner's action. It reflects the learner's actual performance as opposed to the learner's ideal performance. Facts are fed back to the person about his or her performance without the addition of another adult's view of the value of the performance or of how to improve the situation (for example, "You've made thirteen of fifteen foul shots," or, "I wanted my entire audience in rapt attention while I spoke. The videotape shows at least 20 percent of them fidgeting and restless"). The advantage of this orientation to feedback is its emphasis on making feedback clear and self-evident in order to encourage learners' self-assessment and self-direction. For adults from more collectivist cultures and for those of us who desire the inclusion of other perspectives on our work, this orientation to feedback might seem too individualistic or minimalist.

Feedback is probably the most powerful process that teachers and other learners can regularly use to affect a learner's competence. In studies at Harvard, students and alumni overwhelmingly reported that the single most important ingredient for making a course effective is getting rapid instructor response on assignments and exams (Light, 1990). However, feedback is far more complex than a few words about a learner's progress during a learning project or at the end of an assessment. The following paragraphs describe the characteristics of effective feedback:

• Effective feedback is *informational rather than controlling*. As we have already discussed, our feedback should emphasize the learner's increasing effectiveness or creativity and self-determination. For example, we might say, "In your paper you've clearly identified three critical areas of concern; your writing is well organized and vivid; I appreciate how well you've supported your rationale with facts and anecdotes," rather than, "You're making progress and meeting the standards I've set for writing in this course."

• Effective feedback *provides evidence of the learner's effect relative to the learner's intent*. This most often is feedback that is based on *agreed-on* criteria, standards, and models. Learners can compare their work against a standard: a superbly written executive letter, a museum sculpture, a rubric for critical thinking, or a video of a political activist giving a rousing speech. Learners are then in a position to understand clearly what they have done and how it compares to their own goals. They can judge how well they have performed or produced in terms of a specific target. They are clear about the criteria against which their work is being evaluated and can explicitly indicate what needs to be done for further effective learning. Self-assessment leads to self-adjustment. Learners can thus use this information to guide their effort, practice, and performance more accurately. For example, in a welding course, each learner agrees to produce a ninety-degree corner weld to industry specifications. The standards are written out on paper and available. When the learner makes a weld that she judges to be up to this standard, she comes to a table to compare her weld to welds ranging from excellent to poor. Based on this comparison, the learner adjusts the necessary skills and improves the next weld or, if satisfied, moves on to a more advanced task. The instructor may give guidance if the learner requests it.

• Effective feedback is *specific and constructive*. It is difficult to improve performance when one has only a general sense of how well one has done. Most people prefer specific information and realistic suggestions for how to improve: for example, "I found your insights on government spending compelling. To emphasize your conclusion, you might consider restating your initial premise in your last paragraph." When you are giving guidance with feedback, it is important to keep in mind how much the learner *wants to* or *ought to* decide on a course of action relative to the feedback. In general, the more the learner can self-assess and self-adjust, the more self-determined the learner will be.

• Effective feedback can be *quantitative*. In such areas as athletics, quantitative feedback has definite advantages. It is precise and can provide evidence of small improvements. Small improvements can have long-range effects. One way to understand learning is by measuring *rate*, which indicates how often something occurs over a fixed time. For example, learners are told they completed thirty laps during a one-hour swimming practice. Another way is to decide what percentage of learning performance is correct or appropriate. Percentages are calculated by dividing the number of times the learning performance occurs correctly by the total number of times the performance opportunity occurs, as in batting averages and field goal percentages.

Another common form of quantitative feedback is *duration*, which is how long it takes a learning performance to be completed. For example, a lab technician might receive feedback on how long he takes to complete a particular chemical analysis. These are not the only forms of quantitative feedback that are possible, but they are a representative sample. Whenever progress on learning a skill appears to be slow or difficult to ascertain, quantitative feedback may be an effective means to enhance learner motivation.

• Effective feedback is *prompt*. Promptness characterizes feedback that is quickly given as the situation demands rather than immediately. Sometimes a moderate delay in feedback enhances learning because such a delay is simply culturally sensitive or polite. For example, some learners may experience discomfort with direct mention of specific performance judgments shortly after the occasion. Also, a short wait may allow learners to forget incorrect responses more easily or reduce their anxiety, as in the case of a public performance. In general, it is best to be quick with feedback but to pay careful attention to whether any delay might be beneficial.

• Effective feedback is usually *frequent*. Frequent feedback is probably most helpful when new learning is first being acquired. In general, you should give feedback when improvement is most possible. Once errors have accumulated, learners may see improvements as more difficult to accomplish. Also, once multiple errors become established, the new learning encouraged through feedback may seem overwhelming and confusing to learners, making further progress seem even more remote.

• Effective feedback is *positive*. Positive feedback places emphasis on improvements and progress rather than on deficiencies and mistakes. It is an excellent form of feedback because it increases learners' intrinsic motivation, feelings of well-being, and sense of competence and helps learners form a positive attitude toward the source of the information. Adults prefer positive feedback because when they are trying to improve, emphasis on errors and deficiencies (negative feedback) can be discouraging. Even when learners are prone to making mistakes, the instructor's pointing out a *decrease* in errors may be considered positive feedback. Also, positive feedback can be given with constructive feedback. For example, an instructor might say to a learner, "You've been able to solve most of this problem. Let's take a look at what's left and see if we can understand why you are getting stuck."

• Effective feedback is *related to impact criteria*. Impact criteria are the main reasons a person is learning something, the heart of the individual's learning goal (Wiggins, 1998). Often these are unique or strongly related to a cultural perspective. One person may produce a speech or a piece of writing to inspire, arouse, or provoke. Another may wish to create a design or a performance to be a gift for the family or friends. Assessment and feedback should support such goals and respectfully deal with what may be ineffable or accomplished only in a realm beyond mechanistic objectivity. We may need to give feedback that is more akin to dialogue or to what many artists do when they respond to how another's work affects them, rather than "evaluate" that work.

• Effective feedback is usually *personal and differential*. Differential feedback uses self-comparison and focuses on the increment of personal improvement that has occurred since the last time the learning activity was performed. In skill or procedural learning, such as writing, operating a machine, or learning a particular sport, emphasizing small steps of progress can be very encouraging to learner motivation. The amount of time that lapses before we give such differential feedback can be quite important. For example, learners are able to see larger gains and feel a greater sense of accomplishment when their improvement is reviewed on a daily or weekly schedule, rather than after each performance.

In addition to the specific characteristics of feedback just listed, some refinements in the composition and delivery of feedback may be helpful. For many skills, *graphing* or *charting* feedback can be encouraging to learner motivation because it makes progress more concrete and shows a record of increasing improvement.

We should always consider *asking learners what they would like feedback on*, especially when we are working with diverse populations. Their needs and concerns may be different from ours, and the knowledge gained from such discussion can make the feedback more relevant and motivating.

Learners' *readiness to receive feedback* is also important. If people are resistant to feedback, they are not likely to learn or self-adjust. For example, this may mean holding off on feedback until a personal conference can be arranged or until learners are more comfortable with the learning situation.

There are times when *checking to make sure our feedback was understood* can be important. This is certainly true for complex feedback or situations in which English is not the learner's first language.

Everything that has been said about feedback thus far could also apply to *group feedback*. Whether the group involved is a team, a collaborative group, or an entire class, feedback on total performance can influence each individual, and because group feedback consolidates members' mutual identification and sense of connection, it helps enhance group cohesiveness and morale.

As a final point, remember that sometimes the best form of feedback is simply to encourage learners to move forward to the next, more challenging learning opportunity. Too much comment by instructors tends to emphasize our power and can diminish our role as colearners.

STRATEGY 49: *Avoid cultural bias in assessment procedures.*

Probably nothing is more demoralizing to an adult than to realize she does not have a fair chance to demonstrate her knowledge or learning. The reality is that it is difficult to avoid bias in any test or assessment procedure that uses language, because the words and examples sway the learner toward a particular cultural perspective. This is especially true for paper-and-pencil tests. A common example of bias is content that favors one frame of reference over another (Ovando and Collier, 1997). These issues relate not only to ethnicity but also to age and gender. For example, items about baseball averages tend to give males an edge, whereas items of similar difficulty but focusing on child care may favor females (Pearlman, 1987). We need always to examine the assumptions embedded in the materials we create or select for assessment. We do not want to penalize anyone for not having been fully socialized in a particular culture. We know adult learning is derived from multiple sources and varied life experiences (Kasworm and Marienau, 1997). So when we are developing our assessment instruments, it is important to consider the following issues (as we should with all training and curricular materials):

- Invisibility

  Is there a significant omission of women and minority groups in assessment materials? (This implies that certain groups are of less value, importance, and significance in our society.)

- Stereotyping

  When groups or members of groups are mentioned, are they assigned traditional or rigid roles that deny diversity and complexity within different groups? (When stereotypes occur repeatedly in print and other media, learners' perceptions are gradually distorted, making stereotypes and myths seem more acceptable.)

- Selectivity

  Does offering or allowing for only one interpretation of an issue, situation, or group of people perpetuate bias? (We may fail to tap the varied perspectives and knowledge of learners.)

- Unreality

  Do assessment items lack a historical context that acknowledges—when relevant—prejudice and discrimination? (Glossing over painful or controversial issues obstructs authenticity and creates a sense of unreality.)

- Linguistic bias

  Do materials reflect bias in the English language? For example, are masculine examples, terms, and pronouns dominant? (The implication of invisibility is to devalue the importance and significance of women and minorities.)

Even directions for tests can constitute a form of bias. This is especially true for language-minority students. English-language learners of all ages can benefit from test instructions that are direct and simplified. Whenever possible, we want to avoid the passive voice and ambiguous comments. Test instructions should be in short sentences with clear and explicit ground rules. We also should allow adequate processing time for questions and directions to be understood.

STRATEGY 50: *Make assessment tasks and criteria known to learners.*

The time has come. No more secrets. If we genuinely want self-assessing, self-adjusting, and self-directed learners, we must make sure they comprehend the tasks and criteria by which they are assessed. Trainers in the business world do this frequently, and those of us in higher education must evolve in this direction as well. Adults greatly appreciate this approach because becoming competent is then no longer a guessing game, and they can more clearly assess and guide their own learning.

This strategy complements mastery learning, scaffolding, and contracting (see Chapter Five). Using it, we make criteria, examples, and models readily available to learners. Where scoring or grades are necessary, we ensure that all learners clearly understand the rationale for their assignment. In fact, one of the issues we need to consider when using this strategy is the degree to which learners participate in the creation and refinement of the assessment criteria. Certainly, we should discuss criteria and assessment procedures at the beginning of a course or training, remaining open to making changes to the process or criteria, based on the input from the learners. For example, discussion might reveal a lack of time, materials, or opportunities. These conditions may prohibit certain kinds of learning. Therefore, it's quite possible that we could not apply certain criteria fairly.

However, what about revision of criteria or assessment procedures because of differences in the learners' values or perspectives? I don't have an answer that I believe would fit most circumstances, but I do have a procedure that I often find helpful. I offer it not as a formula but as an example of how I have dealt with the complexity of asking adults to participate in shaping assessment criteria.

In a research course, part of the assessment process is for students to critique a research article of their own choosing and also to create a research proposal in an area of interest. The major purpose of the course is for learners to develop an understanding of the primary assumptions, perspectives, and methods that guide research as it can be conducted in the social sciences.

On the first day, I give the learners models of an excellent critique of a research article and an exemplary research proposal. After reading them, the class divides into small groups to discuss why these two examples might be considered commendable. They also reflect on other ways to critique an article or create a proposal that might vary from the examples I offered and still be laudable. During a whole-group discussion, we list both sets of these qualities. I then pass out the criteria I normally use, and we see which of their criteria match mine and which do not match. Then we talk further, and after this discussion, I make the agreed-on revisions to the criteria. Often the changes have to do with adding qualitative pieces, such as interviews and personal histories.

Transforming training and courses into educational settings where learners share responsibility and authority for their learning is an evolving process for learners as well as for instructors. It may often mean coming to the learning environment with a well-considered plan and set of assessment criteria but being willing to reinvent some of these elements according to the learners and situation we find there.

STRATEGY 51: *Use authentic performance tasks to enable adults to know that they can proficiently apply what they are learning to their real lives.*

Authentic performance tasks are one of the oldest forms of assessment and have been commonly used in training and adult education for many years (Knowles, 1980). Today we have a more sophisticated understanding of these procedures and their central idea: that assessment should resemble as closely as possible the ways adult learners will express in their real lives what they have learned. Thus, if a person is learning computer programming skills, we would assess his learning by asking him to program a personal computer in a relevant area.

The closer assessment procedures come to allowing learners to demonstrate what they have learned in the environment where they will eventually use that learning, the greater will be learners' motivation to do well and the more they can understand their competence and feel the self-confidence that emerges from effective performance. Providing the opportunity for learners to complete an authentic task is one of the best ways to conclude a learning activity because it promotes transfer of learning, enhances motivation for related work, and clarifies learner competence. An authentic task directly meets the adult need to use what has been learned for more effective daily living.

According to Wiggins (1998), an assessment task, problem, or project is authentic if it

Is realistic. The task replicates how people's knowledge and capacities are "tested" in their real world.

Requires judgment and innovation. People have to use knowledge wisely to solve unstructured problems, as a carpenter remodeling part of a house must do more than follow a routine procedure.

Asks the learners to "do" the subject. Rather than recite or demonstrate what they have been taught or what is already known, the learners have to explore and work within the discipline, as when they demonstrate their competence for a history course by writing history from the perspective of particular people in an actual historical situation.

Replicates or simulates the contexts that adults find in their workplace, community, or personal life. These contexts involve specific situations and their demands: for example, managers learning conflict resolution skills could apply them to their work situations, with consideration of the actual personalities and responsibilities involved.

Assesses the learners' ability to use an integration of knowledge and skill to negotiate a complex task effectively. Learners have to put their knowledge and skills together to meet real-life challenges. This is analogous to the difference between taking a few shots in a warm-up drill and actually taking shots in a real basketball game, or between writing a paper on a particular law and writing a real proposal to appropriate legislators to change the law.

Allows appropriate opportunities to rehearse, practice, consult resources, and get feedback on and refine performances and products. This is so important. Learning and, consequently, assessment are not one-shot enterprises! Almost all learning is formative, whether one is learning how to repair plumbing, write a publishable article, or bake a pie. We put out our first attempt and see how it looks, sounds, or tastes. We repeatedly move through a cycle of *perform, get feedback, revise, perform.* That's how most high-quality products and performances are attained—especially in real life. *We must use assessment procedures that contribute to the improvement of adult performance and learning over time.* Doing so means that much of the time assessment is separated from grading processes to assure learners that their mistakes are not counted against them but are a legitimate part of the learning process.

Exhibit 7.1 contains Wiggins's description of the differences between typical tests and authentic tasks.

STRATEGY 52: *Provide opportunities for adults to demonstrate their learning in ways that reflect their strengths and multiple sources of knowing.*

As adults, most of us are motivated to accomplish assessments in which we can use our strengths to demonstrate the depth and complexity of our learning. Such opportunities cannot use one-dimensional, high-stakes paper-and-pencil testing formats because, by their very structure, tests of this sort reduce and constrict what we can show about what we know. We need either multiple forms of assessment (tests, products, portfolios, and journals) or multidimensional assessment (such as authentic performance tasks and projects) to adequately reveal the richness of the strengths and sources of our knowing.

At times, the amount of professional time required to accomplish the assessments described here can seem overwhelming. Yet,

Exhibit 7.1. Key Differences Between Typical Tests and Authentic Tasks.

Typical Tests	Authentic Tasks	Indicators of Authenticity
Require correct responses only.	Require quality product or performance (or both) and justification.	We assess whether the learner can explain, apply, self-adjust, or justify answers, not just the correctness of answers using facts.
Must be unknown in advance to ensure validity.	Are known as much as possible in advance; involve excelling at predictable demanding and core tasks; are not "gotcha!" experiences.	The tasks, criteria, and standards by which work will be judged are predictable or known to the learner—as a recital piece, a play, an engine to be fixed, or a proposal to a client can be clearly understood and anticipated prior to assessment.
Are disconnected from a realistic context and realistic constraints.	Require real-world use of knowledge: the learner must "do" history, science, and so on in realistic simulations or actual use.	The task is a challenge with a related set of constraints that are authentic—likely to be encountered by the professional, citizen, or consumer. (Know-how, not plugging in, is required.)
Contain isolated items requiring use or recognition of known answers or skills.	Are integrated challenges in which knowledge and judgment must be innovatively used to fashion a quality product or performance.	The task is multifaceted and nonroutine, even if there is a "right" answer. It thus requires problem clarification, trial and error, adjustments, adapting to the case or facts at hand, and so on.
Are simplified so as to be easy to score reliably.	Involve complex and nonarbitrary tasks, criteria, and standards.	The task involves the important aspects of performance or the core challenges of the field of study (or both), not the easily scored; it does not sacrifice validity for reliability.
Are one-shot.	Are iterative: contain recurring essential tasks, genres, and standards.	The work is designed to reveal whether the learner has achieved real versus pseudo mastery and understanding versus mere familiarity over time.
Depend on highly technical correlations.	Provide direct evidence, involving tasks that have been validated against core adult roles and discipline-based challenges.	The task is valid and fair on its face. It thus evokes student interest and persistence and seems apt and challenging to learners and instructors.
Provide a score.	Provide usable (sometimes concurrent) feedback; the learner is able to confirm results and self-adjust as needed.	The assessment is designed not merely to audit performance but to improve future performance. The learner is seen as the primary beneficiary of information.

Source: Wiggins, 1998, p. 23.

if we make assessment a partner to exciting learning and continuing motivation for adults, rather than merely audits by which to assign grades or scores, assessments become important learning activities in and of themselves, worthy of everyone's time and effort. Nonetheless (I know you are thinking), time constraints will still be a challenge. With this problem in mind, here are some worthwhile activities and methods to support the use of authentic tasks or to be transformed into authentic tasks.

Assessment options based on Gardner's multiple intelligences. Adults have different profiles of intelligences. Their having the opportunity to select an assessment process that reflects their particular intellectual strengths should encourage their participation and enthusiasm for demonstrating their competence. The following menu of options, adapted from *Teaching and Learning Through Multiple Intelligences* (Campbell, Campbell, and Dickinson, 1992), is categorized by each intelligence (see Chapter One).

Linguistic

Tell or write a short story to explain . . .	Keep a journal to illustrate . . .
Write a poem, myth, play, or editorial about . . .	Create a debate to discuss . . .
Create an advertising campaign to depict . . .	Create a talk show about . . .

Logical-Mathematical

Complete a cost-benefit analysis of . . .	Write a computer program for . . .
Design and conduct an experiment to . . .	Create story problems for . . .
Induce or deduce a set of principles on . . .	Create a time line for . . .

Musical

Create a song that explains or expresses . . .

Revise lyrics of a song to . . .

Collect and present music and songs to . . .

Create a musical piece to . . .

Create a music video to illustrate . . .

Use music to . . .

Spatial

Create a piece of art that demonstrates . . .

Create a poster to . . .

Create a videotape, collage, photo album of . . .

Chart, map, or graph . . .

Design a flag or logo to express . . .

Create a scale model of . . .

Bodily-Kinesthetic

Perform a play on . . .

Build or construct a . . .

Role-play or simulate . . .

Use puppets to explore . . .

Create a sequence of movements to explain . . .

Create a scavenger hunt to . . .

Interpersonal

Participate in a service project that will . . .

Offer multiple perspectives of . . .

Contribute to resolving a local problem by . . .

Teach a group to . . .

Use what you've learned to change or influence . . .

Conduct a discussion to . . .

Intrapersonal

Create a personal philosophy about . . .

Discern what is essential in . . .

Explain your intuitive hunches about . . .

Explain your emotions about . . .

Explain your assumptions in a critical incident . . .

Use a journal to . . .

Naturalist

Discover and describe the patterns in . . .

Create a typology for . . .

Relate and describe the interdependence of . . .

Create a flow chart for . . .

Use a field trip to analyze . . .

Observe and describe . . .

In addition to accommodating multiple intelligences, this assessment menu offers a range of performance actions that require higher-order thinking—*design, teach, discern, explain, analyze, write,* and the like. For example, a learner in a science course might *design* an experiment to analyze the chemicals in the local water supply and *write* an editorial based on the results for the local paper. These assessments provide opportunities for imaginative experiences that allow adults to use their unique preferences and strengths. Furthermore, with these assessments adults can develop deeper relationships between new learning and their cultural backgrounds and values.

Portfolios and process folios. Regardless of its purpose, a portfolio is a sample of a person's work or learning. It can provide more diverse evidence and an array of performance examples incorporating a longer time frame than a single test. Multiple indicators, such as tests, products, media, and self-assessments, can make up a portfolio and contribute to a deeper understanding of an adult's learning. Portfolios are an excellent means of assessing an adult's personal goals as they mesh with course goals in such programs of study as the arts and in vocational and graduate schools. The contents of a portfolio and the assessment criteria used to evaluate it will differ depending on the portfolio's purpose. The following is a list of some of the possible ways a portfolio can be used (Wiggins, 1998):

As a display of the learner's best work, as chosen by the learner, the instructor, or both

As a display of the learner's interests and goals

As a display of the learner's growth or progress

As documentation of self-assessment, self-adjustment, self-direction, and learning

As evidence for professional assessment of learner performance

A *process folio* (Gardner, 1993) goes beyond a traditional portfolio: it layers elements of the entire learning experience so that learners are able to document and reflect on challenges and understandings that emerge over time. The process folio documents three primary considerations: the content of learning (what is being learned), the context of learning (how what is being learned fits into a larger framework, possibly the learner's life and experiences), and perceptions of the process of learning (perceptions about various influences on the student's learning and ways in which learning was enhanced). This type of portfolio is a powerful tool for responding to the interests and concerns of diverse learners (Wlodkowski and Ginsberg, 1995).

The following are some guidelines to consider when working with portfolios:

1. Involve learners in the composition and selection of what makes up the portfolio.

   A. Learners may want to explore different aspects of a particular discipline. In a research course, for example, the learner might design an ethnographic study *and* an experimental study for her portfolio.

   B. Learners may choose among different categories, such as most difficult problem, best work, most valued work, most improved work, a soulful or spiritual experience, and so forth.

2. Include information in the portfolio that shows learner's self-reflection and self-assessment.

   A. Learners may include a rationale for their selections.
   B. Learners may create a guide for their portfolio offering interpretations, commentary, critique, and matters of contextual importance.
   C. Learners may include self- and peer assessments indicating strengths, areas for improvement, and relationships between earlier and later works.

3. Be clear about the purpose of the portfolio.

   A. Learners should be able to relate their goals for learning to the contents of the portfolios.
   B. Learners should be able to provide a fair representation of their work.
   C. Rubrics and their models for assessing portfolio contents should be clearly understood and available (see Strategy 53).

4. Exploit the portfolio as a process to show learner growth.

   A. Learners may submit the original, the improved, and the final copy or draft of their creation or performance.
   B. Using specific works, learners may make a history of their "movement" along certain dimensions in their growth.
   C. Learners may include feedback from outside experts or descriptions of outside activities that reflect the growth illustrated in the portfolio.

5. Teach learners how to create and use portfolios.

   A. Offer models of excellent portfolios for learners to examine but stress that each portfolio is an individual creation.
   B. Review portfolios regularly and give feedback to learners about them, especially early in the term or year when learners are initially constructing their portfolios.

Projects. We often use the term *project* to describe the major undertakings of businesses and institutions ("We're working on a new project," or, perhaps more critically, "This thing is turning into a project"). In education and training, it is magnitude and complexity that afford something the status of a project. From performing community service to making dramatic presentations, projects offer the multiple challenges, meanings, and creative resolutions that make learning motivating and capable of embracing cultural diversity. Because of their size and duration, projects provide the opportunity for active immersion across disciplines and the use of a wide range of profiles of intelligences. They easily can connect new concepts and skills with the real lives and goals of learners.

The investigation conducted by Daniel Solorzano (1989) and his students is a classic example of a collaborative project carried out with critical consciousness. In the late 1970s, Solorzano offered a sociology course at East Los Angeles College. Beginning with a discussion centering on the negative stereotypes of Chicanos in Hollywood gang movies, Solorzano and his students arrived at two questions: Why are Chicanos portrayed negatively in the mass media? and, Whose interests are served by these negative portrayals of Chicanos?

To conduct extensive research on these queries, the class divided itself into three research groups: (1) a library group to research contemporary and historical images of Chicanos in the media, (2) a group to research public information data on youth gangs in East Los Angeles, and (3) a group to research the film industry. After analyzing and discussing their research, the learners more clearly understood how film companies were exploiting Chicano stereotypes. Consequently, they organized a boycott against these films. Collaborating with outside organizations for assistance led to the founding of the ad hoc Gang Exploitation Committee. Solorzano reports that no new Chicano youth gang movies appeared in the decade after this class. Student learning was extensive, and the students succeeded in doing something they considered important and positive.

In the same vein, the investigation of learning styles designed and executed by Yolanda Scott-Machado (see Strategy 25 in Chapter Five) is a fine representation of an individual project. Some guidelines to keep in mind for creating and carrying out projects are as follows:

- Whether the project is individual or collaborative, learners should be involved in its conception and planning.

- Consider goal setting (see Strategy 25 in Chapter Five) or some of its elements as a means to explore and plan the project.

- Request an outline of the project that includes some schedule of agreed-on documentation and a completion date.

- Arrange for the presentation of the project to a relevant audience who can offer authentic acknowledgment and feedback.

- Assess the project from numerous perspectives, including a learner's self-assessment (see Strategy 54). Overall, assessment may involve the quality of project planning, execution, and presentation; the challenge level; creativity and originality; the employment of resources; what was learned. It may also incorporate the evaluation of other learners and knowledgeable people outside the course or training.

STRATEGY 53: *When using rubrics, make sure they assess the essential features of performance and are fair, valid, and sufficiently clear so that learners can accurately self-assess.*

When it comes to assessment, rubrics are "where the rubber meets the road." That is because rubrics often mean more than assessment; they mean evaluation. Assessment describes or compares, but evaluation makes a value judgment. In evaluation, we fix passing scores or criteria that determine how acceptable or unacceptable a given performance is. Grades or scores may be assigned and recorded according to the rubric. Evaluations often significantly affect an adult's promotion to or qualification for particular programs or positions.

A rubric is a set of scoring guidelines for evaluating a learner's work. It strongly *controls* learning because, as Wiggins (1998, p. 154) points out, many instructors use rubrics to answer the following questions:

By what criteria should performance be judged?

What should we look for to judge performance success?

What does the range in quality of performance look like?

How do we determine validly, reliably, and fairly what score should be given and what that score should mean?

How should the different levels of quality be described and distinguished from one another?

I've been carefully and cautiously using rubrics for about three years, and they can be deceptive even though they do not appear that way at first glance. They remind me of a large wall from a distance. You can't see the cracks until you get closer. Baseball averages afford a good example of the complexity and elusiveness of rubrics. A rubric comprises a scale of possible points along a continuum of quality. Batting average is a rubric in the sense that we evaluate how good batters are by their percentage of hits for times at bat. The higher the average, the better the player. But is a .300 hitter a good hitter? Well, that depends: How many times has the player been to bat? Does she get extra base hits? How does she hit when players are on base? At night? With two strikes? When the team is behind? Against left-handed pitching? As many managers know, you don't use batting average alone to evaluate a player—not even to judge only hitting. And that's how it is with rubrics: they may seem concrete, specific, and telling, but life's contexts and complexity can make the simplest performance a puzzle.

Yet rubrics answer a question that counts for many adults: What are you going to use to judge me? If rubrics are fair, clear, reliable, and valid and get at the essentials of performance, and learners can self-assess with them to improve before performance is evaluated, they enhance motivation because they significantly increase the probability of learners' achieving competence. However, rubrics need models and indicators to make each level of quality concretely understandable. And they need to be created or revised with input from learners if they are to be culturally sensitive. For example, if we use *smiles frequently* as one indicator for *very good* presentation style, we penalize someone who tends to be droll or someone from a culture where smiling frequently is more an indication of anxiety than of ease. Excellent rubrics are valuable but flawed assistants in making judgments about learning—flawed because language at best renders, but never duplicates, experience.

Let's look at one straightforward rubric for judging the clear expression of a main idea in an essay (Exhibit 7.2). (Other rubrics would be necessary for evaluating other dimensions of performance

Exhibit 7.2. A Rubric for Expressing an Idea Clearly.

Rating	Descriptor with Indicators
Exemplary = 4	Clearly communicates the main idea or theme and provides support that contains rich, vivid, and powerful detail.
Competent = 3	Clearly communicates the main idea or theme and provides suitable support and detail.
Acceptable with flaws = 2	Clearly communicates the main idea or theme, but support is sketchy or vague.
Needs revision = 1	The main idea or theme is not discernible.

in the essay, such as critical thinking or writing skills.) This rubric will help us better understand some of Wiggins's guidelines (1998) for creating effective rubrics. These guidelines follow Exhibit 7.2.

If I were using this rubric (and had a model for the descriptor of each level of performance) to evaluate twenty essays *only for the main idea*, I should be able to

Use this rubric to discriminate accurately among the essays by assessing the essential features of performance. This makes the rubric valid.

Rely on the rubric's descriptive language (what the quality or its absence looks like), as opposed to relying on merely evaluative language, such as "excellent product," to make the discrimination.

Use this rubric to consistently make fine discriminations across four levels of performance. When a rubric can be repeatedly used to make the same discriminations with the same sample of performances, it is reliable. To maintain reliability, rubrics seldom have more than six levels of performance.

Make sure learners can use this same rubric and its descriptors (and models) of each level of performance to accurately self-assess and self-correct their work.

See that this rubric is parallel. Each descriptor generally matches the others in terms of criteria language used.

See that this rubric is coherent. The rubric focuses on the same criteria throughout.

See that this rubric is continuous. The degree of difference between each descriptor (level of performance) tends to be equal.

There is a cottage industry in books about how to write rubrics. At this time, I find most of these books overly linear and not culturally sensitive. However, I do find reading them helpful for understanding the creative variety of rubrics that are possible and for deepening my critical awareness about the uses, value, and possible harm of rubrics. Right now, the discipline of assessment and evaluation reminds me of the computer industry: there are vast changes and better models ahead.

STRATEGY 54: *Use self-assessment methods to improve learning and to provide learners with the opportunity to construct relevant insights and connections.*

In addition to the type of self-assessment in which learners compare their work against rubrics and make self-adjustments, there are reflective assessment methods that enable adults to understand themselves more comprehensively as learners, knowers, and participants in a complex world. These methods help learners weave relationships and meanings between academic and technical information and their personal histories and experiences. These forms of self-assessment allow adults to explore their surprises, puzzlement, and hunches, to explore the tension they feel when they experience something that does not fit with what they already know. Because integration of learning with identity and values is essential to adult motivation, this kind of self-assessment is a key process for deepening adult learners' feelings of competence: it can create the bridge that unites formal learning with learners' subjective world.

In general, learners appreciate clearly knowing what to focus on (and what might possibly be learned) in the process of self-assessment. It's a good idea to explain how we as instructors will evaluate or respond to self-assessments. Our interest and timely feedback encourage learners. Not everything needs to be read or commented on, but learners are more likely to strengthen their reflective skills if they receive expected, supportive, and specific feedback from us (or other learners). This is especially so in the beginning phases of any self-assessment process.

Self-assessment can be superficial when it is appended to a training or class as a single episode at the end of a long term. MacGregor (1994) advises instructors to build self-assessment into longer learning situations as an ongoing activity. There are several approaches we can use throughout a learning experience and then summarize from a longer perspective. Among them, I have found journals, post-writes, closure techniques, and the Critical Incident Questionnaire to be very beneficial.

Journals. Journals can take a number of forms. Consider, for example, a journal that is used in a science course to synthesize lab notes, address the quality of the work, examine the process(es) on which work is based, and address emerging interests and concerns. Journals document risk, experimentation with ideas, and self-expression. They are an informative complement to more conventional forms of assessment.

With respect to sensitivity to cultural differences and encouraging critical awareness of the origins and meanings of subject-specific knowledge, learners can use journals to address the following questions: From whose viewpoint am I seeing or reading or hearing? From what angle or perspective? How do I know what I know? What is the evidence, and how reliable is it? Whose purposes are served by this information?

Journals can address interests, ideas, and issues related to course material and processes, recurring problems, responses to questions from the instructor, responses to questions generated by the learner, and important connections that the learner is making. These important connections may be the learner's observations in the classroom, but optimally, connections are meanings that emerge as the learner applies course work to past, present, and future life experiences. If we wish to promote this level of reflection, then we must make the classroom a place where this can happen. Providing time in class for learners to respond in their journals to readings, discussions, and significant questions builds community around the journal process and sends yet another message that the classroom is a place in which the skills of insight and personal meaning are valued.

Journals require time and effort. Initially, it may be best for learners to pay less attention to the mechanics and organization and to whether or not their writing makes sense; they should simply try to get their thoughts and feelings down on paper where they can learn from them. Having sufficiently incubated, this material can be reorganized and summarized later.

Post-writes. Post-writes are reflections that encourage learners to analyze a particular piece of work, how they created it, and what it may mean to them (Allen and Roswell, 1989). For example, you might say, "Now that you have finished your essay, please answer the following questions. There are no right or wrong answers. We are interested in your analysis of your experience writing this essay."

What problems did you face in the writing of this essay?

What solutions did you find for these problems?

Imagine you had more time to write this essay. What would you do if you were to continue working on it?

Has your thinking changed in any way as a result of writing this essay? If so, briefly describe.

It is easy to imagine ways in which this technique could be applied across disciplines. Consider, for example, slightly redesigning the previous questions to allow learners in math or science to identify and reflect on a problem that posed a particular challenge.

Closure techniques. Closure activities are opportunities for learners to synthesize—to examine general or specific aspects of what they have learned, to identify emerging thoughts or feelings, to discern themes, to construct meaning, to relate learning to real-life experiences, and so forth. Essentially, learners articulate their subjective relationship with the course or training material. For example, at the end of a workshop, we might ask participants to formulate an action plan to apply what they have learned. Closure, then, becomes a way of building coherence between what people have learned in the workshop and their personal experience beyond the workshop. Another example of this might be to ask participants to identify one particular obstacle they must still overcome to be more proficient with what they have learned. Additional suggestions for positive and constructive closure follow.

• *Head, heart, hand* is a closure activity that allows learners to integrate different dimensions of a learning experience. After learners have had a short time for reflection, the activity may be conducted as a small- or large-group experience in which all learners have a chance to hear each other's voices. Learners may report out one or more of the following possibilities. For *head*, learners identify something they will continue to think about as a consequence of the learning experience. For *heart*, learners identify a feeling that has emerged as a result of the learning experience. For *hand*, learners identify a desired action they will take that has been stimulated by the learning experience.

• *Note-taking pairs* is a technique that can be used intermittently during a lecture or as a culminating activity (Johnson, Johnson, and Smith, 1991). Either way, two learners work together to review, add to, or modify their notes. This is an opportunity to cooperatively reflect on a lesson, review major concepts and pertinent information, and illuminate unresolved issues or concerns. It is especially beneficial after a lecture. Many learners, including but certainly not limited to students who speak English as a second language, benefit by summarizing their lecture notes to another person or vice versa. Students may ask each other such questions as, What have you got in your notes about this particular item? What are three key points made by the instructor? What is the most surprising thing the instructor said today? What is something that you are feeling uncertain about? and the like.

• *Summarizing questions* are informative questions for reflecting on an entire course or training program. The following are some examples (Elbow, 1986):

What have you accomplished that you are proud of?

Compare your accomplishments with what you had hoped for and expected at the start.

Which kinds of things were difficult or frustrating? Which were easy?

What is the most important thing you did during this program?

Think of some important moments from this learning period: your best moments, typical moments, crises, or turning points. Tell about five or six of these, using a sentence or two for each.

Who is the person you studied whom you cared the most about? Be that person and write that person's letter to you, telling you whatever it is they have to tell you.

What did you learn throughout? Skills and ideas? What was the most important thing? What idea or skill was hardest to really "get"? What crucial idea or skill came naturally?

Describe this period of time as a journey: Where did the journey take you? What was the terrain like? Was it a complete trip or part of a longer one?

You learned something crucial that you won't discover for a while. Guess it now.

Tell a few ways you could have done a better job.

What advice would some friends in the course give you if they spoke with 100 percent honesty and caring? What advice do you have for yourself?

Critical Incident Questionnaire. I have adapted this self-assessment approach from the work of Brookfield (1995, p. 115). In training and teaching, it allows me to be more responsive as an instructor and helps learners be more reflective about their significant experiences.

The Critical Incident Questionnaire is made up of five questions, each of which asks learners to write details about important events that took place while they were learning. For college courses,

Brookfield uses it at the end of each week. For intensive workshops and seminars, I have found value in using it at the end of each session (four hours or longer). The questions are printed on a form; there is space below each question for the learner's responses. Learners complete the questions anonymously and retain a photocopy or carbon copy of their answers for their own benefit.

The Critical Incident Questionnaire

1. At what moment in this workshop did you feel most engaged with what was happening?

2. At what moment in this workshop did you feel most distanced from what was happening?

3. What action that anyone (instructor or learner) took in the workshop did you find most affirming and helpful?

4. What action that anyone (instructor or learner) took in the workshop did you find most puzzling or confusing?

5. What about the workshop surprised you the most? (This could be something about your own reactions to what went on, or something that someone did, or anything else that occurs to you.)

I explore the papers looking for themes, patterns, and, in general, learners' concerns or confusions that need adjustments and responses on my part. I also look for the part of our learning and instruction that has been affirmed. I find hints and suggestions for areas to probe or deepen. Most important, my experience has been that this questionnaire gives me a more sensitive reading of the emotional reactions of learners and of those areas that may create controversy or conflict. However, I do realize that for some students, writing may inhibit their responses, and I publicly acknowledge this shortcoming of the process.

For the beginning of the session immediately following the distribution of the questionnaire, I outline the results in short phrases on an overhead projection and have a dialogue with the learners about these responses. This tends to build trust, further communication, and deepen learning. What I like most is that this form of self-assessment can be so fluidly used to build community. Brookfield (1997) has also developed the Critical Practice Audit, which uses a critical analysis approach to self-assessment for such practitioners as instructors and nurses.

A Few Words About Grades, Assessment, and Motivation

Although they serve no legitimate teaching purpose and do not accurately predict educational or occupational achievement, grades receive very high status in U.S. society (Wlodkowski and Ginsberg, 1995). For most adults, low grades, because they are threatening and stigmatizing, do more to decrease motivation to learn than they do to enhance it. For poor and working-class people, grades as an indication of intellectual merit reduce accessibility to higher education (American Association of University Women Educational Foundation, 1992). Topping off a thirty-year trend, grade inflation is growing at a rapid rate (Astin, 1998) and further eroding the worth of grades.

Yet, until we reform the grading system, many of us will have to give grades. Because contracts have a structure that allows for mutual understanding and agreement and a dialogue about the content, process, criteria, and outcomes of learning, I recommend using them to arrive at grades (see Chapter Five). If you are not able to use contracts but can use the assessment strategies described in this chapter to assign grades that stand for something fair, clear, stable, and valid, then the more pernicious motivational consequences of grading should be minimal.

In fact, as a set of interdependent practices, Strategies 48 through 54 align extremely well with the guiding principles for assessment of adult learning offered by Kasworm and Marienau (1997). In general, adults become more competent, feel more confident, and look forward to assessment when assessment procedures are

Related to goals they understand, find relevant, and want to accomplish

Reflective of growth in learning

Indicative of clear ways to improve learning without penalty

Expected

Returned promptly

Permeated with instructor and peer comments that are informative and supportive

Used to encourage new challenges in learning

Communicating to Engender Competence

The rest of the motivational strategies found in this chapter also enhance competence but are frequently used apart from assessment. Often they are straightforward communications given as the situation demands.

STRATEGY 55: *When necessary, use constructive criticism.*

Constructive criticism is similar to feedback but has a few more qualifications. It does emphasize errors and deficiencies in learning, but unlike basic criticism, it does not connote expressions of disapproval, disgust, or rejection. In general, criticism does not have to be used as often as we may think. Instructors may tend to overuse criticism when they do not know how to use feedback properly or have to work with learners who do not have proper entry-level skills for the learning task they are *required* to perform. The latter condition is best alleviated through more appropriate selection and guidance procedures, such as pretesting and interviews. However, there are still circumstances in which giving constructive criticism may be a necessary strategy for engendering competence:

When the learning process is extremely costly or involves a threat to human safety, mistakes cannot be afforded. Training with a particular machine, weapon, chemical, or medical procedure are examples of this type of situation.

When the learning performance is so poor that to emphasize success or improvement would be ridiculous or patronizing.

When the learning performance has significant errors and there are only a few remaining chances for improvement in the training or course.

When a learner directly requests criticism.

Constructive criticism may be a helpful and motivating way to deal with these situations. Like feedback, constructive criticism has the following qualities: it is informational, based on performance criteria, behavior specific, corrective, and prompt, and when possible, it provides efficient opportunities for improvement. Unless a state of emergency exists, it is given privately. In addition, where appropriate, constructive criticism has the following characteristics:

• It helps the learner see performance in the context of overall progress and not as an isolated failure: for example, "Your science exam indicates that 70 percent of the concepts are still unclear to you. I hope you keep in mind that you've already progressed through four units, and although this one may seem difficult, that's a pretty good indication you can more fully understand these ideas. Let's go over the material."

• It respectfully informs the learner of the conditions that lead to the emphasis on mistakes or deficiencies: for example, "This machine can be quite dangerous. For your own safety, before you get another chance to operate it, I think we'd better take a look at any mistakes you might have made," or, "You've got only one more chance to practice before you meet with the review committee. I think the best use of our time would be to check your performance on the last case study and to concentrate on any parts that may need improvement."

• It acknowledges the learner's effort: for example, "There's no doubt you've put a great deal of work into this report. Just the number of references you cite testifies to the effort and comprehensive research that went into this project. Yet it seems to need more organization. There's no unifying theme that ties all this evidence together. What generalization could you think of that might serve this purpose?"

• It provides emotional support: for example, "At the end of your last session, your client stated he felt frustrated as he left. Do you think you may have been trying too hard? You sounded a bit strident and didn't respond to the client's stated needs. We can analyze the videotape to see just where this happened. However, you did very well with the other two clients you worked with. Since you have only one more chance to practice in this seminar, let's be as careful as possible to understand what might not have worked so well. It's obvious you want to do your best, and I feel confident you'll learn from this situation."

When you are giving feedback and constructive criticism, adults benefit from knowing when more effort on their part or another learning strategy could significantly contribute to their learning. Strategy 20 (Chapter Five) explains why and how to make these attributions.

Strategy 56: *Effectively praise and reward learning.*

In this book, the term *praise* has the same meaning it usually has in everyday language: to commend the worth of or to express approval or admiration (Brophy, 1981). It is an intense response on the part of an instructor, one that goes beyond positive feedback to include such emotions as surprise, delight, or excitement as well as sincere appreciation for the learner's accomplishment. ("That's a remarkable answer. It's comprehensive, insightful, and extremely precise.")

As a strategy, the use of praise has had a controversial history. Some scholars have opposed praise and rewards on principle, viewing them as bribes for doing something that is often in the learners' best interest or in the best interest of society (Kohn, 1993). Others are critical of praise because it may contribute to a hierarchical relationship between learners and instructors. Instructors distribute praise because they are the judges and experts who deem learners as praiseworthy. This kind of social exchange may diminish the chances for colearning and for a more egalitarian relationship.

Although praise can enhance learners' motivation, there is considerable research to show it often does not serve this purpose (Kohn, 1993). Praise is frequently ineffective because it is not related to exemplary achievement, it lacks specificity (the learner does not know exactly why it was given), and it is not credible. For example, sometimes we may give it because learners seem happy and enthusiastic about their work and show it to us, and we do not know what else to say (*awkward-moment praise*). Other times we may give it because we feel sorry for learners who are having difficulty and use it to boost their morale (*mercy praise*).

Many competent adults do not want or expect praise. They want clear, positive feedback about their progress and may experience praise as annoying or patronizing (*snob praise*). Furthermore, praise given too frequently and indiscriminately may begin to seem perfunctory and predictable to learners, encouraging them to interpret it as a form of instructor small talk or flattery (*jabber praise*). The focus of praise on form rather than substance can cause a problem as well. Praise for turning in an assignment or for learning responses that agree with instructor values may seem controlling and manipulative (*puppet praise*). In some instances, instructors have even used praise to *end* learner behavior: perhaps a discussion initiated by a learner has, in our opinion, gone on a bit too long; we toss out a compliment about what has been said to provide pleasant closure, and move on to something else (*terminator praise*).

In general, to praise effectively we need to praise *well*, rather than necessarily *often*. The same could be said about rewarding effectively. In fact, praise is often considered to be a verbal reward (Pittman, Boggiano, and Ruble, 1983). Whether the reward is verbal (praise) or tangible (money, promotions, privileges) or symbolic (grades, trophies, awards), there are guidelines that can ensure the positive effects of these rewards on learner motivation. The six suggestions that follow are based on a continuing analysis by Brophy (1998), which has largely used studies done with children and adolescents. However, this material is supported by research with young adults (Morgan, 1984) and adults learning in the workplace (Keller, 1992).

Effective praise and rewards are

1. *Given with sincerity, spontaneity, variety, and other signs of credibility.* These characteristics may be more pertinent for praise than for other rewards. Rewards are often known ahead of time and given with more uniformity of procedure. However, the affect with which a reward is given is critical to its impact on the learner. An insincerely given reward or form of praise is really an insult to an adult. (A personal note: I have conducted hundreds of workshops in which I have asked instructors to volunteer the guidelines for effective praise. Without exception, sincerity has been listed as the number one guideline.)

2. *Based on the attainment of specific performance criteria.* This means that the learner has achieved a standard and can clearly understand what particular personal behaviors are being acknowledged. This approach not only makes the reward or praise informational but also significantly increases the person's chances of learning exactly which behaviors are important. For example, "Nice

job" written on a paper is not as helpful as, "This paper has not a single spelling or grammatical error in it. I appreciate the meticulous editing this so obviously reflects."

3. *Adapted in sufficiency, quantity, and intensity to the accomplishments achieved.* Rewards that are less than what is merited can be insulting and demeaning. Rewards that are too much for what has been accomplished are excessive and disturbing. There are common expressions in everyday language to reflect adult embarrassment in response to inadequate or undeserved praise: "Damning with faint praise" (too little praise) and "Gushing over trivia" (too much praise).

4. *Given to attribute success to the apparent combination of the personal effort, knowledge, and capabilities of the learner.* Emphasizing these attributes increases the learner's sense of internal causality and implies the learner can continue such accomplishments in the future: for example, "Your design of this model is exceptional. It meets all the criteria for strength, durability, and esthetics. Would you mind sharing how you created it with the rest of the team? I think we could all learn from your approach."

5. *Given contingent on success at a challenging task.* This makes the learner's task *praiseworthy* and testifies to the competence of the learner. The praise implies that the learner overcame a real difficulty and deserves the recognition. If the task were not challenging, then the praise would be indiscriminate, and a reward, if given, would tend to be seen as likewise.

6. *Adapted to the preference of the individual.* Again, this characteristic may be more applicable to praise than to other rewards. Rewards are often given in a ritualistic manner, as in award ceremonies. However, one would certainly want rewards to be attractive and valued in relation to the learner's cultural preferences. For example, more collectivist cultures may prefer to receive praise indirectly rather than directly. In one study, Jones, Rozelle, and Chang (1990) found that Chinese adults did not want to be used as "good examples for others," whereas the group from the United States

found that to be quite acceptable. When in doubt, it is probably best to give praise and other rewards privately.

There is a mnemonic device for remembering these six guidelines: 3S-3P, which stands for Sincere, Specific, Sufficient, Properly attributed, Praiseworthy, and Preferred. In sentence form, the mnemonic can be stated this way: praise (or other rewards) should be Sincere, Specific, Sufficient, and Properly attributed for genuinely Praiseworthy behavior, in a manner Preferred by the learner. In general, it is important to remember that the subjective viewpoint of the learner and the context in which praise and other rewards are given will immensely influence their effect (Morgan, 1984). As of now, there are no ways to accurately prescribe these conditions, except to encourage instructors to remain continually sensitive to their impact.

Further Means of Affirming Learner Competence

There are important strategies to enhance aspects of adult competence that may not easily be measured by performance criteria but that are critical nonetheless, such as creativity or cooperation. In some instances, these aspects of competence emerge out of the human experience learners and instructors share from having worked and accomplished something together. The following strategies accommodate these less easily categorized outcomes of learning.

STRATEGY 57: *Acknowledge and affirm the learners' responsibility and any significant actions or characteristics that contributed to individual or group learning.*

The idea behind this strategy is as follows: if there is anything significant the learner has done or exemplified that has contributed to the individual's or group's learning, we want to reflect this back to the learner. The implication of this strategy is that standard means of providing feedback, assessment, praise, or other rewards were not sufficient to adequately reveal the learner's assets. Some specific ways to carry out this strategy are as follows:

• Interview learners for their opinions as to what the critical processes were that helped them to learn successfully. This method is especially useful with self-directed individual and small-group learning projects. It offers an excellent opportunity to include self-assessment materials, such as post-writes, journals, and closure techniques (see Strategy 54). A more formative approach to competence in ongoing self-directed learning activities is this set of four questions asked at an appropriate interval: What is your evaluation of what you have done so far? How can you still improve? How can you help yourself? How can I help you?

• Acknowledge the risk taking and challenge involved in the learning accomplishment. When adults deliberately choose a challenging learning goal, the process of learning becomes even more special because they have knowingly placed themselves at risk. This condition intensifies what they can learn about themselves. With further reflection, learners can build their self-confidence and experience the merit of their talents, strategies, and effort. If they do not accomplish the learning goal, the process can be a lesson in reality testing and self-appraisal. Learners can explore related issues through questions like these: What has been learned from attempting to accomplish the goal? Does the goal remain worthwhile? Is it reasonable to continue to strive for the goal? If not, what is a desirable next step? And so forth.

Taking on learning challenges that are reasonable and personally valued is a form of courage—the courage to persevere in the midst of ambiguity, the courage to extend personal boundaries, the courage to embrace learning for its own sake. These are not spontaneous human qualities. They are cultivated, and they evolve. As instructors, we can provide opportunities for adults to reflect on where these aspects of their learning occur and what their value may be.

• Affirm the strengths and assets of the learner that contribute to the learner's own achievements or to the accomplishments of others. When instructors and learners work together for a period of time, they begin to recognize in each other various qualities that are beneficial not only to learning but also to people's well-being. Many of these characteristics may not be easily classified under the performance criteria being applied. Also, they may not be praise-worthy by definition. However, they are significant enough to be recognized and influential enough to be appreciated. Helping learn-ers see that they possess these assets can raise their self-awareness and make these strengths more available to them in future learning and work situations. Stating such an appreciation can be quite sim-ple. For example, "I just wanted you to know I really enjoyed your sense of humor in this course" could suffice. We can make this kind of statement informally, one-on-one with the learner, or as part of a concluding group exercise in which each member of the learning group is allowed two statements of appreciation to anyone about anything that has occurred during the course or training.

The following are some strengths and assets learners often pos-sess, and it may benefit learners to know they possess them:

Writing skills	Thinking skills
Physical skills	Integrity
Multiple intelligences	Cooperativeness
Personal traits	Creativity
Verbal skills	Math skills
Knowledge base	Sense of humor
Organizational skills	Kindness
Significant actions	Leadership skills

This list is more suggestive than exhaustive. The main point is not to miss the opportunity to give learners important information derived from the human interaction in a learning experience. Also, this approach encourages learner-to-learner feedback, which might have more impact on a person than anything an instructor could communicate.

STRATEGY 58: *Use incentives to develop and maintain adult motivation in learning activities that are initially unappealing but personally valued.*

One of the insights Peters and Waterman (1982) made about the use of positive rewards is that rewards are an excellent means to help people move in directions they are already headed. Positive reinforcement can be a gentle and precise way to develop and maintain adult motivation for learning that is personally valued but not initially appealing.

An *incentive* may be defined as an anticipated reward. It serves as a goal we expect to achieve as a result of some specific behavior. Incentives take many forms, such as recognition, money, relationships, and privileges. Incentives are frequently used in the workplace (Kemmerer and Thiagarajan, 1992). However, I use this concept only as it can be understood to support intrinsic motivation while learning—as a means to assist adults in becoming more effective at what they personally value. Incentive systems in the workplace are not necessarily created or implemented with this orientation as an essential element.

Adults' lives are filled with incentives. We frequently use rewards for performing activities we value but find tedious, difficult, or perhaps even painful—exercising easily comes to mind, but there's also dieting, studying, budgeting, and cleaning. We reward ourselves at certain points for performing these activities. The reward may be a piece of chocolate, a massage, a movie, a long distance call, or a walk outside. Knowing these kinds of incentives are coming at the end of our task makes the tedium or effort a little more bearable. Regardless of how many times I tell myself it's great to get my heart rate up and sweat like a steam whistle, seeing my favorite cold drink at the end of the workout is a far more fetching notion to keep me working out. But please keep in mind that I chose the activity, I value the activity, and I want to be competent at it. I'm using a reward to help me sustain an activity I'm intrinsically motivated to perform. And make no mistake about it: in my mind, the reward makes the whole experience better.

There are at least two situations in which incentives may be an effective and inviting means to encourage adult participation in a valued learning activity:

1. *The adult has had little or no experience with the learning activity.* Maybe the training or instructional program is very new or unique. Lack of experience can prevent the learner from enjoying or valuing what he is learning or cause him to feel cautious and apprehensive. Or perhaps the person is learning how to use a new machine or how to apply a different auditing process or how to work with recently invented technology. In this case, the learner anticipates the value of the activity but has not yet realized that value. Under such circumstances, incentives could actually contribute to the awakening of intrinsic motivation in the learner because there is no prior negative experience to lead the learner to believe that the incentive is being used as compensation for participation in an unpleasant learning task (Lepper and Greene, 1978). The learner is more likely to see the incentive as a reward for "trying out" or becoming competent in a new learning opportunity.

2. *The adult has to develop a level of competence before the learning activity can become enjoyable or interesting.* Some sports, such as tennis and swimming, are good examples of this situation, but the same could be said for learning to speak a foreign language or use a personal computer or play the trumpet. There are so many things that are valuable to learn but just not that appealing to do until the learner has achieved a level of competence. In such situations, incentives may be the only positive means available to sustain effort

until the necessary level of proficiency provides its own pleasure and satisfaction. That is why parents applaud vigorously and unashamedly for their children at those, to say the least, imperfect music recitals and why an instructor might have to give extra attention and recognition to a struggling student in an adult basic education course.

One of the things we're learning from studies of the situated nature of learning (Greeno, Collins, and Resnick, 1996) and the sociocultural perspective is that we can't separate learning from its context, certainly not in the mind of the learner. So when rewards are external to the activity but enable adults to become competent in learning they value, they may see those rewards as necessary and functionally a very real part of the learning process. For example, I love basketball and want to improve my free-throw shooting average, and I have a coach who will take me out to lunch if I practice five hundred extra free throws. To some people, lunch and free throws seem unrelated, but to me they are part of the same idea: getting better at basketball while having a fun way to make the grueling monotony of practicing free throws more immediately worth it. When it comes to intrinsic motivation and incentives, the paramount issues to consider are the learners' value for the activity or for what the activity leads to, the probability of increasing competence through the activity, and the learners' view of the overall process.

Promoting Natural Consequences and Positive Endings

The concept of natural consequences comes out of reinforcement theory (Vargas, 1977). Natural consequences are changes in a person resulting from learning. Reading a book may have the natural consequence of producing new insights and expanded awareness in an adult. When working with natural consequences, we emphasize the result of learning (insights) more than the process of learning (reading). Sociocultural theory takes the perspective that both of these elements are intimately related and cannot be arbitrarily divided. For example, a person is motivated to solve a problem by both the pleasure of analyzing it and the satisfaction of arriving at a solution. In other words, it's both the trip and the destination that are motivating. Yet emphasizing natural consequences is an effective motivational strategy, because like a good tour guide, it helps adults more vividly understand the importance of their destination.

Strategy 59: *When learning has natural consequences, help learners to be aware of them and of their impact.*

One can see that natural consequences and feedback go hand in hand. However, because using natural consequences as a strategy includes *every* consequence that an adult can perceive as a result of learning, it encourages instructors to *make learning active as soon as possible* so that adults can quickly have natural consequences to increase and maintain their motivation. The remarkably successful Suzuki violin method does this for children, but so might any instructor of adults teaching any skill, ranging from sailing to surfing the Internet.

Many learning activities have natural consequences for adults that are not included in the performance criteria. To miss these would be a shame. It would be like serving a cake without the frosting. People often do not realize some of the consequences of their learning. In these situations, instructors can act as mirrors or magnifying glasses to reveal relevant consequences not readily apparent. The guiding question is, As a result of this learning activity, what else does the learner know or what else can the learner do that is important and worth pursuing? Suppose, for example, that an adult takes a course in technical report writing. The standard of performance is based on a readability index that is precise and provides excellent informational feedback. The adult achieves the standard of performance and successfully completes the course. It is also possible that because of the learning in this course, the adult is more confident as a writer, enjoys writing in general more than ever before, can more clearly communicate verbally, sees improvement in personal letter writing, and will now pursue a career in which writing is a requisite skill. When the instructor takes some time at the end of this course to discuss with the learners what other outcomes may have been achieved by them, they are likely to deepen their motivation and broaden their transfer of learning.

Discussion is not the only means of making natural consequences more conspicuous. Authentic performance tasks and simulations often reveal more than the specific expected learning. Using self-assessment strategies as well as videotapes and audiotapes to record progress and demonstrate before and after effects, we can highlight a variety of natural consequences. There is also the possibility of using examples in which a given skill or concept is applied outside the expected context, such as asking how a communication skill might be used with a learner's family as well as on the job.

STRATEGY 60: *Provide positive closure at the end of significant units of learning.*

A significant unit of learning can be determined by length or importance. In terms of length, when any entire course, seminar, or training program is terminating, a significant unit of learning has occurred. In longer courses there may be segments based on content or skill that each have a clearly delineated beginning and ending. For example, a course in marketing might be divided into units on promotion, sales, and contracts.

In terms of importance, a significant unit of learning is any segment of learning that has some characteristic that makes it special: the level of difficulty, cohesiveness, or creativity; the type of learning situation, structure, or process (special equipment, materials, location, grouping, or task); or the presence of such prominent individuals as an esteemed audience, lecturer, or evaluator.

In all these cases, something notable is coming to an end. Positive closure enhances learners' motivation because it affirms the entire process, verifies the value of the experience, directly or indirectly acknowledges competence, increases cohesiveness within the group, and encourages the surfacing of inspiration and other beneficial emotions in the learners themselves. Positive closure can be a small gesture, such as thanking learners for their cooperation, or something much more extravagant, such as an awards ceremony. Some ways to achieve positive closure are as follows:

• Celebrations. For people all over the world, festivals and holidays have been a joyous means of acknowledging the ending of seasons, religious periods, and harvests. There is no valid reason to avoid this in learning. Savor with learners their moment of triumph and accomplishment. This can be a pleasurable discussion, a party, a round of applause, sitting back and reliving the experience through "remember when" statements, or mild congratulations. But let the moment linger and enjoy it together. It is a happy occasion, not to be taken for granted. Celebrations are a wonderfully inclusive metaphor. They allow people to feel pleasure for whatever they personally accomplished or valued during the entire learning experience.

• Acknowledgments. These can be simple statements of gratitude and appreciation or more formal and ritualized awards. The goal is to recognize any learner contributions or achievements that were noteworthy during the span of the learning event (see Strategy 57). Depending on the situation, acknowledgments can be given by the instructor, the learners, or both.

• Sharing. Sharing is anything the instructor and learners might do to show their caring and sensitivity to the special quality of the learning experience and those involved in it. Some have cooked dinner for their learning group. Others have brought in personal collections or demonstrated their musical or artistic abilities. More frequently, this type of sharing takes the form of a poignant final statement that may include an eloquent poem or an inspirational quotation. When something has gone well, it deserves a fitting form of closure.

8

Building Motivational Strategies into Instructional Designs

When we do the best we can, we never know what
miracle is wrought in our life, or in the life of another.
Helen Keller

W hen it is very good, instruction is technical excellence under the command of artistic expression. For no matter how many fixed rules, precise definitions, and logical strategies we establish in learning, the process remains embedded in a human context that is open ended, subjective, unique, and constantly changing. For this reason, instruction remains a science within an art, more akin to communication than to engineering. In fact, instruction may never be a sure thing, because what makes people learn is beyond guarantee or total prediction. Therefore, it will always need the timeliness, sensitivity, and vision that any effective relationship contributing to human growth demands. Among the many important aspects of instruction, none seem more deserving of this perspective than those that deal with motivation.

At our current level of understanding, human motivation in learning is too complex and indomitable to lend itself to easy panaceas. But we can plan for it. A logical and seductive assumption is that if instruction itself is well planned and efficient, motivation for what is being learned should neatly and nicely come along as well. In some instances this is true, especially when adults feel respected and know that what they are learning is relevant and when the instructional process increases their effectiveness. However, the longer the instructional sequence or the more complicated the human factors within it, the easier it is for motivation to diminish—which it seems to do with regularity. If this were not so, motivation would not be the epidemic concern it is for instructors.

Industry and business are filled with well-designed, efficient instructional programs that are not very motivating. Part of the problem is efficiency itself. Motivation takes people-to-people skills and time. Like a good conversation, it cannot be rushed. The best way to see a motivational strategy is as an investment. It pays dividends but often not immediately. Also, because what motivates people is often beyond the inherent structure of the knowledge or skill they are learning, instructors have to plan for motivation in its own right. It cannot be taken for granted. If we look at the motivational conditions and strategies described in the other chapters, most of them address cultural and internal human influences in learning, such as inclusion, attitude, meaning, and competence. Many instructional formats do not address these influences (Yelon, 1992; Rothwell and Kazanas, 1992). Yet they are essential to motivated learning, and planning for them, at the very least, seems sensible.

The Motivational Framework for Culturally Responsive Teaching can be used as an organizational aid for instructional planning. It is a systemic structure for applying motivational strategies throughout a learning sequence. Instruction is a complex network of influences and interactions whose results are produced by the total system of such influences, not by its individual parts (Wlodkowski and Ginsberg, 1995). With this motivational framework we can design instruction so that the development and enhancement of learners' *intrinsic motivation* is an essential part the plan. The framework and its related strategies enable us to programmatically combine a series of learning activities from the beginning to the end of an instructional sequence so that they create a network of mutually supportive motivational conditions. These conditions—inclusion, attitude, meaning, and competence—work in concert to elicit adult motivation for learning for the entire learning sequence. It may be helpful to review the discussion of this framework in Chapter Three before reading further sections of this chapter.

Increasing Motivational Self-Awareness

In preparation for our effective use of the Motivational Framework for Culturally Responsive Teaching, a few considerations may increase our sensitivity to how the framework will be most helpful to us. The first is to conduct an analysis of our roles as instructors, our assumptions about the motivation of adults, and our instructional situation relative to motivation. Many times instructors apply a new method in education and training without reflecting on how well this approach fits their philosophy, style, and professional environment. This can be a mistake because, rather than fluidly integrating the new method, it attempts to inject the new method among other professional habits and circumstances that seriously limit its effectiveness. Exhibit 8.1 lists three areas significantly related to an instructor's approach to learner motivation.

Having conducted the reflections outlined in Exhibit 8.1, you may wish to review all the strategies discussed in this book before proceeding to the instructional planning section of this chapter. Table 8.1 is a summary of the motivational strategies contained in the four previous chapters. It includes the four major motivational conditions and a listing of specific related strategies and the purposes they serve. For instructional planning, which tends to be linear, you may want to assign these strategies to the particular time phase suggested in Table 8.1. My experience over the last thirteen years and the experiences of the numerous instructors who have corresponded with me indicate that these strategies do indeed have their maximum impact when timed in this way. However, my experience also tells me that the creativity and complexity of teaching and learning make the strategies processes *not* to be simply circumscribed by time.

Exhibit 8.1. Instructor Self-Assessment Regarding Motivation.

Reflecting on the three areas listed here can help you be more aware of the extent to which the motivational approach offered in this book can be of use to you. Take a few minutes for each section and give yourself time to answer the questions and to reflect on your responses. Writing out responses to each section may clarify your thoughts and make the entire process a deeper experience.

1. *Your Perception of Your Role as an Instructor*

This approach to instruction is generally incompatible with roles that are authoritarian and directive but very effective with those that are collaborative, egalitarian, and consultative. How appropriate and natural does it feel for you to be a colearner among adults? What generally have been your reactions to your experiences when you are a guide and facilitator of adult learning rather than a director or lecturer? How comfortable are you when you respect the voices of others as you teach? Is this an area for greater professional growth? Consider three things you most often do to enhance learner motivation. What do these habits tell you about the kind of role you prefer as an instructor?

2. *Your Assumptions About the Motivation of the Adults You Teach or Train*

Another critical reflection is to become aware of your assumptions about the motivation of the adults you teach or train. How do you understand the relationship between how these adults have been socialized and their motivation to learn? What are your thoughts about the importance of teaching or training in ways that engage the motivation of *all* learners? This approach to motivation respects cultural diversity and assumes that learning situations for adults should model equitable learning environments and promote an understanding of how what is learned relates to a more equitable society. What is your thinking on these matters? How important are they to you?

3. *Your Perceptions of Your Instructional Situation*

Finally, think about your instructional situation. When you consider the organization you work for, what are its highest priorities for your instruction? How are these compatible with your own goals and the goals of the motivational approach in this book? What are the areas in which you have the most freedom to be flexible and self-directed? Are there parts of your instructional program that need a change? Has any of the information in the previous chapters helped in this regard? If so, how? Where would be the best place to begin to make a few changes? And just as important, what material in this book has affirmed your teaching or training? Please conclude this section by completing the following sentence as you think your learners would (listing as many answers as are applicable): My instructor helps me feel motivated because he or she . . .

According to need and situation, they may be a positive motivational influence at any moment, hour, or day.

The review you perform using Table 8.1 has a number of purposes. First, it will give you a more immediate sensitivity to all the possible strategies that can be used for instructional planning. Second, you can use the table as a checklist of all the strategies you are currently employing. Many instructors are not aware of all the things they do to enhance adult motivation for learning. This kind of inventory may give you a more concrete awareness of your repertoire of current motivational strategies. The summary will also probably list strategies that are not part of your repertoire, some of which you might want to include in your instructional efforts. If you find more than a few motivational strategies that you would like to initiate, rank these strategies in terms of their personal value to you as well as their probability of being successful. Using these two criteria for selection will increase the chances that the new strategies you finally choose will be effective and adaptable to your instructional situation.

Designing an Instructional Plan

After the review of the sixty strategies listed in Table 8.1, the next step is to consider some ways to design an instructional plan based on the Motivational Framework for Culturally Responsive Teaching. These methods can be adapted to more prescriptive approaches to instructional design (Rothwell and Kazanas, 1992). The first step is to clarify the learning objective. A clear understanding of the proposed learning outcome will suggest the sequence of instruction and its relationship to a larger instructional unit (if there is one). When needs assessments are used to develop learning objectives, they can be either a prior step or part of the first step in this planning.

Once the learning objective is well understood, the next step is to determine the amount of time available to help learners achieve it. This length of time will have a strong influence on the kind and

Table 8.1. Summary of Motivational Strategies.

Major Motivational Condition	Motivational Purpose	Motivational Strategy
Inclusion (beginning learning activities)	To engender an awareness and feeling of connection among adults	1. Allow for introductions.
		2. Provide an opportunity for multidimensional sharing.
		3. Concretely indicate your cooperative intentions to help adults learn.
		4. Share something of value with your adult learners.
		5. Use collaborative and cooperative learning.
		6. Clearly identify the learning objectives and goals for instruction.
		7. Emphasize the human purpose of what is being learned and its relationship to the learners' personal lives and contemporary situations.
	To create a climate of respect among adults	8. Assess learners' current expectations and needs and their previous experience as it relates to your course or training.
		9. Explicitly introduce important norms and participation guidelines.
		10. When issuing mandatory assignments or training requirements, give your rationale for these stipulations.
		11. To the degree authentically possible, reflect the language, perspective, and attitudes of adult learners.
		12. Introduce the concepts of comfort zones and learning edges to help learners accommodate more intense emotions during episodes of new learning.
		13. Acknowledge different ways of knowing, different languages, and different levels of knowledge or skill to engender a safe learning environment.

Attitude (beginning learning activities)	To build a positive attitude toward the subject	14. Eliminate or minimize any negative conditions that surround the subject.
		15. Ensure successful learning with mastery learning conditions.
		16. Positively confront the erroneous beliefs, expectations, and assumptions that may underlie a negative learner attitude.
		17. Use assisted learning to scaffold complex learning.
	To develop positive self-concepts for learning	18. Encourage the learner.
		19. Promote the learner's personal control of the context of learning.
		20. Help learners accurately attribute their success to their capability, effort, and knowledge.
		21. When learning tasks are suitable to learners' capability, help learners understand that effort and knowledge can overcome their failures.
	To establish expectancy for success	22. Make the criteria of assessment as fair and clear as possible.
		23. Use relevant models to demonstrate expected learning.
		24. Announce the expected amount of time needed for study and practice for successful learning.
		25. Use goal-setting methods.
		26. Use contracting methods.
	To create relevant learning experiences	27. Use the five entry points suggested by multiple intelligences research as ways of learning about a topic or concept.
		28. Make the learning activity an irresistible invitation to learn.
		29. Use the K-W-L strategy to introduce new topics and concepts.

Table 8.1. Summary of Motivational Strategies, cont'd.

Major Motivational Condition	Motivational Purpose	Motivational Strategy
Meaning (during learning activities)	To maintain learners' attention	30. Use brainstorming webs to develop and link new information.
		31. Provide frequent response opportunities to all learners on an equitable basis.
		32. Help learners realize their accountability for what they are learning.
		33. Provide variety in personal presentation style, modes of instruction, and learning materials.
		34. Introduce, connect, and end learning activities attractively and clearly.
		35. Selectively use breaks, physical exercises, and energizers.
	To invite and evoke learners' interest	36. Relate learning to adult interests, concerns, and values.
		37. When possible, clearly state or demonstrate the benefits that will result from the learning activity.
		38. While instructing, use humor liberally and frequently.
		39. Selectively induce parapathic emotions.
		40. Selectively use examples, analogies, metaphors, and stories.
		41. Use uncertainty, anticipation, and prediction to the degree that learners enjoy them with a sense of security.
	To develop engagement and challenge with adult learners	42. Use critical questions to stimulate learner engagement and challenge.
		43. Use relevant problems to facilitate learning.
		44. Use an intriguing problem to make instructional material meaningful.
		45. Use case study methods to enhance meaning.

Competence (ending learning activities)		46. Use simulations and role playing to enhance meaning with a more realistic context.
		47. Use invention, artistry, imagination, and enactment to render meaning and emotion in learning.
	To engender competence with assessment	48. Provide effective feedback.
		49. Avoid cultural bias in assessment procedures.
		50. Make assessment tasks and criteria known to learners.
		51. Use authentic performance tasks to enable adults to know that they can proficiently apply what they are learning to their real lives.
		52. Provide opportunities for adults to demonstrate their learning in ways that reflect their strengths and multiple sources of knowing.
		53. When using rubrics, make sure they assess the essential features of performance and are fair, valid, and sufficiently clear so that learners can accurately self-assess.
		54. Use self-assessment methods to improve learning and to provide learners with the opportunity to construct relevant insights and connections.
	To engender competence with communication	55. When necessary, use constructive criticism.
		56. Effectively praise and reward learning.
		57. Acknowledge and affirm the learners' responsibility and any significant actions or characteristics that contributed to individual or group learning.
		58. Use incentives to develop and maintain adult motivation in learning activities that are initially unappealing but personally valued.
		59. When learning has natural consequences, help learners to be aware of them and of their impact.
		60. Provide positive closure at the end of significant units of learning.

number of motivational strategies chosen. For example, because processing a lengthy case study takes much longer than conducting a short role play, the role play may have to be selected for the instructional plan.

The next step is to analyze the inherent structure of the material, knowledge, or skill to be learned. This structure itself may determine the order of content or the sequence of steps to be followed if the material is to be adequately learned, as is often the case in math or a foreign language. In addition to analyzing the structure of the material, we need to consider the assessment process. Often we mentally have to go back and forth between understanding the flow of the content and the type of assessment we desire in order to work out what sequence of learning activities will lead to evidence that satisfactorily establishes the competence of the learners.

There is no one way to sequence learning. For example, should learning activities make content flow from the general to the specific, or vice versa? Or should we begin with a concrete experience of the content, move to reflective observation, then to abstract conceptualization, and, finally, to active experimentation, as Smith and Kolb (1986) have proposed? Or we might problem-pose the content and codevelop the sequence with learners, as Paulo Freire (1970) has espoused. In this book, I advocate following a motivational framework to teach content. I suggest beginning a new course or training with learning activities based on strategies to establish inclusion, followed by activities sequenced according to strategies to develop attitude, enhance meaning, and engender competence, respectively. However, once learning has started, it may be an experience much more like playing jazz than playing classical music, with many unexpected but desired twists and turns. Then we can use the strategies for each of the four motivational conditions in a less linear order, on an "as-wanted" basis.

Nonetheless, we may be concerned about ordering content per se, relatively independent of pedagogical theory. If so, we can consider the more technical design guidelines offered by Tracey (1992, p. 242):

- Start the sequence with materials that are familiar to the learners and then proceed to new materials (integrating the familiar with the new).

- Give learners a context or framework to use in organizing what they are to learn.

- Place easily learned tasks early in the sequence.

- Introduce broad concepts and technical terms that have application throughout the instructional process early in the sequence.

- Place practical application of concepts and principles close to the point of the initial discussion of the concepts and principles.

- Place prerequisite knowledge and skills in the sequence prior to the point where they must be combined with subsequent knowledge and skills.

- Provide for practice and review of skills and knowledge that are essential parts of tasks to be introduced later in the activity.

- Introduce a concept or a skill in the task in which it is most frequently used.

- Structure learning objectives in closely related, self-contained groups.

- Avoid overloading any task with elements that are difficult to learn.

- Place complex or cumulative skills late in the sequence.

- Provide support or coaching for practice of required skills, concepts, and principles in areas where transfer is likely to occur.

When it comes to the assessment component of instructional planning, I have a bias. Because of my experience and understanding of adult motivation, I plan for some kind of authentic performance task as soon as possible. I believe that competence is such a high priority and so motivating for adults that the sooner they experience it, the deeper their learning and motivation will be. Therefore, once I have ascertained the learning objective and the content, I begin imagining what kind of performance task could creatively and clearly reveal to learners that they are becoming more effective at what they value. Once I settle on the performance task, I go back to sequence the course content so that it can lead learners to successful accomplishment of the task. For example, in a research course, one learning objective is to critique a research article effectively. The performance task is pretty straightforward: learners choose a relevant research article to critique. Now I'm back to content; I have to ask myself, What must learners know to make a basic critique, and in what order must they know it? The concepts of reliability and validity come to mind (teach reliability before validity). Now I return to the performance task to consider what the criteria and indicators should be. Once this is settled, I can begin to select motivational strategies to teach reliability and validity. And so it goes.

In this scheme, using assessment to enhance learning, motivation, and learners' self-direction is on an equal footing with using assessment to audit learning. Therefore, it is very important to make the learning objective something *that can be assessed in measurable terms by the learner.* Accuracy is always important, but comprehensiveness may have to wait for a later, more summative assessment. In motivation workshops, for example, I often give participants an instructional scenario to critique for teaching errors. They are requested to find the possible errors and indicate why these actions might be motivational errors. But the participants are not requested to modify the teacher's behavior. They haven't had a chance to learn the content to do this. However, in finding and explaining the errors, the participants discover that their learning about motivation is measurably increasing. This so deepens their motivation that I have made working with this scenario a standard practice.

Superimposing the Motivational Framework

For instructors who are more experienced and possess well-developed instructional plans or who are instructional designers who follow a strictly defined sequence for learning, the best use of the motivational framework may be the *superimposed* method of instructional planning. In this approach, we use the four questions from the Motivational Framework for Culturally Responsive Teaching like a template, together with a previously completed instructional plan.

By asking these questions *with close attention to the diversity of our learners* as we peruse our instructional plan, we can estimate where our instructional activities fulfill the intent of these questions and where they do not. For those questions that are not adequately answered, we can develop learning activities based on the strategies (found in Table 8.1) related to the motivational conditions the specific questions represent. The two main criteria for successful instructional planning based on the motivational framework are as follows: (1) the instructional plan establishes all four of the motivational conditions, and (2) each time phase (beginning, during, and ending) has activities in its sequence of instruction to elicit significant motivation among learners.

The Four Questions for Instructional Planning

1. *Establishing inclusion:* How does this learning sequence create or affirm a learning atmosphere in which we feel *respected* by and *connected* to one another? (Emphasis on beginning activities)

2. *Developing attitude:* How does this learning sequence make use of personal relevance and learner choice to create or affirm a favorable disposition toward learning? (Emphasis on beginning activities)

3. *Enhancing meaning:* Are there *engaging* and *challenging* learning experiences that include learners' perspectives and values in

this learning sequence? (Emphasis on main activities during the instructional plan)

4. *Engendering competence:* How does this learning sequence create or affirm an understanding that learners have *effectively learned something they value* and perceive as *authentic to their real world*? (Emphasis on ending activities)

One of the problems with instructional planning is the struggle to deal with the complexity and nuance of real, live teaching in a two-dimensional format. In this struggle, it helps to remember that most of the sixty strategies are applicable *throughout* a teaching or training experience. For example, we might begin an instructional plan with an authentic performance task to estimate learners' competence for the skill to be taught, or we might start a course with a role play to evoke emotional relevance. The most important aspect of this approach is establishing the four motivational conditions as we instruct. The strategies are a means to this essential goal.

You may also be wondering about the specificity of calibration for each time phase. When does the beginning phase end and the during phase begin? When does the during phase end and the ending phase begin? Beyond individual judgment, there is no precise way of determining this because of the diversity in learners, content, learning situations, and learning objectives. In this respect, the time phases are analogous to the broad way in which we divide a day—morning, afternoon, and evening—imprecise segments of time that give order to our day and help us understand that some activities are more appropriate at certain times than at others.

The length of any time phase can range from a few minutes to a few days, depending on the situation. For example, the beginning phase for a particular learning objective with a group of highly motivated and self-directed adult learners may be very short. However, for a group of restless and resistant adult learners, the beginning phase for the same objective may have to be quite a bit longer to develop positive attitudes toward learning.

My experience with instructional design formats is that the beginning phase is frequently too short, and the motivational condition of inclusion is often only slightly developed. Creating a climate of respect and connection with a group of diverse adults takes some time. For the courses and training I've conducted, establishing inclusion takes, on the average, about 20 percent of total instruction time. The benefits are well worth that time. The quality of the dialogue and the depth of the thinking, the sincerity and realism of people's perspectives, the connections made, and the awareness that, at times, we're a living, breathing democracy of learning in which our respect is deeply felt and mutual—all have made the learning vital and the future hopeful.

Using the Motivational Framework as a Source for Instructional Planning

Another approach to instructional planning is to begin with learner motivation as central to the instructional process. We will still have to respect the parameters of the learning objective, the structure of the content to be learned, and the time available, but we can focus on instructional planning that considers motivation and culture as essential to the entire process.

The learning objective remains a top priority because without it, the motivation of the learners has no direction. However, once we understand the objective, we then reflect on the learners, their culture, and their expected motivation regarding the learning objective. Next, we review the motivational purposes (listed in the second column of Table 8.1) to select motivational strategies to guide our choice of learning activities that will fit these considerations as well as the structure of the content and the time available for learning. In this manner, we do not merely add on or blend in motivational strategies but use them as the *source* for learning activities that fulfill the four motivational conditions and achieve the learning objective.

Having selected the most relevant strategies for each time phase (beginning, during, and ending), we then reflect on each strategy to create a learning activity that will carry out the essence of the strategy. Because design is a creative process and an act of composing, ideas for activities will sometimes emerge before we select strategies, in which case the strategies can be suitable afterthoughts that confirm the motivational intent of the activities. In fact, having conducted hundreds of workshops for the source approach has taught me that the creativity of teachers and trainers can justifiably obliterate any set method of instructional planning. Creating an instructional plan from the framework and its related motivational strategies can be a very idiosyncratic process. However conceived, the plan should respect the cultural, structural, and temporal considerations for learning, establish the four motivational conditions, and achieve the learning objective.

Examples of Instructional Planning Using the Motivational Framework

Whether developed using the superimposed method or the source method, an instructional plan contains an alignment of motivational purposes with motivational strategies and their related learning activities or instructor behaviors in a time framework. The examples of instructional plans that follow will begin with simple and short units of learning and move toward longer and more complex units of learning. (Note that in all the examples, the numbers of the motivational strategies correspond to those used in Table 8.1 and in Chapters Four through Seven.)

Example 1

An instructor is conducting a three-hour class session in a college extension course titled the Modern American Novel. The topic for the evening is Alice Walker and her novel *The Color Purple*. The learners have been requested to complete the reading of this novel prior to this course session.

Type and number of learners: twenty men and women ranging in age from twenty-five to fifty-nine. There is considerable diversity of ethnicity and race among the students in the class. Most of them have had at least a few extension courses previous to this class.

Learning objective: learners will communicate their perspective and understanding of the novel through participation in discussion and a short written critique. (Writing samples and related rubrics were passed out and discussed at the first class session.)

The instructional plan for Example 1 is illustrated in Table 8.2.

Example 1 contains at least one motivational purpose for each of the four major motivational conditions. In this example, the instructor used nine motivational strategies out of a possible sixty. Because the example is only illustrative, it is conceivable that more or fewer strategies could be used. The particular learning activities or instructor behaviors are what the instructor would do to carry out the motivational strategies. Note that one activity can carry out more than one strategy, as one does in this example, carrying out Strategies 5 and 28. This is common. In fact, one elaborate activity might represent as many as ten strategies. Also, a strategy can appear more than once in an instructional plan, as providing feedback (Strategy 48) does twice in this short plan.

Example 2

A trainer is conducting a ninety-minute training session on how to use e-mail.

Type and number of learners: fourteen men and women ranging in age from twenty-five to fifty (each is seated at a personal computer). There is considerable diversity of ethnicity and race among the trainees. There also appear to be significant differences in their individual experience with personal computers.

Learning objective: trainees will learn to retrieve and send e-mail. By the end of the session, each person will edit a received e-mail and forward it to two other trainees and the trainer.

The instructional plan for Example 2 is illustrated in Table 8.3.

Example 2 contains at least one motivational purpose for every major motivational condition. Example 2 also illustrates combining two motivational strategies (Strategies 1 and 8) to fulfill both

Table 8.2. Instructional Plan for Example 1.

Motivational Purpose	Motivational Strategy	Learning Activity or Instructor Behavior
(Inclusion—beginning)		
To engender an awareness and feeling of connection	4. Share something of value with your adult learners.	Share reactions when first reading the novel over fifteen years ago: discomfort with the roles of the men in it but attraction to the idea of redemptive love.
To create a climate of respect	12. Introduce the concepts of comfort zones and learning edges to help learners accommodate more intense emotions during episodes of new learning.	Acknowledge some of the potentially controversial issues dealt with in the novel: abuse, incest, violence, racism, and its vision of the liberation of women from men—areas where strong feelings and new learning may emerge.
(Attitude—beginning)		
To create relevant learning experiences	5. Use collaborative or cooperative learning.	Divide the learners into small groups to share (to the extent they are comfortable) any situations in the novel that they relate to their personal experiences—areas that have a resonance with their own reality.
	28. Make the learning activity an irresistible invitation to learn.	
(Meaning—during)		
To develop engagement and challenge	42. Use critical questions to stimulate learner engagement and challenge.	Conduct a whole-group discussion with the following questions. Probe for assumptions: Based on your reading, what do you think are Alice Walker's assumptions about the relations between men and women? Women and women? Men and men? Please offer evidence from the book for each of these assessments.

To maintain learner attention	Compare and contrast: What are some of the similarities and differences between this book's perspective of humanity and what we've read by Flannery O'Connor?
	Critically assess: A hundred years from now, will this book remain a classic? In this regard, what are its strengths and weaknesses?
32. Help learners realize their accountability for what they are learning.	To encourage equitable responding, at times randomly select students, but only on those occasions when you have initially used *think-pair-share* to process the question.
(Competence—ending)	
To engender competence with assessment	Request learners to write a short critique of the novel as they might for a newspaper or newsmagazine.
51. Use authentic performance tasks to enable adults to know that they can proficiently apply what they are learning to their real lives.	
48. Provide effective feedback.	After learners have completed writing their critiques, pass out copies from the *New York Times* and *Newsweek* of the actual reviews the novel received in 1982.
54. Use self-assessment methods to improve learning and to provide learners with the opportunity to construct relevant insights and connections.	Ask learners to compare the reviews to their critiques, then to select one review and write answers to the following questions: How has this review informed my thinking? And how might my critique have informed this reviewer?
48. Provide effective feedback.	Collect learner critiques and self-assessments. Return with feedback at the next class meeting.

Table 8.3. Instructional Plan for Example 2.

Motivational Purpose	Motivational Strategy	Learning Activity or Instructor Behavior
(Inclusion—beginning)		
To engender an awareness and feeling of connection and to create a climate of respect	1. Allow for introductions.	Ask people to briefly introduce themselves and to mention any experience they've had with e-mail and how they see themselves using it in the future.
	8. Assess learners' current expectations and needs and their previous experience as it relates to your course or training.	
	4. Share something of value.	With the overhead projector, share a few important or interesting e-mails received from peers in exotic locales across the globe. Explain how efficient and inexpensive this system of communication is.
(Attitude—beginning)		
To build a positive attitude toward the subject	17. Use assisted learning to scaffold complex learning.	Having estimated the zone of proximal development of the learners from their introductions and working with one of the trainees as a *model*, project her computer screen for the rest of the learners to see and *coach* her through the steps to access the Internet and retrieve, store, send, and trash mail. Learners practice with their computers as they observe her screen. Conclude this segment by asking a volunteer to take the role of trainer and coach the other learners through these steps with her projected computer screen.

(Meaning—during)

To develop engagement and challenge

47. Use invention, artistry, imagination, and enactment to render meaning and emotion in learning.

Post the e-mail addresses of all learners on the overhead screen. Trainees practice sending, receiving, and replying to imagined business, community, or family messages from one another.

48. Provide effective feedback.

During the practice session, provide coaching and feedback as necessary.

(Competence—ending)

To engender competence with assessment

51. Use authentic performance tasks to enable adults to know that they can proficiently apply what they are learning to their real lives.

52. Provide opportunities for adults to demonstrate their learning in ways that reflect their strengths and multiple sources of knowing.

As a concluding activity, each learner is sent an e-mail by the trainer that contains ten possible uses of e-mail. Upon receiving the message, the learner edits the list of ten to indicate those uses she believes will be true for her and adds others not described in the list. This e-mail is then forwarded to the trainer and two other learners. When each of these individuals confirms receiving this message with a reply, the learner has completed the training.

purposes for the motivational condition of inclusion. Thus we see that a combination of strategies can be used to fulfill a combination of motivational purposes.

The scaffolding strategy (Strategy 17) has a number of sequenced activities aligned with it, which demonstrates that several learning activities can together carry out a single motivational strategy. *Instructors need not concern themselves that every instructional behavior or learning activity in a learning sequence has listed next to it every possible motivational strategy corresponding to it.* Creating too specific a breakdown in instructional planning can become confusing and unnecessarily labor intensive (Gronlund, 1978). The instructional plan should be sufficient and effective so long as we have listed the most important strategies and related activities, and the necessary structural components of the concept or skill are evident and linked in the sequence of learning activities.

The scaffolding strategy (Strategy 17) to carry out the motivational purpose of building a positive attitude toward the subject is also a good example of a series of activities that start at the beginning phase for learning and carry over well into the during phase.

Please also note one more intention of this example: that although the skill learned is technical, most of the activities are socially constructed learning experiences that elicit student perspectives, modeling, interaction, and colearning.

Example 3

A faculty development specialist is conducting a seven-hour workshop on the management of strong emotions during classroom controversy.

Type and number of learners: fifteen faculty members ranging in age from thirty to sixty. Six of the faculty are women, and five are people of color. All participants have had at least three years of college teaching experience.

Learning objective: faculty will identify and practice teaching and communication methods that support learners' emotions in a manner that allows for both individual expression and continuing mutual respect.

The instructional plan for Example 3 is illustrated in Table 8.4.

In Example 3, the beginning of the workshop has three consecutive small-group activities with intermittent whole-group discussions. Starting the during phase with a minilecture and overheads may be a welcome change of pace.

The activities for Strategies 43 (journaling responses to the video) and 46 (role playing) obviously include feedback during the related discussions and develop learner competence. I emphasize this relationship to point out that frequently in instructional planning, a learning activity corresponding to one major motivational condition (in this case, meaning) will contain elements for developing another major motivational condition (in this case, competence). Thus we see that a learning activity can comprise characteristics that simultaneously engender more than one motivational condition (in this case, meaning and competence). We can safely generalize that such activities are relatively strong sources of motivational influence because they have multiple positive effects. For purposes of planning, we should consider the flow of content and the primary motivational condition we wish to establish, and use this relationship as a guide to selecting and placing activities that may have multiple motivational influences. We should be aware of these additional influences but not restricted or burdened by them.

Example 4

A trainer is conducting a two-day job-search workshop in Denver for dislocated workers. (This example is adapted from the instructional plan of René Preston, agency trainer for the Mayor's Office of Employment and Training.)

Type and number of learners: twelve men and women ranging in age from twenty-eight to fifty-six. There is considerable diversity of occupation, socioeconomic status, ethnicity, and race among the trainees.

Table 8.4. Instructional Plan for Example 3.

Motivational Purpose	Motivational Strategy	Learning Activity or Instructor Behavior
(Inclusion—beginning)		
To engender an awareness and feeling of connection	1. Allow for introductions.	The specialist asks people to briefly introduce themselves.
	6. Clearly identify learning goals.	The specialist describes learning goals for workshop.
	2. Provide an opportunity for multidimensional sharing.	Participants form small groups to share a topic or skill they value teaching that also elicits strong emotions in them because of their cultural or social background.
To create a climate of respect	5. Use collaborative and cooperative learning.	In the same groups, participants brainstorm particular student words, actions, triggers, or incidents they find very challenging to manage. Groups report out and the specialist records these items on a flip chart.
	8. Assess learners' current expectations and needs and their previous experience as it relates to your course or training.	
	11. To the degree authentically possible, reflect the language, perspective, and attitudes of adult learners.	
(Attitude—beginning)		
To create relevant learning experiences	28. Make the learning activity an irresistible invitation to learn.	Participants form triads and volunteer methods each has used effectively to respond to one or more of the challenges listed on the flip chart. Triads report out and the specialist lists these methods next to the indicated challenges. The specialist surveys the group about the extent to which participants know these methods and about which of the methods they would like to learn more in depth. Two of the highest rated are added to the workshop content. The specialist invites faculty to continue to share their insights and experience throughout the workshop.
	29. Use the K-W-L strategy to introduce new topics and concepts.	

(Meaning—during) To maintain learners' attention and to develop engagement and challenge	33. Provide variety in personal presentation style, modes of instruction, and learning materials.	The specialist uses an overhead projector and handouts to deliver a minilecture on participation guidelines and their use. She asks participants to think of the perspectives and language of their students and to revise or add to the participation guidelines to make them more understandable and culturally respectful for personal application.
	34. Introduce, connect, and end learning activities attractively and clearly.	
	42. Use critical questions to stimulate learner engagement and challenge.	The specialist uses a simulation to teach and practice the think-pair-share strategy.
To develop engagement and challenge	46. Use simulations and role playing to enhance meaning with a more realistic context.	
	43. Use relevant problems to facilitate learning.	The specialist shows a video of students at different points in an argument and asks participants to journal their possible responses if they were the teacher. The specialist uses a whole-group dialogue to process the various responses.
	46. Use simulations and role playing to enhance meaning with a more realistic context.	Participants role-play a learning group in conflict over a controversial court decision involving gender issues. Faculty take turns practicing methods to lessen conflict in this group while maintaining communication and mutual respect. Activity concludes with a whole-group discussion of the role play.

Table 8.4. Instructional Plan for Example 3, cont'd.

Motivational Purpose	Motivational Strategy	Learning Activity or Instructor Behavior
(Competence—ending)		
To engender competence with assessment	51. Use authentic performance tasks to enable adults to know that they can proficiently apply what they are learning to their real lives.	In small groups, participants respond to a case study in which a faculty member loses control of a culturally diverse class in conflict over recent campus politics. Participants conceptualize what might have been done in the moment as well as what might have been done to prevent this incident.
	52. Provide opportunities for adults to demonstrate their learning in ways that reflect their strengths and multiple sources of knowing.	
	48. Provide effective feedback.	Participants compare their responses to the case study with the written suggestions of three faculty members (not present) who are experienced multicultural educators.
To engender competence with communication	59. When learning has natural consequences, help learners to be aware of them and of their impact.	The workshop concludes with each participant writing and posting an action plan for his or her own course based on learning from the workshop. The specialist and participants visit the posters, in carousel fashion, to offer supportive comments and suggestions.
	60. Provide positive closure at the end of significant units of learning.	

Learning objective: by the end of the workshop, participants will (1) understand a selected body of knowledge to more effectively manage their transition to another job, and (2) write their first draft of an informative and professionally suitable résumé. (In the ensuing weeks, consultation with the trainer or a follow-up workshop is available for participants to refine and advance the skills they learned in this workshop.)

The instructional plan for Example 4 is illustrated in Table 8.5.

In Example 4, please note how short the beginning phase of the second day is. There is a goal review and one multidimensional sharing activity to renew a feeling of connection in the group; then it's on to new content. There are no activities to establish attitude because that appears to have been well done on the first day. When the activities for meaning and competence are collaborative and engaging, the need for strategies to sustain inclusion and attitude is oftentimes considerably less.

Also note that with the exception of the activities, which need a longer narrative to exemplify their tone and context, I've begun to shorten the strategies and combine the purposes. This is to model what I've seen in the field for the last ten years: most instructors develop a shorthand of phraseology for the various purposes, strategies, and learning activities, so as to increase their efficiency in planning.

On day two, the trainer used a self-assessment strategy activity (head, heart, hand) to sustain inclusion; she used assisted learning, originally aligned with building a positive attitude, to enhance meaning. This flexible placement of the strategies and activities illustrates the numerous motivational purposes they can serve.

Example 4 is the last of the examples of motivation planning in this book. I treated each example as a learning sequence that is a complete unit with beginning, during, and ending time phases so that it could exemplify as many aspects of the Motivational Framework for Culturally Responsive Teaching as possible. A complete learning unit can comprise minutes, hours, days, or weeks. The time and qualitative differences between a short presentation and a long-term

Table 8.5. Instructional Plan for Example 4.

	Day One (Seven Hours)	
Motivational Purpose	Motivational Strategy	Learning Activity or Instructor Behavior
(Inclusion—beginning)		
To engender an awareness and feeling of connection and to create a climate of respect	1. Allow for introductions.	Trainer and participants briefly introduce themselves and mention how long they've lived in the area.
	2. Provide an opportunity for multi-dimensional sharing.	Group divides into triads. Using a Venn diagram to highlight common ground among them, group members share jobs they've held all the way back to high school, places they've lived, the type of work they are interested in, and their expectations for the workshop. The expectations are reported out and listed by the trainer on a flip chart.
	8. Assess learners' current expectations and needs and their previous experience as it relates to your course or training.	
	6. Clearly identify learning goals.	The specialist describes learning goals for workshop, relates them to expectations on the flip chart, and describes her own experience as a dislocated worker. She expresses her own enthusiasm for the workshop and gives brief histories of some of the people who have found satisfying work after completing the workshop.
	3. Concretely indicate your cooperative intentions.	
	13. Acknowledge different ways of knowing, different languages, and different levels of knowledge or skill to engender a safe learning environment.	The specialist notes the diversity in the room and discusses how there may be a variety of experiences, skill levels, and perspectives for dealing with the content in the workshop: "a real benefit for what we can learn from each other."

(Attitude—beginning)		
To build a positive attitude toward the subject	16. Positively confront erroneous beliefs.	The trainer introduces the Core and Contingent Workforce data showing how in the last decade the majority of new jobs have shifted from positions with a regular forty-hour week and full benefits to more entrepreneurial, consulting, service, and part-time or temporary positions.
To develop a positive self-concept for learning	20. Help learners accurately attribute success to their capability, effort, and knowledge.	The trainer emphasizes how most of the workshop content is about strategies (that succeed) for finding satisfying work: networking, résumé writing, and so on.
(Meaning—during)		
To evoke interest and to develop engagement and challenge	36. Relate learning to adult concerns.	The trainer gives minilecture on seven possible reactions to loss such as disbelief, anger, hope, and so forth. Then she divides participants into small collaborative groups to review this material with a few critical questions and to apply this understanding to their own lives: for example, What might someone do who was in a state of disbelief? What are the implications? How does any of this make sense to you?
	42. Use critical questions to stimulate learner engagement and challenge.	
	5. Use collaborative and cooperative learning.	
	45. Use case study methods.	The trainer introduces the stages of transition for change and gives the participants a case study to deliberate in small groups. Their goal is to identify the stages of transition in the case and to suggest how some of the reactions to loss might serve to facilitate the worker's progress from one stage to another—for example, transferring anger into action.

Table 8.5. Instructional Plan for Example 4, cont'd.

Motivational Purpose	Motivational Strategy	Learning Activity or Instructor Behavior
	33. Provide variety in learning materials. 54. Use self-assessment methods.	Participants conduct a self-assessment with a short personal styles inventory. They discuss with a partner how the results of this assessment make sense to them.
(Competence—ending)	52. Provide opportunities for adults to demonstrate their learning in ways that reflect their strengths and multiple sources of knowing. 59. When learning has natural consequences, help learners to be aware of them.	Participants create an action plan to apply to their families, to their educational futures, or to their job searches based on the information and learning in today's workshop. The day concludes with those participants who wish to volunteer and share one important aspect of their action plan.

Day Two (Seven Hours)

Motivational Purpose	Motivational Strategy	Learning Activity or Instructor Behavior
(Inclusion—beginning) To engender an awareness and feeling of connection	2. Provide an opportunity for multidimensional sharing. 6. Clearly identify learning goals.	Participants introduce themselves again and do one cycle of head, heart, hand regarding a thought, feeling, or action from yesterday's workshop that left a strong impression. The trainer reviews learning goals and how some were met by yesterday's work.

(Meaning—during)

To develop engagement and challenge

43. Use a relevant problem. 46. Use a simulation.	The trainer discusses the problem of needing about a thirty-second introduction for purposes of networking and interviewing. She listens to participants' views about what might be essential to such a brief introduction. Most participants think some version of where you've been, what you did, and where you're going might suffice. Each participant writes out a personal version of this introduction and practices it with three other participants in a classroom *walkabout*. Activity concludes with participants privately giving each other feedback.
40. Selectively use examples, analogies, metaphors, and stories. 46. Use a role play.	The trainer introduces the short story technique for responding in interviews—a way to give evidence of one's competence by tying a skill to the place where it was used and the successful results that occurred. This information is delivered as a very short story. The trainer demonstrates with a couple of stories from her own professional history. After conceptualizing two such stories, participants practice them in a role-playing format and receive feedback from the interviewer and observer.
33. Provide variety in modes of instruction. 38. Use humor.	Participants view and discuss a humorous video on the how, what, and why of networking.
17. Use assisted learning to scaffold complex learning. 23. Use relevant models to demonstrate expected learning.	With an exemplary model of a résumé on the overhead projector, the trainer reviews its format and thinks out loud through anticipated difficult areas. She provides a checklist of ten steps for writing an excellent résumé. She also provides examples of professionally done résumés from former participants of this workshop who have found satisfying work.

Table 8.5. Instructional Plan for Example 4, cont'd.

Motivational Purpose	Motivational Strategy	Learning Activity or Instructor Behavior
(Competence—ending)		
To engender competence with assessment	51. Use authentic performance tasks.	Participants write the first draft of their résumé. In addition to the ten-step checklist for writing the résumé, they have a handout describing and exemplifying the qualities of an excellent résumé. When finished with the first draft, they find a partner. Each reads the other's draft and provides feedback based on the qualities highlighted in the handout. At this point they can make revisions or bring their draft to the trainer for another round of feedback or do both.
	53. When using rubrics, make sure they assess the essential features of performance and are fair, valid, and sufficiently clear so that learners can accurately self-assess.	
	48. Provide effective feedback.	
To engender competence with communication	60. Provide positive closure.	Participants gather their chairs in a circle with the trainer and have the opportunity to briefly share one thing they are genuinely glad they've learned and to extend an appreciation to the group or any member of it. It is well understood that it is certainly agreeable for any member to pass on either opportunity.

course are immense. However, even in the latter instance, there will be separate units that can be planned. No matter what the length of a particular learning unit, we will need to apply strategies with a sense of timing if we are to establish the four motivational conditions and evoke continuing intrinsic motivation among diverse adults.

These examples are meant to show what might be possible and what is structurally necessary for instructional planning. They are not intended as precise models to follow. It is quite possible that better and more creative means could be found to approach learner motivation for each of the particular learning objectives.

It is important to note there is a practice effect to planning with the framework. The more often it is done, the more familiar the motivational conditions and their related strategies become. Practice significantly lessens the time required for instructional planning and makes the process more fluid. In my experience, most instructors need to practice applying the framework about six times before their planning with it becomes more intuitive and automatic.

In review, the lists that follow summarize the basic steps for each of the two types of planning with this motivational framework.

Superimposed Method

1. Consider who the learners will be, paying particular attention to their experience and diversity.

2. Clarify the learning objective(s) with diligent regard for the learners and the learning situation.

3. Estimate the amount of time available for instruction.

4. Consider the inherent structure of the content or skill to be learned.

5. Examine the established curricular or instructional design to be followed for the learning unit.

6. Superimpose the four questions for instructional planning (listed earlier) based on the Motivational Framework for

Culturally Responsive Teaching onto the indicated format of instruction to see where the predetermined instructional activities positively respond to these questions and where they do not.

7. For any of the four questions that remain inadequately answered, select appropriate motivational strategies from Table 8.1 and develop related learning activities or instructor behaviors. (Because the total time allowed for instruction may limit these selections, it may be necessary to reduce or revise other predetermined learning activities.)

8. The ultimate criteria are as follows: (1) the instructional plan establishes all four of the motivational conditions, and (2) each time phase (beginning, during, and ending) has activities in its sequence of instruction to elicit significant motivation among learners.

Source Method

1. Consider who the learners will be, paying particular attention to their experience and diversity.

2. Clarify the learning objective(s) with diligent regard for the learners and the learning situation.

3. Estimate the amount of time available for instruction.

4. Consider the inherent structure of the content or skill to be learned and its relationship to intended assessment activities.

5. Review the motivational purposes listed in Table 8.1 as they align with the four motivational conditions and select motivational strategies to guide the development of learning activities.

6. Use the selected motivational strategies to choose or create learning activities that fit the flow of content or skill development and their assessment. Be reasonably certain this instructional plan can be carried out in the time available.

7. Ultimate criteria are as follows: (1) the instructional plan establishes all four of the motivational conditions, and (2) each time phase (beginning, during, and ending) has activities in its sequence of instruction to elicit significant motivation among learners.

When either method is used effectively, the adult's perspective while learning is likely to be as follows:

1. I am a member of a learning community in which I feel a mutual sense of care and respect.
2. I am freely and successfully learning something I find relevant.
3. I am engaged in a challenging learning experience where my experience and perspective can inform as well as be informed.
4. I am becoming more effective in something I value.

These four statements represent what is possible when adults learn in a situation where the four motivational conditions—inclusion, attitude, meaning, and competence—are fully present. If adults can honestly make these statements, they will be motivated to learn and to continue learning. This does not mean adults bear no responsibility for their own motivation for learning. It does mean that we as instructors have optimally exercised our professional skill to respect adults as they are at that moment and to make instruction an experience that enhances their motivational resources.

Motivation is dynamic. It grows or diminishes as learners engage in learning and are influenced by instruction. Like communication, motivation works reciprocally, and instructors are the lead communicators. Our responsibility is to maximally support and nourish the motivational capacities adults bring with them to the learning experience. Just as a dinner host provides the best setting possible to elicit conversation among all guests, we provide the best possible learning situation to evoke motivation among all learners. Having done so, we can reasonably expect adults to do what adults have done naturally under these circumstances for centuries—willfully learn what they value.

Assessing Learner Motivation

We have done our planning. We have a comprehensive, motivating instructional sequence from the beginning to the end of the learning unit. We are carrying it out. Now, how do we know if and when the learners are motivated? Of all the questions in this book, this is one of the most difficult to answer. Because scientists do not have an adequate theory to explain the exact nature of motivation and the operation of the motivational processes, we have not been able to develop precise measures of motivation to learn (Pintrich and Schunk, 1996). Issues of reliability and validity remain significant challenges for developing any motivation index. One of the main problems is that motivation as a concept is difficult to operationalize. The choices people make in life and the degree of effort they will exert relative to those choices are influenced by myriad cultural, personal, and environmental variables. Also, motivation is unstable. People not only vary in their commitment to the choices they have made but also to the degree of persistence they will expend on behalf of those choices. This is as true in learning as it is in work, play, or intimate relationships. To a large extent, many societies have developed oaths and contracts in respect for and fear of the instability of personal motivation. Because motivation fluctuates on a minute-to-minute basis (I'm paying attention . . . I'm distracted . . . I'm paying attention again . . .) we probably need a measuring instrument more akin to a thermometer than any paper-and-pencil test can be.

Although we cannot precisely assess the motivation of adult learners, there are several approaches we can use to estimate the presence and quality of their motivation as they are learning. But first, a cautionary note: frequently, instructors use exams and other indicators of *learning accomplishment* as evidence of learner motivation. Intuitively we think, "If students are motivated, they will learn." However, learning achievement is strongly influenced by capability and opportunity (instructional design, materials, time available, and so forth) as well as motivation. At best, learning is an indirect indicator of motivation, and unless we can carefully separate capability and opportunity for measurement purposes, it can be a misleading indicator.

Among the possible means of evaluating learner motivation are self-report instruments—questionnaires, rating scales, checklists, and the like—that elicit the learners' assessment of their own behavior, beliefs, or perceptions. Instructor-developed self-reports can be very helpful as estimating and feedback devices. However, they have disadvantages. One is that learners may bias their responses for reasons that range from social desirability to grades they received, and another is that learners are not always aware of their motives or how to explain them. When well constructed and used with other indicators of motivation, such as observation ratings, self-reports can be informative (Assor and Connell, 1992). I often ask learners to complete the self-report shown here to give me their perceptions of how well the course or workshop is fulfilling the four motivational conditions of the framework. (Learners rate each of the following items on a four-point scale from *strongly disagree* to *strongly agree*.)

1. The workshop climate is friendly and respectful. (Inclusion)

2. This workshop is relevant to my life. (Attitude)

3. This workshop is challenging me to think. (Meaning)

4. This workshop is helping me be effective at what I value. (Competence)

5. The teacher respects learners' opinions and ideas. (Inclusion)

6. In this workshop, I can use my experience and ways of knowing to support my learning. (Attitude)

7. Most of the time during this workshop I feel engaged in what's going on. (Meaning)

8. I can actually use the information or skills I am learning in this workshop. (Competence)

Probably the best moment-to-moment method of assessing learner motivation is personal observation. This too is an imperfect method. Our biases and mood can contaminate what we perceive as well as what we select to perceive. (Focusing on one resistant adult learner seems to make the whole classroom picture bleak.) It is also difficult to be totally sure that what we see is a real indicator of motivation. For example, it is possible that signs of learners' intensity might be nothing more than their obvious reactions to physical or mental discomfort. Understanding and assessing effort are also very tricky. Culturally speaking, when tasks become difficult, some people are socialized to be calm and contemplative so as to let the light of learning emerge, rather than to become intense and more active. Looking for vigor to assess motivation in learners can be deceptive. That's why, especially over time, I prefer to use persistence as an indicator of motivation. Even though the kind of behaviors may vary, do learners continue to engage in actions aimed at accomplishing the learning task? Other observable indicators of intrinsic motivation, supported by personal experience and also research (Stipek, 1998), are that learners

Begin learning activities without resistance

Prefer the challenging aspects of tasks

Spontaneously relate learning to outside interests

Ask questions to expand their understanding beyond the learning at hand

Go beyond required work

Find joy in the process of learning—the studying, writing, reading, and so forth

Are proud of their learning and its consequences

I pay very close attention to learners' physical energy. Most adults are capable of being in a state of flow when their activity level ranges some place between relaxed and alert and excited and involved (Csikszentmihalyi, 1997).

By keenly and continually observing to assess these indicators of motivation, we can adjust our teaching or training to the benefit of learner motivation. Also, as discussed in Chapter Six, I believe we need minimum standards for the quality of motivation we observe in our courses and training. This standard may be the percentage of people who willingly begin a learning task, the percentage of people who persist to overcome a learning obstacle, the percentage of people who appear relaxed and alert while learning, or some combination of these. Possessing such standards enables us to be both aware and responsive, to steer a course while teaching that brings to life the instructional plan we so carefully designed.

Margery Ginsberg has developed an observation guide to assess how an instructor has established the four motivational conditions from the Motivational Framework for Culturally Responsive Teaching. Using this "Observation Guide for Culturally Responsive Teaching and Learning," an instructor, colleague, or learner can locate evidence of specific norms and behaviors that indicate the presence of each condition during a learning experience. This information can inform future instruction and planning as well as point out motivational conditions that may need more development. This guide is reproduced in the Appendix.

Encouraging Continuing Adult Motivation

In an increasingly complex society, where the need for continuous education during one's lifetime is a reality, fostering the willingness of adults to learn may be of greater consequence than ensuring that they have learned some specific thing at a certain point in time. People who eventually find reading, writing, calculating, and expanding their knowledge and skills an interesting and satisfying way of being are usually considered *lifelong learners*. The tendency to find these processes worthwhile and compelling is considered the trait of motivation to learn—a propensity for learning, often narrowly conceived as *academic*, that gradually develops over time. As Cross (1981) frames it, these adults are gourmet learners, people who are able to tailor the resources in the learning environment to their own needs. Yet no one has developed an exact method for establishing continuing motivation to learn among people.

Having surveyed the research, McCombs (1991) believes this trait is a naturally occurring capacity in human beings that is nurtured by supportive relationships, opportunities to exert personal choice and responsibility for learning, and personally relevant learning activities. Deci and Ryan (1991), who have spent more than twenty-five years studying the phenomenon of intrinsic motivation, believe the key to acquiring this value—to finding the act of learning worthwhile—is feeling free enough to accept it as one's own. People who embrace this value and can be described as lifelong learners are deeply aware that the fundamental aspects of learning fit who they are. They read, reflect, and purposely seek to deepen their awareness and knowledge.

For example, writing can become one of these aspects of learning and contribute to someone's becoming a lifelong learner. If there is a kind of writing most adults find appealing, it is probably personal letters, notes, and cards. Yet there is a smaller group of people who find writing to be a form of reflection, expression, and connection to the world. It is part of their identity and their motivation to learn. Sometimes I have the privilege of seeing adults cross the bridge to making writing a deeper learning and a continuing worthwhile aspect of their lives. When that happens, the writing is the voice of who they are; they want to say what they have written, and somehow they can now grasp some important meaning that their writing, perhaps only their writing, enabled them to express.

For teaching and training, the Motivational Framework for Culturally Responsive Teaching is ideally suited to encourage continuing adult motivation to learn. Beginning with a plan, we create, as a community of learners, compelling experiences to attain relevant learning with our integrity intact.

To round out the picture of what we need to do to enhance continuing adult motivation to learn, we can ask two questions: (1) How can adults maintain and sustain their own motivation to learn? and (2) How can we assist adults in transferring what they've learned, in using new learning in the community or workplace?

Self-Regulation

Although entire books have been written about how people can foster their own motivation to learn (Smith, 1982; Zimmerman and Schunk, 1989), this process remains a challenge to understand and explain. The approach that has been researched the most is self-regulated learning (Pintrich, 1995). *Self-regulation* is a process by which learners control their behavior, feelings, and thoughts to attain academic goals. Many adults have the idea that after they make up their mind to learn something, willpower and persistence will accomplish it. However, *one can have the will yet lack the way.* There is such a thing as *ineffective effort,* as occurs when people set unrealistic deadlines or become so anxious trying to learn something that they are unable to concentrate (Trawick and Corno, 1995). Adults may enthusiastically and sincerely agree to a learning contract, yet they may be thwarted by a lack of skills—for how to deal with distractions, how to organize their work, how to correct mistakes, and how to boost their self-confidence. These kinds of skills are part of a constellation of *self-regulation strategies* that lead to successful learning and can be directly taught to learners.

Although many people seem to have attained these skills without direct instruction, most are unlikely to use them unless they believe the learning task is interesting or important and are confident they can achieve the learning goal (Schunk and Zimmerman, 1994). These skills are an example of something socioculturally learned (through social-familial practices and modeling) but individually and cognitively applied.

Self-regulation strategies are an extensive and complex lot. They range from something as simple as telling yourself to ask for assistance when you don't understand something (self-instruction) to assessing the steps and resources necessary to complete an assignment on time (a metacognitive skill). Using findings from research of self-regulated learning, Trawick and Corno (1995) developed a volitional enhancement program for urban community college students. Among the strategies included were those to manage distractions, to monitor one's attention while learning, and to maintain a suitable state of mind for learning by controlling negative emotions and self-defeating motivational patterns. Interviews with the students indicated that as a result of this short-term intensive training experience, the students became increasingly knowledgeable about appropriate study environments, useful strategies for handling distractions, and self-coaching. (A forty-page outline and supplementary materials describing this program are available from Trawick, 1990).

One of the most practical day-to-day approaches to teaching self-regulation strategies is to assess how adults currently use them by sensitively asking direct questions—for example, What steps did you take to learn this? What did you do when you became distracted? What did you tell yourself when you realized this might have been a mistake? What are you telling yourself to sustain your motivation?

What follows is an example of how we can work with this last question.

Introduce the strategy and explain its usefulness. For example, "It helps to talk to yourself a bit about your own motivation, to let yourself realize why this is important to you. Sometimes we need to remind ourselves. What are some things you might reflect on that would encourage you to do this work?"

Use scaffolding techniques (see Chapter Five).

Model the strategy: for example, "Sometimes when I feel my enthusiasm for writing diminishing, I remind myself how much I've learned through writing, how my ideas become clearer, how fine a way it is to communicate with another person, and that if I don't continue writing I would have to give up what I'm doing for a living. That's something I sure don't want to do."

Give guided practice, use reminders and hints, coach a bit, and gently withdraw: for example, "You've been doing so well with self-motivation, I don't think any questions I might ask would be of any significant assistance. It's a real pleasure to see you taking charge of your learning."

In this way we help learners to be self-conscious—in the best sense of that expression—about their learning, to realize they have the power to employ their own motivational skills.

Transfer

When we talk about *transfer,* we are usually concerned with how well adults can apply what they have learned to their life, community, or workplace. The majority of studies suggest that transfer is not easily achieved, but a closer examination of the conditions under which transfer does occur offers a more optimistic picture (Perkins and Solomon, 1996). We will concern ourselves mainly with positive transfer, the constructive application of what someone has learned to new contexts or new purposes. For example, learning to use the motivational framework for planning instruction in classrooms helps an instructor use it effectively for planning instruction for distance learning (a new context).

It is worthwhile to note the distinction between near transfer and far transfer. *Near transfer* describes taking a routine use of a knowledge or skill and applying it in a similar context—for example, learning to shift with a four-speed manual transmission in one car and then using that learned procedure to shift proficiently with a four-speed manual transmission in *another* car. *Far transfer* is the successful application of learning to a more remote context or a novel situation—for example, applying the understanding and skill of shifting gears on a bike to understanding and shifting gears in a car. For the rest of this discussion we will focus on far transfer, because most of us are responsible for learning that is applied to complex situations.

From her experience and her review of the literature, Caffarella (1994) has developed a typology of key factors influencing the transfer of learning. An adaptation of these six key factors follows; it includes Caffarella's perspective (pp. 110–111) on how the key factors can work as enhancers of the transfer process.

1. *Program participants or learners:* their culture, experiences, attitudes, and values will influence what they learn and whether they can or want to apply it to their personal, work, or public lives. As enhancers, program participants or learners (1) have useful prior knowledge and experiences to link to what they have learned, (2) are willing to apply that learning, and (3) view the learning content as relevant and practical.

2. *Instructional design and execution:* the learning activities include methods or strategies for the transfer of learning. As enhancers, instructional design and execution (1) include authentic application exercises, (2) use self-assessment to understand what learners believe they can apply from what they have learned, and (3) directly teach transfer-of-learning strategies, such as action planning and how to develop a support group to maintain transfer in the workplace.

3. *Content:* the knowledge, skills, and values learned. As an enhancer, the content (1) is relevant and practical; (2) connects with the knowledge, experience, and ways of knowing of the learners; (3) is competently learned; and (4) is practiced in relevant contexts.

4. *Change process:* the complexity and nature of the changes required in the people, professional practices, organizations, and communities to apply the new learning and endure the consequence of that learning and change. As an enhancer, the change process (1) is doable and realistic, (2) is allotted enough time to develop, (3) is supported in a caring and equitable manner, and (4) involves key players in the follow-up activities.

5. *Organizational context:* the people, structures, and cultural milieu of an organization as it can support or inhibit transfer of learning. As an enhancer, the organizational context (1) involves key people in planning and preparing for the transfer of learning (for example, by pretraining administrators of learners in new learning), (2) offers support from important leaders, (3) makes incentives apparent, and (4) adapts to new structures and norms caused by application of the new learning.

6. *Community and societal forces:* the social, economic, and political conditions that can influence transfer of learning. As enhancers, community and societal forces (1) provide economic conditions that are favorable, (2) offer support from key leaders, and (3) create a receptive political climate.

Other practical strategies to enhance transfer of learning (Caffarella, 1994) are providing mentors, offering a session in the instructional sequence to discuss transfer, supplying job aids and resources to promote transfer, creating a peer coaching system, and scheduling refresher or follow-up sessions.

Although Broad and Newstrom (1992) report that as much as 80 percent of learning and training is not fully applied in the workplace, there is obviously a great deal that can be done to promote transfer of learning. Thinking that adults will voluntarily transfer their learning because they value it is probably a misguided assumption. We can do more. Caffarella's words (1994, p. 109) beckon our commitment.

There are many issues and concerns related to the lives of adults that can and should be at least partially addressed through educational programs—health care reform, violence in our communities, restructuring of public education, world peace, and environmental concerns, just to name a few. What is critical about so many of these issues and concerns is that solutions were needed yesterday. Therefore, what has so often been left to chance by educators—whether people, as a result of attending a variety of educational programs, can apply what they have learned to solving these complex problems—is no longer either a viable or ethical option.

Epilogue

Being an Effective Instructor of Adults

In recognizing the humanity of our fellow beings, we
pay ourselves the highest tribute.

Thurgood Marshall

It is probably only fair that what works so well for the learner works just as well for the instructor. To experience our jobs as intrinsically satisfying, we need to feel respected where we work, to believe what we do is relevant, and to have a sense that we can effectively accomplish the challenges we value. If these conditions are met, we live a professional life in which we breathe the air of vital meaning. In reality, we need the same conditions adults need to optimally learn. Senge's idea (1990) of the learning organization supports this notion as well.

Yet this book has sought something more than deep self-satisfaction for the instructor. It has connected teaching and training with a meaning surpassing work well done. Guiding this revision are the value of respect for cultural diversity among the adults we teach and train and the belief that a learning environment should be a model of equitable opportunity where the motivation and learning of every adult is supported and where learning is connected to an encompassing ethical purpose beyond successful achievement. The last idea has been the most difficult to communicate because I am simply not certain what the guiding moral purpose for every reader of this book should be. I have alluded to the common good and the social benefits of what we teach but have said nothing singularly directive.

What I do feel adequately prepared to assert is that as teachers and trainers we have a responsibility to consider the content and purpose of our instruction from an ethical perspective. We need to be engaged in an abiding moral reflection on our work. We teach people to do things and to want to do the things we teach them. That is power and responsibility. What are the potential consequences of what we teach? Whose perspective are we fostering? What system is perpetuated by what we do?

As I complete this revision, the tobacco industry has been engaged in litigation of historic significance. It has been exposed for its decades of deception and ill gain. Yet there were researchers, lawyers, business people, advertisers, and instructors involved in this enterprise. To what extent did they or do they still promote and create a product so directly connected to damaging people's health? I raise this issue because it represents so many other similar concerns and requires me to ask where in my own professional life I deny the consequences of my actions and rationalize the moral responsibility I hold, especially if I am a masterful teacher.

In an odd way, this dilemma reflects the progress we have made in adult education. We have become more effective in our instructional methods and means of enhancing adult motivation to learn. Training and development clearly make a difference. We have a place at the corporate table and in the college boardroom. Now we need to cast our net wider—to enable *all* adults to learn well. As we continue to make progress toward this goal, we are obliged to consider more carefully the consequences of what we teach or train others to know.

Our work distinctly serves an age-old question: What is worth knowing and perpetuating? Our craft carries the responsibility to wrestle with this question just as medical doctors carry the obligation to know what life is and when it is worth saving. This duty does not lessen the joy of being an instructor. It is what gives our profession a soul.

When Garfield (1986) studied older *peak performers*—adults who were sixty or older who loved their work and in the eyes of their peers were excellent at what they did, whatever the occupation—they had one thing in common. They saw their work as part of something greater than themselves. Garfield called this quality a sense of mission, a belief that one's work contributes to something transcendent. For some it was connected to a spiritual belief, for others to a social contribution or to the beauty of the work itself. To have this quality for ourselves as instructors, we need to realize and question the worth of what we teach or train, to inform our faith with reason.

In learning, there is a unity among worth and meaning and joy. As motivationally sound instruction becomes an inherently rewarding experience for both the learner *and* the instructor, it enables optimal learning. How much of this is science, or art, or intuition, I'm still not completely sure. But when it flows, when learning between instructor and learner is reciprocal and respectful, it is an inspired dimension of being: not something one practices or performs but something one enters and lives.

Appendix

Observation Guide for Culturally Responsive Teaching and Learning (Adult Version)

Margery B. Ginsberg

This guide is organized to identify elements that support intrinsic motivation. It is not an assessment tool but an instrument to promote dialogue about instruction and to affirm what is working to foster the four motivational conditions.

Establishing Inclusion

How does the learning experience contribute to developing a community of learners who feel respected and connected to one another?

Norms are visible and understood by all:

__ Norms are in place that help everyone feel that he or she belongs.

__ Learners and instructor have opportunities to learn about each other.

__ Learners and instructor have opportunities to learn about each other's unique backgrounds.

__ Course agreements are negotiated.

Evidence:

All learners are equitably and actively participating and interacting:

__ Instructor directs attention equitably.

__ Instructor interacts respectfully with all learners.

__ Learners talk to and with partner or small group.

__ Learners know what to do, especially when making choices.

__ Learners help each other.

Evidence:

Developing a Positive Attitude

How does this learning experience offer meaningful choices and promote personal relevance?

Instructor works with learners to personalize the relevance of course content:

__ Learners' experiences, concerns, and interests are used to develop course content.

__ Learners' experiences, concerns, and interests are addressed in responses to questions.

__ Learners' prior knowledge and learning experiences are explicitly linked to course content and questions.

__ Instructor encourages learners to understand, develop, and express different points of view.

__ Instructor encourages learners to clarify their interests and set goals.

__ Instructor maintains flexibility in pursuit of emerging interests.

Evidence:

Instructor encourages learners to make real choices regarding such issues as

__ How to learn (multiple intelligences)

__ What to learn

__ Where to learn

__ When a learning experience will be considered to be complete

__ How learning will be assessed

__ With whom to learn

__ How to solve emerging problems

Evidence:

Enhancing Meaning

How does this learning experience engage participants in challenging learning?

The instructor encourages all learners to learn, apply, create, and communicate knowledge:

__ Instructor helps learners activate prior knowledge and use it as a guide to learning.

__ Instructor in concert with learners creates opportunities for inquiry, investigation, and projects.

__ Instructor provides opportunities for learners to actively participate in challenging ways.

__ Instructor asks higher-order questions of all learners throughout instruction.

___ Instructor elicits high-quality responses from all learners.

___ Instructor uses multiple *safety nets* to ensure learner success (for example, not grading all assignments, allowing learner to work with a partner, and so forth).

Evidence:

Engendering Competence

How does this learning experience create an understanding that learners are becoming more effective in learning that they value and perceive as authentic to their real-world experience?

There is information, consequence, or product that supports learners in valuing and identifying their learning:

___ Instructor clearly communicates the purpose of the lesson.

___ Instructor clearly communicates criteria for excellent outcomes.

___ Instructor provides opportunities for a diversity of competencies to be demonstrated in a variety of ways.

___ Instructor helps all learners identify accomplishments.

___ Instructor offers options for assessment.

___ Instructor provides opportunities for continual feedback for individual learning.

___ Instructor provides opportunities for learners to make explicit connections between new and prior learning.

___ Instructor provides opportunities for learners to make explicit connections between their learning and the real world.

___ Instructor provides opportunities for learners to self-assess their learning and to adjust or reflect.

__ Instructor provides opportunities for learners to self-assess their personal responsibility for contributing to the course or training.

__ Instructor provides opportunities for learners to give each other feedback.

Evidence:

References

Adams, M., Bell, L. A., and Griffin, P. (eds.). *Teaching for Diversity and Social Justice: A Sourcebook*. New York: Routledge, 1997.

Adams, M., and Marchesani, L. S. "Curricular Innovations: Social Diversity as Course Content." In M. Adams (ed.), *Promoting Diversity in College Classrooms: Innovative Responses for the Curriculum, Faculty, and Institutions*. New Directions for Teaching and Learning, no. 52. San Francisco: Jossey-Bass, 1992.

Albanese, M. A., and Mitchell, S. "Problem-Based Learning: A Review of Literature on Its Outcomes and Implementation Issues." *Academic Medicine*, 1993, 68(1), 52–81.

Allen, M. S., and Roswell, B. S. "Self-Evaluation as Holistic Assessment." Paper presented at the annual meeting of the Conference on College Composition and Communication, Mar. 1989. (ED 303 809) .

Alley, R. "Simulation Development." In D. S. Hoopes and P. Ventura (eds.), *Intercultural Sourcebook: Cross-Cultural Training Methodologies*. Washington, D.C.: Intercultural Network, 1979.

American Association of University Women Educational Foundation. *The AAUW Report: How Schools Shortchange Girls*. Washington, D.C.: National Education Association, 1992.

Andersen, P. A. "Explaining Intercultural Differences in Nonverbal Communication." In L. A. Samovar and R. E. Porter (eds.), *Intercultural Communication: A Reader*. (5th ed.) Belmont, Calif.: Wadsworth, 1988.

Andersen, P. A. "Cues of Culture: The Basis of Intercultural Differences in Nonverbal Communication." In L. A. Samovar and R. E. Porter (eds.), *Intercultural Communication*. (8th ed.) Belmont, Calif.: Wadsworth, 1997.

Andersen, P. A., and Bowman, L. "Positions of Power: Nonverbal Influence in Organizational Communication." In J. A. DeVito and M. L. Hecht (eds.), *The Nonverbal Reader*. Prospect Heights, Ill.: Waveland Press, 1990.

Anderson, L. *International Encyclopedia of Teaching and Teacher Education*. (2nd ed.) New York: Pergamon Press, 1995.

Apter, M. J. *The Experience of Motivation*. Orlando, Fla.: Academic Press, 1982.

Association for Supervision and Curriculum Development. "Effective Teaching Redux." *ASCD Update*, 1990, *32*(6), 5.

Assor, A., and Connell, J. P. "The Validity of Students' Self-Reports as Measures of Performance Affecting Self-Appraisals." In D. H. Schunk and J. L. Meece (eds.), *Student Perceptions in the Classroom*. Hillsdale, N.J.: Erlbaum, 1992.

Astin, A. W. "The Changing American College Student." *Review of Higher Education*, 1998, *21*(2), 115–135.

Baldwin, A. L. *Theories of Child Development*. New York: Wiley, 1967.

Bandura, A. "Self-Efficacy Mechanism in Human Agency." *American Psychologist*, 1982, *37*(2), 122–147.

Bandura, A. *Social Foundations of Thought and Action: A Social Cognitive Theory*. Upper Saddle River, N.J.: Prentice Hall, 1986.

Belenky, M., Clinchy, B., Goldberger, N., and Tarule, J. *Women's Ways of Knowing: The Development of Self, Voice, and Mind*. New York: Basic Books, 1986.

Bellah, R. N., Madsen, R., Sullivan, W. M., Swidler, A., and Tipton, S. *Habits of the Heart: Individualism and Commitment in American Life*. New York: HarperCollins, 1985.

Berliner, D. "But Do They Understand?" In V. Richardson-Koehler (ed.), *Educators' Handbook: A Research Perspective*. New York: Longman, 1987.

Berliner, D. "The Development of Expertise in Pedagogy." Charles W. Hunt Memorial Lecture. American Association of Colleges for Teacher Education, New Orleans, Feb. 17, 1988.

Beyer, B. K. *Practical Strategies for the Teaching of Thinking*. Needham Heights, Mass.: Allyn & Bacon, 1987.

Bloom, B. S. *All Our Children Learning*. New York: McGraw-Hill, 1981.

Bredo, E. "Reconstructing Educational Psychology: Situated Cognition and Deweyian Pragmatism." *Educational Psychologist*, 1994, *29*(1), 23–35.

Broad, M. L., and Newstrom, J. M. *Transfer of Training*. Reading, Mass.: Addison-Wesley, 1992.

Brockett, R. G., and Hiemstra, R. *Self-Direction in Adult Learning: Perspectives on Theory, Research, and Practice*. New York: Routledge, 1991.

Brookfield, S. D. *Understanding and Facilitating Adult Learning: A Comprehensive Analysis of Principles and Effective Practices*. San Francisco: Jossey-Bass, 1986.

Brookfield, S. D. "Using Critical Incidents to Explore Learners' Assumptions." In J. Mezirow and Associates (eds.), *Fostering Critical Reflection in Adulthood: A Guide to Transformative and Emancipatory Learning*. San Francisco: Jossey-Bass, 1990.

Brookfield, S. D. *Becoming a Critically Reflective Teacher*. San Francisco: Jossey-Bass, 1995.

Brookfield, S. D. "Adult Learning: An Overview." In A. C. Tuijnman (ed.), *International Encyclopedia of Adult Education and Training*. (2nd ed.) New York: Pergamon Press, 1996.

Brookfield, S. D. "Assessing Critical Thinking." In A. D. Rose and M. A. Leahy (eds.), *Assessing Adult Learning in Diverse Settings: Current Issues and Approaches*. New Directions for Adult and Continuing Education, no. 75. San Francisco: Jossey-Bass, 1997.

Brooks, J. G., and Brooks, M. G. *The Case for Constructivist Classrooms*. Alexandria, Va.: Association for Supervision and Curriculum Development, 1993.

Brophy, J. "Teacher Praise: A Functional Analysis." *Review of Educational Research*, 1981, *51*(1), 5–32.

Brophy, J. "Conceptualizing Student Motivation." *Educational Psychologist*, 1983, *18*(3), 200–215.

Brophy, J. "On Motivating Students." In D. Berliner and B. Rosenshine (eds.), *Talks to Teachers*. New York: Random House, 1988.

Brophy, J. *Motivating Students to Learn*. New York: McGraw-Hill, 1998.

Brown, L. R., Kane, H., and Roodman, D. M. *Vital Signs 1994: The Trends That Are Shaping Our Future*. New York: Norton, 1994.

Brundage, D. H., and MacKeracher, D. *Adult Learning Principles and Their Application to Program Planning*. Toronto: Ministry of Education, Ontario, 1980.

Buck, R. *The Communication of Education*. New York: Guilford Press, 1984.

Burgoon, J. K., Buller, D. B., and Woodall, W. G. *Nonverbal Communication: The Unspoken Dialogue*. New York: HarperCollins, 1989.

Buzan, T. *Use Both Sides of Your Brain*. New York: Dutton, 1979.

Caffarella, R. S. "Self-Directed Learning." In S. B. Merriam (ed.), *An Update on Adult Learning Theory*. New Directions for Adult and Continuing Education, no. 57. San Francisco: Jossey-Bass, 1993.

Caffarella, R. S. *Planning Programs for Adult Learners: A Practical Guide for Educators, Trainers, and Staff Developers*. San Francisco: Jossey-Bass, 1994.

Campbell, B., Campbell, L., and Dickinson, D. *Teaching and Learning Through Multiple Intelligences*. Seattle: New Horizons for Learning, 1992.

Campbell, D. P., and Hansen, J.I.C. *Manual for the SVIB-SCII*. Stanford, Calif.: Stanford University Press, 1981.

Chapell, M. S. "Brief Report: Changing Perspectives on Aging and Intelligence: An Empirical Update." *Journal of Adult Development*, 1996, *3*(4), 233–239.

Checkley, K. "The First Seven . . . and the Eighth: A Conversation with Howard Gardner." *Educational Leadership*, 1997, *55*(1), 8–13.

Chi, M.T.H., Glaser, R., and Farr, M. J. (eds.). *The Nature of Expertise*. Hillsdale, N.J.: Erlbaum, 1988.

Christensen, C. R., and Hansen, A. J. *Teaching and the Case Method*. Boston: Harvard Business School Press, 1987.

Clarke, J. H. *Patterns of Thinking*. Needham Heights, Mass.: Allyn & Bacon, 1991.

Clifford, J. "Introduction: Partial Truths." In J. Clifford and G. E. Marcus (eds.), *Writing Culture: The Poetics and Politics of Ethnography*. Berkeley: University of California Press, 1986.

Costa, P. T., Jr., and McCrae, R. R. "Personality Continuity and the Changes of Adult Life." In M. Storandt and G. R. Vanden Bos (eds.), *The Adult Years: Continuity and Change*. Washington, D.C.: American Psychological Association, 1989.

Courtney, S. *Why Adults Learn: Toward a Theory of Participation in Adult Education*. New York: Routledge, 1991.

Cross, K. P. *Adults as Learners: Increasing Participation and Facilitating Learning*. San Francisco: Jossey-Bass, 1981.

Cruickshank, D. R., and others. *Teaching Is Tough*. Upper Saddle River, N.J.: Prentice Hall, 1980.

Csikszentmihalyi, M. *Finding Flow: The Psychology of Engagement with Everyday Life*. New York: Basic Books, 1997.

Csikszentmihalyi, M., and Csikszentmihalyi, I. S. *Optimal Experience: Psychological Studies of Flow in Consciousness*. New York: Cambridge University Press, 1988.

Cunningham, P. M. "Making a More Significant Impact on Society." In B. A. Quigley (ed.), *Fulfilling the Promise of Adult and Continuing Education*. New Directions for Continuing Education, no. 44. San Francisco: Jossey-Bass, 1989.

Darkenwald, G. G., and Valentine, T. "Factor Structure of Deterrents to Public Participation in Adult Education." *Adult Education Quarterly*, 1985, *35*(4), 177–193.

Davies, D. R., Shackleton, V. J., and Parasuraman, R. "Monotony and Boredom." In R. Hockey (ed.), *Stress and Fatigue in Human Performance.* New York: Wiley, 1983.

Day, H. I. (ed.). *Advances in Intrinsic Motivation and Aesthetics.* New York: Plenum, 1981.

Deci, E. L. "The Relation of Interest to the Motivation of Behavior: A Self-Determination Theory Perspective." In K. A. Renninger, S. Hidi, and A. Krapp (eds.), *The Role of Interest in Learning and Development.* Hillsdale, N.J.: Erlbaum, 1992.

Deci, E. L., and Ryan, R. M. "A Motivational Approach to Self: Integration in Personality." In R. Dienstbier (ed.), *Nebraska Symposium on Motivation,* Vol. 38: *Perspectives on Motivators.* Lincoln: University of Nebraska Press, 1991.

Deshler, D. "Metaphor Analysis: Exorcising Social Ghosts." In J. Mezirow and Associates (eds.), *Fostering Critical Reflection in Adulthood: A Guide to Transformative and Emancipatory Learning.* San Francisco: Jossey-Bass, 1990.

Deshler, D. "Participation: Role of Motivation." In A. C. Tuijnman (ed.), *International Encyclopedia of Adult Education and Training.* (2nd ed.) New York: Pergamon Press, 1996.

Dewey, J. *How We Think.* (Rev. ed.) Lexington, Mass.: Heath, 1933.

Dick, W., and Carey, L. *The Systematic Design of Instruction.* (3rd ed.) Glenview, Ill.: Scott, Foresman and Little, Brown Higher Education, 1990.

Dillon, C., and Smith, P. L. *A Review of the Literature of the Learning Benefit of Video-Based Distance Education Systems: Distance Education Effectiveness Study.* IBM Corp., contract no. 11203LKI, 1992.

Dillon, J. T. *Questioning and Teaching: A Manual of Practice.* New York: Teachers College Press, 1988.

Dixon, R. A., and Baltes, P. B. "Toward Lifespan Research on the Functions and Pragmatics of Intelligence." In R. J. Sternberg and R. K. Wagner (eds.), *Practical Intelligence: Nature and Origins of Competence.* Cambridge, England: Cambridge University Press, 1986.

Duke, C. "Adult Tertiary Education." In A. C. Tuijnman (ed.), *International Encyclopedia of Adult Education and Training.* (2nd ed.) New York: Pergamon Press, 1996.

Eisner, E. W. *The Educational Imagination.* (2nd ed.) Old Tappan, N.J.: Macmillan, 1985.

Elbow, P. *Embracing Contraries: Explorations in Learning and Teaching.* New York: Oxford University Press, 1986.

Ellis, A. "Rational-Emotive Therapy." In R. J. Corsini and D. Wedding (eds.), *Current Psychotherapies*. Itasca, Ill.: Peacock, 1989.

Engel, J. "Not Just a Method But a Way of Learning." In D. J. Boud and G. Feletti (eds.), *The Challenge of Problem-Based Learning*. New York: St. Martin's Press, 1991.

Feldman, K. A. "Identifying Exemplary Teachers and Teaching: Evidence from Student Ratings." In R. P. Perry and J. C. Smart (eds.), *Effective Teaching in Higher Education: Research and Practice*. New York: Agathon Press, 1997.

Fisher, C., and others. "Teaching Behaviors, Academic Learning Time and Student Achievement: An Overview." In C. Denham and A. Lieberman (eds.), *Time to Learn*. Washington, D.C.: National Institute of Education, 1980.

Ford, M. *Motivating Humans: Goals, Emotions, and Personal Agency Beliefs*. Thousand Oaks, Calif.: Sage, 1992.

Frederick, P. "Diversity Dimensions." *Professional and Organizational Development (POD) Network in Higher Education News*, Dec. 1997, p. 2.

Freire, P. *Pedagogy of the Oppressed*. New York: Seabury Press, 1970.

Freud, S. "Letter to C. G. Jung, December 6, 1906." In E. Jones, *Life and Work of Sigmund Freud*. Vol. 2: *Years of Maturity, 1901–1919*. New York: Basic Books, 1955.

Fuhrmann, B. S., and Grasha, A. F. *A Practical Handbook for College Teachers*. Boston: Little, Brown, 1983.

Gage, N. L. "The Generality of Dimensions of Teaching." In P. O. Peterson and H. J. Walberg (eds.), *Research and Teaching: Concepts, Findings, and Implications*. Berkeley, Calif.: McCutchan, 1979.

Gage, N. L., and Berliner, D. C. *Educational Psychology*. (6th ed.) Boston: Houghton Mifflin, 1998.

Gardner, H. *Multiple Intelligences: The Theory in Practice*. New York: Basic Books, 1993.

Gardner, H., and Hatch, T. "Multiple Intelligences Go to School." *Education Researcher*, 1989, *1*(8), 4–10.

Gardner, J. W. *On Leadership*. New York: Free Press, 1990.

Garfield, C. *Peak Performers*. New York: Morrow, 1986.

Gephart, W. J., Strother, D. B., and Duckett, W. R. (eds.). "Instructional Clarity." *Practical Applications of Research*, 1981, *3*(3), 1–4.

Gergen, K. J., Gulerce, A., Lock, A., and Misra, G. "Psychological Science in Cultural Context." *American Psychologist*, 1996, *51*(5), 496–503.

Gilligan, C. *In a Different Voice: Psychological Theory and Women's Development.* Cambridge, Mass.: Harvard University Press, 1982.

Ginsberg, M. B. "Observation Guide for Culturally Responsive Teaching and Learning." Unpublished manuscript, 1998.

Goleman, D. *Emotional Intelligence.* New York: Bantam, 1995.

Good, T., and Brophy, J. *Looking in Classrooms.* (6th ed.) New York: Harper-Collins, 1994.

Goodman, J. "Humor, Creativity, and Magic: Tools for Teaching and Living." Unpublished manuscript, Sagamore Institute, Saratoga Springs, N.Y., 1981.

Greeno, J. G., Collins, A. M., and Resnick, L. B. "Cognition and Learning." In D. C. Berliner and R. C. Calfee (eds.), *Handbook of Educational Psychology.* Old Tappan, N.J.: Macmillan, 1996.

Griffin, P. "Facilitating Social Justice Education Courses." In M. Adams, L. A. Bell, and P. Griffin (eds.), *Teaching for Diversity and Social Justice: A Sourcebook.* New York: Routledge, 1997a.

Griffin, P. "Introductory Module for Single Issue Courses." In M. Adams, L. A. Bell, and P. Griffin (eds.), *Teaching for Diversity and Social Justice: A Sourcebook.* New York: Routledge, 1997b.

Gronlund, N. E. *Stating Objectives for Classroom Instruction.* Old Tappan, N.J.: Macmillan, 1978.

Hall, C. "Cultural Malpractice: The Growing Obsolescence of Psychology with the Changing U.S. Population." *American Psychologist,* 1997, *52,* 642–651.

Hall, E. T. *Beyond Culture.* Garden City, N.Y.: Anchor, 1976.

Hall, E. T. *The Dance of Life: The Other Dimension of Time.* Garden City, N.Y.: Anchor, 1984.

Hall, E. T. "A System of the Notation of Proxemic Behavior." *American Anthropologist,* 1996, *65,* 1003–1026.

Hattie, J., Marsh, H. W., Neill, J. T., and Richards, G. E. "Adventure Education and Outward Bound: Out-of-Class Experiences That Make a Lasting Difference." *Review of Educational Research,* 1997, *67*(1), 43–87.

Hayes, E. R., and Darkenwald, G. G. "Attitudes Toward Adult Education: An Empirically-Based Conceptualization." *Adult Education Quarterly,* 1990, *40*(3), 156–168.

Hecht, M. L., Andersen, P. A., and Ribeau, S. A. "The Cultural Dimensions of Nonverbal Communication." In M. K. Asante and W. B. Gudykunst (eds.), *Handbook of International and Intercultural Communication.* Thousand Oaks, Calif.: Sage, 1989.

Hickey, D. T. "Motivation and Contemporary Socio-Constructivist Instructional Perspectives." *Educational Psychologist*, 1997, *32*(3), 175–193.

Hiemstra, R., and Brockett, R. G. (eds.). *Overcoming Resistance to Self-Direction in Adult Learning*. New Directions for Adult and Continuing Education, no. 64. San Francisco: Jossey-Bass, 1994.

Highwater, J. "Imagination as a Political Force." General session address given at the annual conference of the Association for Supervision and Curriculum Development, Chicago, Mar. 1994.

Hockey, R. (ed.). *Stress and Fatigue in Human Performance*. New York: Wiley, 1983.

Hockey, R., and Hamilton, P. "The Cognitive Patterning of Stress States." In R. Hockey (ed.), *Stress and Fatigue in Human Performance*. New York: Wiley, 1983.

Hofstede, G. *Culture's Consequences*. (Abridged ed.) Thousand Oaks, Calif.: Sage, 1982.

Hofstede, G. "Cultural Differences in Teaching and Learning." *International Journal of Intercultural Relations*, 1986, *10*(3), 301–320.

Hurt, H. T., Scott, M. D., and McCroskey, J. C. *Communication in the Classroom*. Reading, Mass.: Addison-Wesley, 1978.

Hutchings, P. *Using Cases to Improve College Teaching: A Guide to More Reflective Practice*. Washington, D.C.: American Association for Higher Education, 1993.

Hyerle, D. *Visual Tools for Constructing Knowledge*. 1996. Alexandria, Va.: Association for Supervision and Curriculum Development, 1996.

Jarvis, P. *Adult Learning in the Social Context*. London: Croom Helm, 1987.

Johnson, D. W. "Attitude Modification Methods." In F. H. Kanfer and A. P. Goldstein (eds.), *Helping People Change*. New York: Pergamon Press, 1980.

Johnson, D. W., and Johnson, F. P. *Joining Together: Group Theory and Group Skills*. (6th ed.) Needham Heights, Mass.: Allyn & Bacon, 1996.

Johnson, D. W., and Johnson, R. T. *Cooperative, Competitive, and Individualistic Procedures for Educating Adults: A Comparative Analysis*. Minneapolis: Cooperative Learning Center, University of Minnesota, 1995.

Johnson, D. W., Johnson, R. T., and Smith, K. A. *Active Learning: Cooperation in the College Classroom*. Edina, Minn.: Interaction, 1991.

Johnson-Bailey, J., and Cervero, R. M. "Negotiating Power Dynamics in Workshops." In J. Anderson Fleming (ed.), *New Perspectives on Designing and Implementing Effective Workshops*. New Directions for Adult and Continuing Education, no. 76. San Francisco: Jossey-Bass, 1997.

Jones, A. P., Rozelle, R. M., and Chang, W. "Perceived Punishment and Reward Values of Supervisor Actions in a Chinese Sample." *Psychological Studies*, 1990, 35, 1–10.

Jones, S. E. *The Right Touch: Understanding and Using the Language of Physical Contact.* Cresshill, N.J.: Hampton Press, 1994.

Jourard, S. *The Transparent Self.* New York: Van Nostrand Reinhold, 1964.

Kasworm, C. E., and Marienau, C. A. "Principles of Assessment for Adult Learning." In A. D. Rose and M. A. Leahy (eds.), *Assessing Adult Learning in Diverse Settings: Current Issues and Approaches.* New Directions for Adult and Continuing Education, no. 75. San Francisco: Jossey-Bass, 1997.

Keller, J. M. "Motivational Design of Instruction." In C. M. Reigeluth (ed.), *Instructional-Design Theories and Models: An Overview of Their Current Status.* Hillsdale, N.J.: Erlbaum, 1983.

Keller, J. M. "Motivational Systems." In H. D. Stolovitch and E. J. Keeps (eds.), *Handbook of Human Performance Technology: A Comprehensive Guide for Analyzing and Solving Performance Problems in Organizations.* San Francisco: Jossey-Bass, 1992.

Kemmerer, F. N., and Thiagarajan, S. "Incentive Systems." In H. D. Stolovitch and E. J. Keeps (eds.), *Handbook of Human Performance Technology: A Comprehensive Guide for Analyzing and Solving Performance Problems in Organizations.* San Francisco: Jossey-Bass, 1992.

Kerman, S. "Teacher Expectation and Student Achievement." *Phi Delta Kappan*, 1979, 60, 716–718.

King, A. "Inquiry as a Tool in Critical Thinking." In D. F. Halpern and Associates (eds.), *Changing College Classrooms: New Teaching and Learning Strategies for an Increasingly Complex World.* San Francisco: Jossey-Bass, 1994.

Kinsella, K. "Instructional Strategies Which Promote Participation and Learning for Non-Native Speakers of English in University Classes." *Exchanges*, 1993, 5(1), 12.

Kitayama, S., and Markus, H. R. (eds.). *Emotion and Culture: Empirical Studies of Mutual Influence.* Washington, D.C.: American Psychological Association, 1994.

Knowles, M. S. *The Modern Practice of Adult Education: From Pedagogy to Audiogogy.* (Rev. ed.) Chicago: Follett, 1980.

Knowles, M. S. *Using Learning Contracts: Practical Approaches to Individualizing and Structuring Learning.* San Francisco: Jossey-Bass, 1986.

Knowles, M. S. *The Making of an Adult Educator: An Autobiographical Journey.* San Francisco: Jossey-Bass, 1989.

Knox, A. B. *Adult Development and Learning: A Handbook on Individual Growth and Competence in the Adult Years*. San Francisco: Jossey-Bass, 1977.

Kogan, N. "Personality and Aging." In J. Birren and K. Schrie (eds.), *Handbook of the Psychology of Aging*. (3rd ed.) Orlando, Fla.: Academic Press, 1990.

Kohn, A. *Punished by Rewards*. Boston: Houghton Mifflin, 1993.

Kosnik, W., and others. "Visual Changes in Daily Life Throughout Adulthood." *Journal of Gerontology*, 1988, *43*, 63–70.

Krapp, A., Hidi, S., and Renninger, K. A. "Interest, Learning, and Development." In K. A. Renninger, S. Hidi, and A. Krapp (eds.), *The Role of Interest in Learning and Development*. Hillsdale, N.J.: Erlbaum, 1992.

Kulik, C. L., Kulik, J., and Bangert-Drowns, R. "Effectiveness of Mastery Learning Programs: A Meta-Analysis." *Review of Education Research*, 1990, *60*, 265–299.

LaBouvie-Vief, G., and Schell, D. "Learning and Memory in Later Life." In B. Wolman (ed.), *Handbook of Developmental Psychology*. Upper Saddle River, N.J.: Prentice Hall, 1982.

Lambert, N. M., and McCombs, B. L. "Introduction: Learner-Centered Schools and Classrooms as a Direction for School Reform." In N. M. Lambert and B. L. McCombs (eds.), *How Students Learn: Reforming Schools Through Learner-Centered Education*. Washington, D.C.: American Psychological Association, 1998.

Land, M. L. "Vagueness and Clarity." In M. Dunkin (ed.), *The International Encyclopedia of Teaching and Teacher Education*. New York: Pergamon Press, 1987.

Langer, S. *Philosophy in a New Key*. Cambridge, Mass.: Harvard University Press, 1942.

Larkins, A. G., McKinney, C. W., Oldham-Buss, S., and Gilmore, A. C. *Teacher Enthusiasm: A Critical Review*. Hattiesburg, Miss.: Education and Psychological Research, 1985.

Lather, P. *Getting Smart: Feminist Research and Pedagogy within the Post Modern*. New York: Routledge, 1991.

Lave, J. *Cognition in Practice*. Cambridge, England: Cambridge University Press, 1988.

Lepper, M. R., and Greene, D. (eds.). *The Hidden Costs of Reward*. Hillsdale, N.J.: Erlbaum, 1978.

Light, R. *Explorations with Students and Faculty About Teaching, Learning, and Student Life*. Vol. 1. Cambridge, Mass.: Harvard University Press, 1990.

Locke, E. A., and Latham, G. P. *A Theory of Goal Setting and Task Performance*. Upper Saddle River, N.J.: Prentice Hall, 1990.

Loden, M., and Rosener, J. B. *Workforce America! Managing Employee Diversity as a Vital Resource*. Homewood, Ill.: Business One Irwin, 1991.

Lowe, J. "Time, Leisure, and Adult Education." In A. C. Tuijnman (ed.), *International Encyclopedia of Adult Education and Training*. (2nd ed.) New York: Pergamon Press, 1996.

Lustig, M. L., and Koester, J. *Intercultural Competence: Interpersonal Communication Across Culture*. New York: HarperCollins, 1993.

MacGregor, J. "Learning Self-Evaluation: Challenges for Students." In J. MacGregor (ed.), *Student Self-Evaluation: Fostering Reflective Learning*. New Directions for Teaching and Learning, no. 56. San Francisco: Jossey-Bass, 1994.

Mager, R. F. *Developing Attitude Toward Learning*. Belmont, Calif.: Fearon, 1968.

Marzano, R. J. *A Different Kind of Classroom: Teaching with Dimensions of Learning*. Alexandria, Va.: Association for Supervision and Curriculum Development, 1992.

Maslow, A. H. *Motivation and Personality*. (2nd ed.) New York: HarperCollins, 1970.

Massimini, F., Csikszentmihalyi, M., and Delle Fave, A. "Flow and Biocultural Evolution." In M. Csikszentmihalyi and I. S. Csikszentmihalyi (eds.), *Optimal Experience: Psychological Studies of Flow in Consciousness*. New York: Cambridge University Press, 1988.

McCombs, B. L. "Motivation and Lifelong Learning." *Educational Psychologist*, 1991, *26*(2), 117–127.

McCombs, B. L., and Whisler, J. S. *The Learner-Centered Classroom and School: Strategies for Increasing Student Motivation and Achievement*. San Francisco: Jossey-Bass, 1997.

McKeachie, W. J. "Good Teaching Makes a Difference—And We Know What It Is." In R. P. Perry and J. C. Smart (eds.), *Effective Teaching in Higher Education: Research and Practice*. New York: Agathon Press, 1997.

McLagan, P. A. *Helping Others Learn: Designing Programs for Adults*. Reading, Mass.: Addison-Wesley, 1978.

Merriam, S. B., and Brockett, R. G. *The Profession and Practice of Adult Education: An Introduction*. San Francisco: Jossey-Bass, 1997.

Merriam, S. B., and Caffarella, R. S. *Learning in Adulthood: A Comprehensive Guide*. San Francisco: Jossey-Bass, 1991.

Meyers, C., and Jones, T. B. *Promoting Active Learning: Strategies for the College Classroom*. San Francisco: Jossey-Bass, 1993.

Mezirow, J. "Transformative Learning: Theory to Practice." In P. Cranton (ed.), *Transformative Learning in Action: Insights from Practice*. New Directions for Adult and Continuing Education, no. 74. San Francisco: Jossey-Bass, 1997.

Mezirow, J., and Associates. *Fostering Critical Reflection in Adulthood: A Guide to Transformative and Emancipatory Learning*. San Francisco: Jossey-Bass, 1990.

Michelson, E. "Multicultural Approaches to Portfolio Assessment." In A. D. Rose and M. A. Leahy (eds.), *Assessing Adult Learning in Diverse Settings: Current Issues and Approaches*. New Directions for Adult and Continuing Education, no. 75. San Francisco: Jossey-Bass, 1997.

Mills, R. C. *Realizing Mental Health*. New York: Sulzburger and Graham, 1995.

Mordkowitz, E. R., and Ginsburg, H. P. "The Academic Socialization of Successful Asian-American College Students." *Quarterly Journal of Laboratory of Comparative Human Cognition*, 1987, 9, 85–91.

Morgan, M. "Reward-Induced Decrements and Increments in Intrinsic Motivation." *Review of Educational Research*, 1984, 54(1), 5–30.

Nietzsche, F. W. *The Antichrist*. New York: Knopf, 1920.

O'Donnell, J. M., and Caffarella, R. S. "Learning Contracts." In M. W. Galbraith (ed.), *Adult Learning Methods*. Malabar, Fla.: Kreiger, 1990.

Ogle, D. "The K-W-L: A Teaching Model That Develops Active Reading of Expository Text." *The Reading Teacher*, 1986, 39, 564–576.

Okun, B. *Seeking Connections in Psychotherapy*. San Francisco: Jossey-Bass, 1990.

Oldfather, P. "Epistemological Empowerment: A Constructivist Concept of Motivation for Literary Learning." Paper presented at the National Reading Conference, San Antonio, Tex., Dec. 1992.

Olsho, L., Harkins, S., and Lenhardt, M. "Aging and the Auditory System." In J. Birren and K. Shaie (eds.), *Handbook of the Psychology of Aging*. (2nd ed.) New York: Van Nostrand Reinhold, 1985.

Ovando, C. J., and Collier, V. P. *Bilingual and ESL Classrooms: Teaching in Multicultural Contexts*. (2nd ed.) New York: McGraw-Hill, 1997.

Paley, V. G. *The Boy Who Would Be a Helicopter: The Uses of Storytelling in the Classroom*. Cambridge, Mass.: Harvard University Press, 1990.

Patterson, M. L. *Nonverbal Behavior: A Functional Perspective*. New York: Springer-Verlag, 1983.

Paul, R. "Socratic Questioning." In R. Paul (ed.), *Critical Thinking: What Every Person Needs to Survive in a Rapidly Changing World*. Rohnert Park, Calif.: Center for Critical Thinking and Moral Critique, Sonoma State University, 1990.

Pearlman, M. "Trends in Women's Total Score and Item Performance on Verbal Measures." Paper presented at the annual meeting of the American Educational Research Association, Washington, D.C., Apr. 1987.

Pedersen, P. A Handbook for Developing Multicultural Awareness. (2nd ed.) Alexandria, Va.: American Counseling Association, 1994.

Perkins, D. N., Allen, R., and Hafner, J. "Differences in Everyday Reasoning." In W. Maxwell (ed.), Thinking: The Frontier Expands. Hillsdale, N.J.: Erlbaum, 1983.

Perkins, D. N., and Solomon, G. "Learning Transfer." In A. C. Tuijnman (ed.), International Encyclopedia of Adult Education and Training. (2nd ed.) New York: Pergamon Press, 1996.

Perry, R. P., Magnusson, J. L., Parsonson, K. L., and Dickens, W. J. "Perceived Control in the College Classroom: Limitations in Instructor Expressiveness Due to Non Contingent Feedback and Lecture Content." Journal of Education Psychology, 1986, 78, 96–107.

Peters, T. J., and Waterman, R. H., Jr. In Search of Excellence: Lessons from America's Best Run Companies. New York: HarperCollins, 1982.

Pintrich, P. R. (ed.). "Current Issues and New Directions in Motivational Theory and Research." Education Psychologist, 1991, 26, 384.

Pintrich, P. R. (ed.). Understanding Self-Regulated Learning. New Directions for Teaching and Learning, no. 63. San Francisco: Jossey-Bass, 1995.

Pintrich, P. R., and Schunk, D. H. Motivation in Education: Theory, Research, and Applications. Columbus, Ohio: Merrill, 1996.

Pittman, T. S., Boggiano, A. K., and Ruble, D. N. "Intrinsic and Extrinsic Motivational Orientations: Limiting Conditions on the Undermining and Enhancing Effects of Reward on Intrinsic Motivation." In J. M. Levine and M. C. Wang (eds.), Teacher and Student Perceptions: Implications for Learning. Hillsdale, N.J.: Erlbaum, 1983.

Poplin, M., and Weeres, J. "Listening at the Learner's Level." The Executive Educator, 1992, 15(4), 14–19.

Rangachari, P. K. "Twenty-Up: Problem-Based Learning with a Large Group." In L. Wilkerson and W. H. Gijselaers (eds.), Bringing Problem-Based Learning to Higher Education: Theory and Practice. New Directions for Teaching and Learning, no. 68. San Francisco: Jossey-Bass, 1996.

Rendon, L. "Validating Culturally Diverse Students: Toward a New Model of Learning and Student Development." Innovative Higher Education, 1994, 9(1), 33–52.

Renninger, K. A., Hidi, S., and Krapp, A. (eds.). The Role of Interest in Learning and Development. Hillsdale, N.J.: Erlbaum, 1992.

Rich, A. Lecture given at Scripps College, Claremont, Calif., Feb. 15, 1984, the 164th anniversary of Susan B. Anthony's birthday (1820–1906).

Rogers, C. R. Freedom to Learn. Columbus, Ohio: Merrill, 1969.

Rogoff, B., and Chavajay, P. "What's Become of Research on the Cultural Basis of Cognitive Development?" *American Psychologist*, 1995, *50*, 859–877.

Rothwell, W. J., and Kazanas, H. C. *Mastering the Instructional Design Process: A Systematic Approach*. San Francisco: Jossey-Bass, 1992.

Saint-Exupéry, A. de. *The Little Prince*. (K. Woods, trans.) Orlando, Fla.: Harcourt Brace, 1943.

Salthouse, T. A. *Theoretical Perspectives on Cognitive Aging*. Hillsdale, N.J.: Erlbaum, 1991.

Sarason, I. G. (ed.). *Test Anxiety: Theory, Research and Application*. Hillsdale, N.J.: Erlbaum, 1980.

Schaie, K. W. "Perceptual Speed in Adulthood: Cross-Sectional and Longitudinal Studies." *Psychology and Aging*, 1989, *4*, 443–453.

Schaie, K. W., and Willis, S. L. *Adult Development and Aging*. (4th ed.) New York: HarperCollins, 1996.

Schneider, W. J. "Lifespan Development: Memory." In A. C. Tuijnman (ed.), *International Encyclopedia of Adult Education and Training*. (2nd ed.) New York: Pergamon Press, 1996.

Schön, D. A. *Educating the Reflective Practitioner: Toward a New Design for Teaching and Learning in the Professions*. San Francisco: Jossey-Bass, 1987.

Schunk, D. H. "Self-Efficacy and Academic Motivation." *Educational Psychologist*, 1991, *26*(3 & 4), 207–231.

Schunk, D. H., and Zimmerman, B. (eds.). *Self-Regulation of Learning and Performance*. Hillsdale, N.J.: Erlbaum, 1994.

Scott, J. P. "A Time to Learn." *Psychology Today*, 1969, *2*(10), 46–48, 66–67.

Seligman, M. *Helplessness*. San Francisco: Freeman, 1975.

Senge, P. M. *The Fifth Discipline: The Art and Practice of the Learning Organization*. New York: Doubleday, 1990.

Sheik, A. A. (ed.). *Imagery: Current Theory, Research, and Application*. New York: Wiley, 1983.

Shor, I. *Empowering Education: Critical Teaching for Social Change*. Chicago: University of Chicago Press, 1992.

Shor, I. "Education in Politics: Paulo Freire's Critical Pedagogy." In P. McLaren and P. Leonard (eds.), *Paulo Freire: A Critical Encounter*. New York: Routledge, 1993.

Shulman, L. S. "Knowledge and Teaching: Foundations of the New Reform." *Harvard Educational Review*, 1987, *57*(1), 1–22.

Skinner, B. F. *Verbal Behavior*. Englewood Cliffs, N.J.: Appleton-Century-Crofts, 1957.

Smith, B. J., and Delahaye, B. L. *How to Be an Effective Trainer*. (2nd ed.) New York: Wiley, 1983.

Smith, D. M., and Kolb, D. A. *User's Guide for the Learning Style Inventory: A Manual for Teachers and Trainers*. Boston: McBer, 1986.

Smith, R. M. *Learning How to Learn*. Chicago: Follett, 1982.

Smolak, L. *Adult Development*. Upper Saddle River, N.J.: Prentice Hall, 1993.

Solorzano, D. "Teaching and Social Change: Reflections on a Freirean Approach in a College Classroom." *Teaching Sociology*, 1989, *17*, 218–225.

Stacey, N., and le To, D. "Market Concepts in Provision." In A. C. Tuijnman (ed.), *International Encyclopedia of Adult Education and Training*. (2nd ed.) New York: Pergamon Press, 1996.

Stipek, D. *Motivation to Learn: From Theory to Practice*. (3rd ed.) Needham Heights, Mass.: Allyn & Bacon, 1998.

Tatum, B. D. "Talking About Race, Learning About Racism: The Application of Racial Identity Development Theory in the Classroom." *Harvard Educational Review*, 1992, *62*(1), 1–24.

Tennant, M., and Pogson, P. *Learning and Change in the Adult Years: A Developmental Perspective*. San Francisco: Jossey-Bass, 1995.

Tharp, R., and Gallimore, R. *Rousing Minds to Life: Teaching, Learning, and Schooling in Social Context*. Cambridge, England: Cambridge University Press, 1988.

Tinto, V. "Colleges as Communities: Taking Research on Student Persistence Seriously." *Review of Higher Education*, 1998, *21*(2), 167–177.

Tobias, S. "Interest, Prior Knowledge, and Learning." *Review of Educational Research*, 1994, *64*, 37–54.

Tobin, K. "Role of Wait Time in Higher Cognitive Level Learning." *Review of Educational Research*, 1987, *57*(1), 69–95.

Torff, B., and Sternberg, R. J. "Changing Mind, Changing World: Practical Intelligence and Tacit Knowledge in Adult Learning." In M. C. Smith and T. Pourchot (eds.), *Adult Learning and Development: Perspectives from Educational Psychology*. Hillsdale, N.J.: Erlbaum, 1998.

Tough, A. *The Adult's Learning Projects*. (2nd ed.) Austin, Tex.: Learning Concepts, 1979.

Tracey, W. R. *Designing Training and Development Systems*. (3rd ed.) New York: AMACOM, 1992.

Trawick, L. "Effects of a Cognitive-Behavioral Intervention on the Motivation, Volition, and Achievement of Academically Underprepared College Students." Unpublished doctoral dissertation, Teachers College, Columbia University, 1990.

Trawick, L., and Corno, L. "Expanding the Volitional Resources of Urban Community College Students." In P. R. Pintrich (ed.), *Understanding Self-Regulated Learning*. New Directions for Teaching and Learning, no. 63. San Francisco: Jossey-Bass, 1995.

Triandis, H. C. "Motivation and Achievement in Collectivist and Individualist Cultures." In M. L. Maehr and P. R. Pintrich (eds.), *Culture, Motivation, and Achievement*, Vol. 9: *Advances in Motivation and Achievement*. Greenwich, Conn.: JAI Press, 1995.

Tuijnman, A. C. "Introduction: Concepts, Theories, and Methods." In A. C. Tuijnman (ed.), *International Encyclopedia of Adult Education and Training*. (2nd ed.) New York: Pergamon Press, 1996.

U.S. Department of Commerce. *The Statistical Abstract of the United States: 1990*. Washington, D.C.: Government Printing Office, 1990.

Uguroglu, M., and Walberg, H. J. "Motivation and Achievement: A Quantitative Synthesis." *American Educational Research Journal*, 1979, *16*, 375–389.

Vaill, P. B. "The Purposing of High Performance Systems." *Organizational Dynamics*, Autumn 1982, pp. 23–29.

Van der Kamp, M. "Participation: Antecedent Factors." In A. C. Tuijnman (ed.), *International Encyclopedia of Adult Education and Training*. (2nd ed.) New York: Pergamon Press, 1996.

Vargas, J. S. *Behavioral Psychology for Teachers*. New York: HarperCollins, 1977.

Voss, J. F. "Problem Solving and the Educational Process." In A. Lesgold and R. Glaser (eds.), *Foundations for a Psychology of Education*. Hillsdale, N.J.: Erlbaum, 1989.

Vygotsky, L. S. *Mind in Society: The Development of Higher Psychological Processes*. Cambridge, Mass.: Harvard University Press, 1978.

Walberg, H. J., and Uguroglu, M. "Motivation and Educational Productivity: Theories, Results, and Implications." In L. J. Fyans Jr. (ed.), *Achievement Motivation: Recent Trends in Theory and Research*. New York: Plenum, 1980.

Watson, J. S., and Ramey, C. G. "Reactions to Response Contingent Stimulation in Early Infancy." *Merrill Palmer Quarterly*, 1972, *18*, 219–228.

Weiner, B. *Human Motivation: Metaphors, Theories, and Research*. Thousand Oaks, Calif.: Sage, 1992.

Weinstein, M., and Goodman, J. *Playfair*. San Luis Obispo, Calif.: Impact, 1980.

Wertsch, J. V. *Voices of the Mind: A Sociocultural Approach to Mediated Action*. Cambridge, Mass.: Harvard University Press, 1991.

Whaba, M. A., and Bridwell, L. G. "Maslow Reconsidered: A Review of Research on the Need Hierarchy Theory." *Organizational Behavior and Human Performance*, 1976, *15*, 212–240.

White, R. W. "Motivation Reconsidered: The Concept of Competence." *Psychological Review*, 1959, 66, 297–333.

Whitehead, A. N. *Process and Reality.* New York: Free Press, 1979.

Wiggins, G. P. *Assessing Student Performance: Exploring the Purpose and Limits of Testing.* San Francisco: Jossey-Bass, 1993.

Wiggins, G. P. *Educative Assessment: Designing Assessments to Inform and Improve Student Performance.* San Francisco: Jossey-Bass, 1998.

Wilkerson, L., and Gijselaers, W. H. (eds.). *Bringing Problem-Based Learning to Higher Education: Theory and Practice.* New Directions for Teaching and Learning, no. 67. San Francisco: Jossey-Bass, 1996.

Wiske, M. S. (ed.). *Teaching for Understanding: Linking Research with Practice.* San Francisco: Jossey-Bass, 1998.

Wlodkowski, R. J., and Ginsberg, M. E. *Diversity and Motivation: Culturally Responsive Teaching.* San Francisco: Jossey-Bass, 1995.

Woolfolk, A. E. *Educational Psychology.* (7th ed.) Needham Heights, Mass.: Allyn & Bacon, 1998.

Yelon, S. L. "Classroom Instruction." In H. D. Stolovitch and E. J. Keeps (eds.), *Handbook of Human Performance Technology: A Comprehensive Guide for Analyzing and Solving Performance Problems in Organizations.* San Francisco: Jossey-Bass, 1992.

Yum, J. O. "The Impact of Confucianism on Interpersonal Relationships and Communication Patterns in East Asia." In L. A. Samovar and R. E. Porter (eds.), *Intercultural Communication: A Reader.* (8th ed.) Belmont, Calif.: Wadsworth, 1997.

Zimmerman, B. J., and Schunk, D. H. *Self-Regulated Learning and Academic Achievement: Theory, Research, and Practice.* New York: Springer-Verlag, 1989.

Zinker, J. *Creative Process in Gestalt Therapy.* New York: Brunner/Mazel, 1977.

Name Index

Subject Index

Date Due

7/6/00			
MAY 1 5 2001			
NO 5 '02			
AP 8 '0			
JY 11 '04			
SE 30 '04			
NO 12 '04			
MY 13 '05			
AP 09 '08			